University of London School of Advanced Study
Institute of Germanic Studies

From Prague Poet to Oxford Anthropologist: Franz Baermann Steiner Celebrated

Essays and Translations

Edited by Jeremy Adler, Richard Fardon, and Carol Tully

iudicium

Dieses Buch erscheint gleichzeitig als Bd. 80 der Reihe
Publications of the Institute of Germanic Studies
(University of London School of Advanced Study)
ISBN 085457-203-1

Bibliografische Information Der Deutschen Bibliothek

Die Deutsche Bibliothek verzeichnet diese Publikation in der Deutschen
Nationalbibliografie; detaillierte bibliografische Daten sind im Internet über
http://dnb.ddb.de abrufbar.

ISBN 3-89129-685-1
ISBN 0-85457-203-1

© IUDICIUM Verlag GmbH München 2003
Druck- und Bindearbeiten: Difo Druck, Bamberg
Printed in Germany
Imprimé en Allemagne

Jeremy Adler, Richard Fardon, and Carol Tully

From Prague Poet to Oxford Anthropologist:
Franz Baermann Steiner Celebrated
Essays and Translations

Contents

PREFACE:
FRANZ BAERMANN STEINER

His Excellency, the Ambassador of the Czech Republic, London, Dr Pavel Seifter

Prague is said to be a crossroads, a meeting place. But Prague has also always been a place of people and things, past and lost. Even now, if you go to Prague and imagine – a shift in time, you may meet them: Einstein and Winternitz, Meyrink and Rilke and Kafka, Kraus and Werfel and Brod, and Adler and Steiner and Lešehrad, amongst many, many others.

I first met them in that imaginary way. Some of them in Prague, some of them in London after they lost their home. Adler and Steiner lived in Karlin, on the other side of the Vltava from where I am writing these words. These days in London I sometimes pass by Steiner's small flat in Notting Hill Gate. Adler's train and mine also passed in February 1947 – mine on its way to Prague, his going to London. Lešehrad returned to Prague, but not until long after he died, when a little museum in his name opened after 1990. What sense does all this make?

What I find so striking about Steiner and his Prague friends is their 'be-ing-in-between'. 'The poem I write, for me, is something between a piece of music and a confession or something between a commandment and mem-ory,' says Steiner. His 'inbetweenness' is, I feel, of an existential kind, in ten-sion with the business of being an exile and with the special way survivors have of 'being':

Weder via Belsen, noch als dienstmädchen
Kam der fremde, keineswegs ein flüchtling.
Dennoch wars ein trauriger fall:
Die nationalität war strittig,
Die religion umlispelte peinlichkeit. (Kafka in England; AsP: 226–7)

(Neither via Belsen, nor as a maid of all work / The stranger came, by no means a refugee. / And yet the case was a sad one: / His nationality was in doubt. / His religion occasioned lisping embarrassment.)

For Steiner – as for all the refugees and survivors of those years, of the war, the Holocaust – the place and time they were born into had gone. Steiner, we are told, was prone to personal accidents, misfortunes, and disasters. Of course in a very broad sense this was true for many of his generation and the whole of Central Europe. It was true for Prague itself, for its German and Jewish culture, and also for its Czech environment and Czech culture – although in the latter case not to the extent of extinction. Prague's time and location became displaced, moving back in history and East in space. Steiner first lost his home, then his parents in 1942. He famously also lost his work of years, his thesis on slavery. The story of his suitcase lost on the train can be seen not merely as an anecdote of misfortune. It reminds me of the tragedy of the philosopher Walter Benjamin whose suitcase, apparently containing his major work, and which he carried with him all the long journey escaping the Nazis from Germany across France and into Spain, was never found after his suicide in Port Sou.

All that was part of an era of extraordinary intensity in intellectual life in Europe. This intensity was so charged that resistance, an anti-intellectual resistance, had to come from somewhere. Such a concentration of brilliant minds, of ideas and ideals, be it in Prague or elsewhere in Europe and also in exile, was perhaps too much to bear, too much to live with. The poisonous climate of politics and ideology, the totalitarian corruption and eventually the murder of intellect and intellectuals along with millions of people who were part of their natural cultural environment, led to total destruction. We inherited the outcome. After the Holocaust, philosophy, culture, and thought could never be the same again, as became clear in the second half of the century.

What we are nowadays exposed to is therefore the cultural aftermath of that disaster: masses, quantities, numbers, and their culture of banality, sentimentality, and infantility. Also emptiness in glittering packaging. One might see this as a natural state of postmodern and post-postmodern mankind, or, as I think melancholically, as a state of loss. Steiner and his friends were well aware of the tragedy of what was going on in their time and no wonder there was a certain feeling of awkwardness and of not belonging to a place, Steiner's home, in the end, was his intellect.

The London conference on Franz Baermann Steiner and the publication of the *Selected Writings* mark his 'homecoming' in a broader sense. This was – after half a century – the first public celebration of Steiner as an intellectual *par excellence*, as a poet, and as an anthropologist. Interestingly, Steiner remained a Czechoslovak national as long as that was possible, which poses a narrower question of his home and homecoming. The truth is that the country of his birth knows little of him. This difficult relationship is represented in a letter regarding Steiner's grant from the Czechoslovak Government in Exile, in 1941, to support his research:

> I did my government, or rather the Ministry of Education, an injustice (yes, there really is such a thing as doing government an injustice!). The money which was promised me was not intended as a fee for spying. The money was mentioned to me by a slimey subaltern in that disgusting connection, and my over-sensitivity in political matters lent wings to my imagination. The matter has now been put right by a higher authority. I am already in possession of part of the sum, which is higher than expected. It is the first 'grant' that the Ministry has awarded to a Czechoslovak scholar. They have finally seen that it will be much better for the reconstruction of the State to encourage students to pursue the scientific education they cannot complete at home than to force them to join the army. (Unpublished letter from Steiner to Elias Canetti, 2 February 1941)

As for a country that might *want* to be seen as the home of Franz Baermann Steiner, what kind of country, and State, could that be? Some rare moments of history like the Czech Velvet Revolution seem to promise a miracle, for a passing moment. But anyway it might have been a straitjacket because Steiner was more a cosmopolitan than a national. The lack is Prague's. We are the ones who need to invite Steiner to come home.

Prague-London, August 2002

INTRODUCTION

This collection developed from a one-day symposium held in February 2000 at the Institute of Germanic Studies in London under the title 'From Prague Poet to Oxford Anthropologist: Franz Baermann Steiner Celebrated'. Celebration is indeed the driving force behind this collection of essays and translations, which draws together readings and studies of Steiner's work from scholars in numerous fields to reflect Steiner's own wide-ranging knowledge and scholarly achievement. The symposium was originally planned to celebrate Franz Steiner's ninetieth birthday, which fell on 12 October 1999, but this date almost coincided with a reception in Oxford to mark the publication of Steiner's *Selected Writings*, so the symposium was delayed for several months, allowing contributors to benefit from the materials the new edition made available. A particular poignancy was added to symposium by the opening address, delivered by His Excellency Pavel Seifter, the Ambassador of the Czech Republic, who pointed out that Steiner had been the very first recipient of a research grant from the Czechoslovak Government in Exile during the Second World War, which enabled him to pursue his research on slavery.

Although the essays in this volume are presented thematically, the very nature of Steiner's work means there is often an overlap between poetry, anthropology and, indeed, the other areas of scholarship embraced by this enviably erudite man. The first section is devoted to Steiner's anthropology, the second to his cultural context, and the third and final section focuses on his poetry. The volume closes with three contemporary memoirs of Steiner from his friends Elias Canetti, H. G. Adler, and Esther Frank. All three appear here in translation for the first time, the latter two never previously having been published.

Steiner came to Britain to pursue his anthropological studies, and it is in anthropology that he achieved his greatest reputation: notably on account of the posthumous publication of *Taboo* (1956). Before his death, Steiner had become a lecturer in the Institute of Social Anthropology at Oxford University just as it became – for a period after the Second World War – the leading centre of its type in the world. The three essays in the first section address aspects of Steiner's late anthropological scholarship, but they do not, however, explore those issues most conventionally associated with British anthropology of the period. Instead they reveal the extent to which Steiner's anthropology retained qualities of metaphysical and moral enquiry more typical of continental scholarship. To do this, each of the essayists has supplemented Steiner's narrowly anthropological writings with his aphoristic texts or poetic writings in order to realize their full context and significance.

Richard Fardon's essay examines the importance to Steiner and to E. E. Evans-Pritchard, his friend and colleague, the post-war professor of anthropology at Oxford, of the relationship between religious and anthropological understandings. Whereas religion was fundamental to Steiner's project of understanding values comparatively, Evans-Pritchard's programmatic statements treated anthropologists' personal religious views as a private, almost aesthetic, domain. Fardon argues that the differences between the two men's views in this respect may be traced to the contrasting character of British and German societies in the first half of the twentieth century, and their different experience of the war. Although he exerted no influence upon later postcolonial and deconstructive theorists, Steiner's congenital and actual outsidership, and his close identification with Eastern cultures and with the subjects of colonization, cause Steiner's concerns to seem to foreshadow questions that preoccupied later twentieth-century commentators: questions of identity, authenticity, and the politics and violence of difference.

Inspection of Steiner's original documents has allowed Erhard Schüttpelz to resolve the transcription of one Steiner's most important aphoristic statements, reconnect this aphorism with another that explicates several of its points, and use these statements as the platform for a wide-ranging exploration of Steiner's sociological insights. The aphorism states Steiner's key sociological principles to be identification and transformation, and it suggests their mutual implication. Schüttpelz suggests that Steiner adapted his account of status change from Arnold van Gennep's celebrated account of *rites de passage* by extending van Gennep's specialized understanding of the ritual passage between statuses to the movement between social identities more generally. Steiner's methodological aphorisms seem to beg the question: which then is prior in terms of sociological understanding, social identification or transformation? Tracing the recurrence of this question through various areas of Steiner's work, Schüttpelz resists answering the question that Steiner appears to pose, and identifies one of the wells of Steiner's thought in his own recognition of the mutual entailments between these two guiding ideas. Schüttpelz concludes with a challenging comparison between the notions of transformation in Steiner and his friend Elias Canetti, and suggests a hitherto hidden intertextual reference to Steiner in Canetti's *Masse und Macht* (Crowds and Power, 1960).

Michael Mack's essay on value, marginality, and myth relates closely to the two previous studies. Drawing as much upon Steiner's poems as upon his explicitly anthropological writings, Mack explores the linked ideas of value, danger, and suffering that are present in all Steiner's late work. Mack emphasizes the ways in which Steiner recurrently focused upon the violence visited upon the margins: on whoever and whatever is construed strange, primitive, wild or foreign. As he demonstrates, Steiner's poetry graphically instantiates his general sociological arguments, whether in relations between Gods and humans (in the rape of Leda), or in the violence visited by tame animals upon the wild (in his exploration of the sources of Steiner's disturbing meditation on capturing elephants). The same theme is resolved poetically in a more optimistic fashion in Steiner's autobiographical poem, when a wandering sea captain is redeemed because the testimony of a foundling child on a remote island brings him intimations of divine presence. The – quintessentially anthropological – idea of instruction by the marginalized appears here as the antithesis of the 'conquests' that Steiner saw instanced both in European Empire and European knowledge. And this suspension of violence is an aspect of the containment – rather than elimination – of the dangers intrinsic to the human capacity to recognize difference that, without being fully worked through anywhere in his writings, is crucial to many of the most urgently expressed passages of Steiner's thought.

Steiner was a reserved man in many respects, nonetheless throughout his life he associated with numerous contemporary writers, artists, and scholars. This placed him at the heart of European culture at a time when the flow of ideas was particularly strong. The second section of the volume examines three of Steiner's cultural associations, and his roles as translator, subject, and inspiration. In the early part of his career, between 1933 and 1934, Steiner acted as a cultural mediator with his translation of *Planety* (The Planets), the verse drama by Josef Maria Emanuel Lešetický z Lešehradu (1877–1955). Robert Pynsent begins his study by locating Steiner in the context of contemporary Czech literature, highlighting links with authors such as Zeyer and Karásek, who like Steiner, were interested in the life of the Catalan mystic Ramon Lull. This same interest in mysticism and the occult drew Steiner to Lešehrad's work. He saw *Die Planeten* as the Czech poet's response to the failure of religion and as such the translation forms part of the continuum of Steiner's anthropological studies. Pynsent sees Steiner's rendition of Lešehrad's verse as the experimental work of a young poet, testing and challenging his own abilities, often enlivening the rather mundane original in the process. This was to be Steiner's only published translation and its significance lies not only in its role in the development of Steiner's skills as a poet, but also in the mediation between Czech and German culture which foreshadows the tenor of Steiner's later anthropological writings which themselves seek to foster understanding between cultures.

As well as playing an active part in the cultural scene of his day, Steiner also found himself the subject of artistic endeavour in the work of the Austrian artist Marie-Louise von Motesiczky (1906–96). Motesiczky was a student of Max Beckmann and friend of Oskar Kokoschka, and as such is very much part of the Expressionist tradition. Despite living in exile in London for many years, her work is still better known in her native Austria. In her essay, Ines Schlenker introduces the artist's life and work, and focuses on her portrayal of three close friends, Steiner, Canetti, and Iris Murdoch. Although her turbulent friendship with Canetti lasted for almost fifty years, it was perhaps with Steiner that Motesiczky had most in common: both were denied full recognition during their lifetime, both experienced exile, and both suffered the tragic loss of loved ones at the hands of the Nazis. Motesiczky's work reflects the harshness of such experiences, leading some to criticize her style as crude and unforgiving. Yet, for all that, she succeeds in capturing the nature of her sitters, and Schlenker describes how her portraits convey the intellectual as well as the physical presence of these writers by means of honest and often harsh depictions. Of the three paintings reproduced in the volume, perhaps the most moving is *Conversation in the Library* (1950), which depicts Steiner and Canetti involved in a heated discussion in a convincing portrayal of their intense relationship.

The complexity of the relationship between Motesiczky's subjects is highlighted in Peter Conradi's discussion of Steiner and Iris Murdoch where Canetti maintains a constant presence in the background. Steiner and Murdoch grew close in 1951. Theirs was in many ways a truly tragic relationship, cut short by Franz's early death in 1952. Yet, in each other, both writers found an intellectual equal and a source of comfort and support. Murdoch was deeply affected by Steiner's death. Indeed, she tended him in his last days and it is thought that they became engaged. Later, she would describe Steiner as 'the most beloved' of her Jewish teachers. Steiner's impact also extended to Murdoch's work, although she often denied depicting those she knew in her novels. Conradi suggests a number of occasions where characters in Murdoch's novels might have been, in part at least, inspired by Steiner. One such striking character is Willy Kost in Murdoch's 1968 novel, *The Nice and the Good*. This East European not only bears a physical resemblance to Steiner, but also often asks the question 'What ees eet?' which Murdoch fondly remembered as one of Steiner's stock phrases, so typical of his sceptical, enquiring attitude.

As well as inspiring the work of others, such as Murdoch and Motesiczky, Steiner's own work was itself inspired by a number of writers and cultures. This becomes clear in the third section of the volume which focuses on Steiner's poetical oeuvre. His relationship to Spain and Spanish culture, and in particular the influence of the poet Jorge Manrique (1440–79) on the elegiac 'Gebet im Garten' (Prayer in the Garden) is the subject of Carol Tully's study. Steiner fell in love with Spain and its people on two visits during the last years of his life. He saw his time there as a spiritual homecoming in the land of the Sephardic Jews and he identified with the fate of the Jews in Spain after 1492, one which in many ways paralleled the experiences of his people in his own lifetime. Steiner's interest in Spanish culture stretched back over many years. Esther Frank remembers learning Spanish with him in the 1940s and points to his interest in Spain's literary heritage. Steiner drew on Jorge Manrique's elegy, 'Coplas a la muerte de su padre' (Verses on the Death of his Father) both as a model and as a counter-type to create his own poem of remembrance, one which would also become his only poetic response to the Shoah. Tully suggests that both poems are grounded in personal and collective histories, centring on the loss of a parent and the issue of cultural identity. The difference lies in their opposing perspectives: that of oppressor and oppressed, a line of demarcation which, as Steiner's poem makes clear, has divided peoples and cultures for centuries.

The notion of demarcation is the focus of Rüdiger Görner's discussion of the role of borders in Steiner's poetry. Steiner's life is itself defined by a number of borders and boundaries. In his work, for example, there is the boundary between poetry and anthropology: the concept of taboo, which is central to his thought, itself represents the very essence of such limits. In his life, too, there is, as a self-proclaimed 'Oriental in the West', the internal and external border between East and West. It is, then, perhaps no surprise that Görner feels the evocation of the borders surrounding 'the Other' to be most prevalent in the semi-autobiographical cycle *Eroberungen* (Conquests). Görner examines Steiner's poetry in the context of his work as a whole as an example of ethnological poetics. The poet's focus on disciplinary as well as cultural and personal borders highlights once more his role as mediator, this time combining a field of scholarship which seeks to uncover and illuminate the mysteries of cultural boundaries, with an art form which is able to reach out beyond even the boundaries it sets itself, something which Steiner is able to achieve in his own work through his attention to detail and nuance in language and the complex rhythms which underpin his verse.

The correlation between Steiner's study of cultures and his poetry is also central to Katrin Kohl's discussion of *Eroberungen*, in which she examines Steiner's understanding of poetry as a means of defending myth. Steiner found the imposition of Western values on non-Western peoples, very much the Jewish experience in Europe, to be both culturally and ethically abhorrent. As one of the key anchors of any culture, myth represents for Steiner a means to freely explore other cultures. He sees the preservation of myth as a poetic task and this is one of the ideals informing *Eroberungen*. Kohl draws on the use of myth in her discussion of the myriad influences apparent in the cycle: Eliot, Wordsworth, Hölderlin, Klopstock, and Rilke all play a prominent role in Steiner's work. This highlights the richness of allusion in his work and demonstrates the depth of Steiner's literary knowledge. However, as Kohl makes clear, Steiner is not merely influenced by these writers. Instead, he seeks inter-action with their work in a way which is both inquiring and demanding. This interaction is typical of Steiner's means of communicating with culture, a strategy which not only defends myth by confronting its abuses, but also en-riches the literary tradition by taking it beyond its acknowledged boundaries.

The rather fraught issue of Steiner's own place within the literary canon is discussed in the final essay in the volume. Nicolas Ziegler traces the reception of Steiner's poetry and tries to find explanations for its limited success, some-thing made all the more incomprehensible by the unreserved approval of con-temporaries such as Canetti, as well as other commentators such as Stephen Spender. Ziegler points to a combination of back luck and bad timing. Steiner's unfortunate relations with the publishing industry are well-docu-mented, a series of mishaps preventing the publication of any major collec-tions during his lifetime. Yet, there was also the issue of the cultural climate of the post-war era. Ziegler focuses on Steiner's friendship with the editor Ru-dolf Hartung who saw Steiner's work as one of the few valid responses to the so-called 'new world' of the late 1940s and 1950s which dealt cautiously with literature as a whole. Steiner's initial lack of success was something experi-enced by other writers such as Nelly Sachs and Paul Celan, both of whom only came to prominence in the late 1950s, by which time, of course, Steiner had died. That Steiner himself felt his work to be worthy of publication is not in doubt. Despite his often negative self-appraisal he made plans for an edition of collected works intended to fill some 25 volumes. The reception of his work was, with a few exceptions, largely posthumous. Ziegler shows how this has developed to the point that Steiner is now the subject of mainstream cultural comment, something to which this volume itself bears testament.

The volume concludes with biographical pieces by three of Steiner's friends, the first two of which, by H. G. Adler and Esther Frank, appear for the first time in this volume, and the third, by Elias Canetti, is published for the first time in English. H. G. Adler's biographical essay is the longest, most detailed account we have of Steiner written by one of his friends. Adler and Steiner were child-hood friends, growing up in the same Prague neighbourhood of Karlin, and were united by an interest in many topics, including poetry, botany, biology, and the social sciences. Adler's piece is couched in the form of a letter to Steiner's friend and colleague Chaim Rabin, a linguist and fellow Zionist from Steiner's Oxford days, who appears to have written to H. G. Adler requesting some bio-graphical information. The innocent request seems to have touched a nerve, since Adler treated it as the occasion to write a detailed account of Steiner's life, including a review of his intellectual biography.

The letter provides innumerable insights into Steiner's origins and youth, as well as into his literary and intellectual development, and is valuable both for the facts which it preserves, and for the insights that it provides. Esther Frank's contribution was recorded some years later, when Esther visited H. G. Adler from the United States, where (as her notes made clear) she had emigrated after the war. The document, written and typed by H. G. Adler from notes taken during his conversations about Franz with Esther, with the intention of preserving facts and details for posterity, was never intended to be written up as an essay. It proceeds by subject, and concludes with notes on several of Franz's poems, explaining allusions (such as the title of the poem 'Fernando Brumal') that would otherwise be lost. The notes are particularly valuable for the insights that they provide from a fellow-Jew, and because they are provided by a woman. How close her relationship to Franz actually was is more implicit than explicit in her conversations. However, if Canetti's account of the relationship to Jeremy Adler is to be believed, Esther worshipped Franz, and wanted to marry him, but whilst he was intellectually and emotionally close to her, he did not love her as a woman, and had no wish to marry her. This would go some way to explaining the tortured, emotional leave-taking which Esther records, and could even account for her departure to the United States.

Canetti's aphoristic essay was found among his papers after his death. It was first mooted in conversation with Jeremy Adler around 1990, when Canetti promised to write an essay on Steiner for a forthcoming issue of the German literary journal *Akzente* which was planned to have a special focus on Steiner. Canetti felt dissatisfied with his piece and did not release it for publication, despite the best efforts of his editor, Michael Krüger. In the event, the planned number of *Akzente* went ahead including, *inter alia*, a piece by Michael Hamburger, and contributed decisively to the growth of interest in Steiner's work. This interest was further fuelled by the posthumous publication of Canetti's essay in a later issue of the same journal, which had a similar focus on Steiner. Among the many points touched on in Canetti's contribution, perhaps the most important is his emphasis on myth. Whilst myth was clearly central to Steiner's thinking, as Mary Douglas has noted elsewhere, he produced no academic work in this field. Although its significance to him is evident from the poems and aphorisms, Canetti provides an essential illumination on its place in Steiner's thought.

The editors wish to thank Professor Mary Douglas and His Excellency Dr Pavel Seifter (Ambassador of the Czech Republic) both for introducing the symposium 'Franz Baermann Steiner Celebrated' and for their encouragement of this project from conception to publication. We are severally indebted to the *Institute of Germanic Studies* and particularly to its Director Professor Görner: most especially for hosting the original symposium and, through the

IGS publications committee chaired by Professor John Flood, accepting this collection for publication in their series. Karin Hellmer and Jane Lewin organized splendid hospitality for the symposium, and the distinguished actress, Lia Williams, closed a memorable day by reading Steiner's elegiac poem to his father 'Prayer in the Garden'.

We are grateful to the Research Committee of the School of Humanities, King's College London, the Research Committee of the School of Oriental and African Studies, the Centre of Jewish Studies, and Humanities Research Committee of the University of Wales Bangor for their financial support of the event and publication.

We would also like to thank the contributors for their enthusiasm, patience, and encouragement. Adler and Fardon wish to add a special note of thanks to Carol Tully for providing the driving force behind this collection, for bearing the brunt of the editorial work, and for making many of the translations.

Jeremy Adler, Richard Fardon, and Carol Tully.

BIBLIOGRAPHICAL NOTES

References to the following works are given in the main body of the text using the abbreviations indicated in parenthesis:

– Franz Baermann Steiner, *Selected Writings*, ed. by Jeremy Adler and Richard Fardon (New York/Oxford: Berghahn, 1999).
 Volume I: *Taboo, Truth, and Religion* (SWI).
 Volume II: *Orientpolitik, Value, and Civilisation* (SWII).
 References to the foreword of either volume are given with the editors' names.
– Franz Baermann Steiner, *Am stürzenden Pfad. Gesammelte Gedichte*, ed. by Jeremy Adler (Göttingen: Wallstein, 2000) (AsP)
 References to the editor's 'Nachwort' and the accompanying 'Dokumente' and 'Anmerkungen' are also indicated in the text.

Throughout the volume, poems have been given in the original with an accompanying English translation. Anthropological writings and aphorisms are given in English only. Versions of the following poems are taken from *Franz Baermann Steiner*, Modern Poetry in Translation, New Series 2, with translations and an introduction by Michael Hamburger (London: King's College, 1992): 'Elefantenfang', 'Kafka in England', 'Gebet im Garten', 'Zinnen', and 'Spätere Jahre des Dichters'. Versions of parts I-VII from the cycle *Eroberungen* are those provided in SWII, translated by Jeremy Adler. Unless otherwise indicated, all other translations are made by Carol Tully.

The editors would like to express their thanks to the following institutions: the Deutsches Literaturarchiv, Schiller-Nationalmuseum, Marbach am Neckar, where Steiner's papers are held, for their co-operation in supplying material to enable completion of this project; Carl Hanser Verlag, Munich, for permission to publish the translation of Elias Canetti's memoir 'Franz Steiner'; the Marie-Louise von Motesiczky Charitable Trust for permission to reproduce *Self-Portrait with Canetti* and *Conversation in the Library*; and St Anne's College Oxford for permission to reproduce *Portrait of Iris Murdoch*.

I. ANTHROPOLOGY

'RELIGION AND THE ANTHROPOLOGISTS' REVISITED

Reflections on Franz Baermann Steiner, E. E. Evans-Pritchard, and the 'Oxford School' at their Century's End[1]

Richard Fardon

Anthropological theories come and go (and occasionally come again); hot topics go cool; ethnographic regions slip from general concern for a while; could something similar be true of styles of anthropological subjectivity? The thought occurred to me while trying to account for the immediacy I discovered reading Franz Steiner's writings together with Jeremy Adler while editing a two volumed *Selected Writings* in English. Steiner's sense of the potential consequentiality of anthropological theory for his contemporary world seemed hardly to have dated. How the two – academic anthropological theory and worldly mid-century predicaments – were sutured seemed impossible to understand aside from Steiner's subjectivity: his concerns were the upshot of his broad lived experience, the political beliefs he struggled to clarify, and the aesthetic dispositions by which he came. Not just Steiner's problems then, but their intensely lived-in quality persuaded me to read him as a contemporary in a way that I find impossible with Steiner's sometime Oxford mentor and colleague E. E. Evans-Pritchard; this despite the fact that Evans-Pritchard is closer to me in nationality, culture, and language and moreover outlived Steiner by two decades.

Subsequently rereading some of Evans-Pritchard's writings on history and religion reinforced this sense that it is his contemporary – Steiner – more than himself who reads like my contemporary. This is not meant to inflate one man's legacy by disparaging the other: Evans-Pritchard has good claim to be-

---

[1] The title refers to E. E. Evans-Pritchard's 1959 Aquinas Lecture, 'Religion and the Anthropologists', which appeared in his *Essays in Social Anthropology* (London: Faber and Faber, 1962), pp. 29–45. Page references appear in the text.

ing simply *the* pre-eminent social anthropologist of the mid-twentieth century, the late twentieth-century discipline is hardly thinkable without him. Steiner's direct influence is by comparison negligible. My point is rather that the late twentieth-century discipline's concerns are as strikingly absent in Evans-Pritchard as they are present in Steiner. The world, it seems, has gone the way of Steiner's preoccupations rather than Evans-Pritchard's. I shall draw my example from their respective treatments of anthropologists' own religious beliefs. The example is not accidental since the topic is one to which the normally forthright Evans-Pritchard contributed (as my title, borrowed from his essay, indicates) but with uncharacteristic reticence.

It is not just that Evans-Pritchard is dismissive of any effects that studying other religions might have on anthropologists' own beliefs, he also evades detailed discussion of the consequences that any religious beliefs anthropologists might hold would have for their ethnographic accounts of other people's religions. By design as well as default, religious experience is presented as preeminently personal and private – not a subject suitable for analysis in relation to contemporary ethnographic practice. In this, Evans-Pritchard falls into step both with the *public* culture of the mid-twentieth century British state which held confessional identities to be a matter of private conscience, and with an unspoken (at least in quite these terms) tenet of mid-century anthropology which held that ethnography was experience-near and theory experience-far. Or, at least, that personal experience mattered when writing ethnographically but was out of place – unmentionable as Leach would later have it[2] – when writing theoretically. The experiential was a region of uncertainty and so hesitancies (and tales of misconstrual) were allowed (even appropriate) there. Fieldwork could plausibly be construed as a learning process hastened only by allowing others to correct the researcher's inappropriate behaviour.[3] However, experience did not intrude legitimately on matters of theory: how you reasoned was not supposed (at least in print) to make sense in terms of who you were. (Though we shall see that Evans-Pritchard does not apply the same considerations to past sociologists.)

With Steiner matters are reversed: there is little ethnography in his works (though that little has impeccably objectivist credentials), but his theoretical writings barely cohere other than through their writer's subjectivity. And it is the antinomies of his subjecthood, I shall suggest, that make Steiner readable as a contemporary. In the face of some exceptions, I want to propose a general

---

[2] See E. R. Leach, 'Glimpses of the unmentionable in the history of British Anthropology', *Annual Review of Anthropology*, 13 (1984), 1–23.

[3] See L. Holy, 'Theory, methodology and the research process', in *Ethnographic Research: a Guide to General Conduct*, Research Methods in Social Anthropology 1, ed. by Roy Ellen (London: Academic Press, 1984).

argument that an important criterion of authenticity in anthropological writing (not all of it written by anthropologists) shifted during the twentieth century: at the century's beginning and middle, experience authorized ethnographic but not theoretical writing; as the century wore on from its middle to its end, grounding the authenticity of ethnographic writing in experience became intensely problematic; experience was called upon instead to underwrite theoretical writings; and this was particularly so in the case of theoretical writings about the mediation of cultures. One corollary of this is that the iconic intellects of anthropological thought in the late century were not the 'native anthropologists' that some mid-century commentators anticipated but the 'halfies', those qualified by life experience to authenticate their reflections on cultural mediation, such as Abu Lughod,[4] and a new canon of non-anthropologist forebears and contemporaries took shape (many of them Francophone – like Camus, Césaire, Fanon, Senghor, and Mudimbe). Steiner's writings, unlike Evans-Pritchard's (private protestations of Welshness notwithstanding), can be made to prefigure this latter tendency (that is he could join the new canon). I am not, at the risk of repetition, reassessing the intellectual history of my discipline by claiming Steiner's direct influence on anthropologists to have been any more extensive than a few demonstrable debts owed him by particular Oxford-trained scholars. What I do want to suggest is that a genealogy of anthropology's current concerns might be constructed that would accommodate Steiner as an ancestor. However, this would be possible only because his situation – and his appreciation of his circumstances – foreshadowed that of later writers in many respects. An interesting, if counter-factual, question arises of why the path Steiner set out upon became overgrown for some decades after his death. Part of the answer must lie in the unusual character of the man himself.

The range of his work – as anthropologist, poet, aphorist, sometime political activist – and the complexity of his 'native' culture make the German-speaking, Jewish Czech, Franz Baermann Steiner an exceptional figure in British anthropology. However, his short life (1909–52) also spanned the first half of the twentieth century, an exceptional period which saw the birth of modern social anthropology and, in the course of two generations, its establishment in the major British universities either as a new subject or as a successor to evolutionary or diffusionist anthropologies. Uniquely among 'British' anthropologists, Steiner belonged among the mid-twentieth century's Jewish exiles from Central Europe who gave so much to the development of social theory in the countries that received them. Recursive territorial displacement allied

---

[4] Abu Lughod, 'Writing against culture', in *Recapturing Anthropology: Working in the Present*, ed. by R. G. Fox (Santa Fe, New Mexico: 1991).

to a central engagement with the consequences of the twentieth century's intellectual tumult was part of the thrust of the exhibition *Ortlose Botschaft* (Message without Address) mounted at the Schiller Nationalmuseum in Germany which travelled to the Strahov in Steiner's birthplace Prague.[5] Steiner's papers were exhibited alongside those of his childhood friend H. G. Adler – ethnographer of the Theresianstadt concentration camp – and Elias Canetti, fellow social thinker and Bulgarian exile. Copies of Steiner's lectures are in Oxford, his papers are in Germany, and his books were sent to Jerusalem: his partible legacy seems to mirror the loosely articulated identity he represented for himself as poet.

As the reader sees elsewhere in this volume, Steiner was also a German language poet, one singularly unfortunate in his dealings with publishers in his life-time, whose collected poems (some three hundred of which survive from maybe four times this number) have only recently been published. He was also an aphorist, and wrote some thousands of aphorisms on subjects that put one in mind not just of Canetti, but of Horkheimer, Adorno, and the cultural critics of the twentieth century. In a slight way, but one that was important to him, Steiner was also an active Zionist, and he was periodically orthodox in his observance of the prescriptions of a Jewish lifestyle, considering his own inconstancy in this regard a failing.

If Steiner's intellect was unusual among the anthropologists, there is a case to be made, nonetheless, for seeing Steiner primarily as an anthropologist: his imagination was anthropological whether he was writing aphorisms or poems or contributing to Zionist debate, and social anthropology dominated the work of his later years when he was a member of the 'Oxford School' – the leading centre of anthropology in the immediate aftermath of the Second World War. As a Central European Jewish refugee from one of the twentieth century's most virulent ideologies, and an intellectual of such outstandingly broad range, Steiner's Oxford contemporaries seem to have held him in some awe. Not having carried out fieldwork in a conventional sense, however, he remained (even to himself) not quite an anthropologist. Strange that a man who had undergone so much could consider himself deficient in the variety of his experience; though here also we may be encountering a congenital marginality, a not-quite-belonging that circulated between fact and predisposition.

Both by his teaching and by the force of his example, Steiner demonstrably influenced his immediate Oxford contemporaries who admired his sophisticated grasp of classical and contemporary philosophy, and also recognized

---

[5] Atze, *Ortlose Botschaft. H. G. Adler, Elias Canetti, Franz Baermeann Steiner. Ein Freundeskreis im englischen Exil, Marbacher Magazin* 84 (Marbach am Neckar: Deutsche Schiller Gesellschaft, 1998).

what Steiner had sacrificed for this learning. But their admiration does not answer my query about the resonance of Steiner's writings down to the late twentieth century. What seemed *avant garde* about Steiner's ideas to mid-century Oxford anthropologists is not what makes his writings seem contemporary at the century's end. If there are respects in which his writings presage post-colonial writers' ways of posing problems, this must be so – I would argue – because of a structural situation he shares with many of them: an outsider identifying with the powerless and yet ensconced in the institutions of the powerful; an outsider who, while identifying with the cultures of the colonized and oppressed, yet reasons about these cultures in terms provided by an academic culture he presents as part of their antithesis. Put crudely, there is an existential price to pay for such uncomfortable social and cultural doublings, and the discomfort can show up in the homely as well as the elevated: Steiner might castigate a friend, the poet Georg Rapp, for marrying a non-Jew, but this did not prevent Steiner himself having numerous relations with non-Jewish women, becoming engaged to at least one, and desiring to marry another (the non-Jewish, if pro-Semitic, philosopher and novelist-to-be Iris Murdoch). Steiner could complain that England lacked European culture while claiming himself to be an Oriental colonized internally within the West. Caught between values constitutively, Steiner frequently entertained two, opposed views on any given subject. The tensions were sometimes amusing but as often agonizing.

It is likely that Steiner felt more ambivalently than other contemporary contributors towards that multi-national and multi-cultural melting pot known – more on account of the ownership of the pot than the nationality of the chefs – as British social anthropology. He saw respects in which British anthropology represented a continuation of the long historical engagement between (facets of) European social thought and European colonialism, and he argued that the expansive character of the social formation within which it arose differentiated it from American anthropology (the product of immigrant cultures keenly attentive to cultural difference) (SWI: 194). Attuned to the importance of what we nowadays call identity politics, Steiner had experienced the little chill that comes from finding himself objectified within a collectivity subject to anthropological interpretations (for instance in his comment 'so we primitives think' with reference to Jewish beliefs about holiness in *Taboo* [SWI: 163], or a note to his diary about Malinowski's, one hopes ironic, application of the phrase 'objects of enquiry' to 'Negroes, Chinese etc.' attending the famed LSE seminar [Adler and Fardon SWI: 63]). Yet Steiner endorsed the method of social contextualization typical of the Oxford School from the time of Evans-Pritchard's predecessor, Radcliffe-Brown, presented it to public audiences and defended it against American cultural anthropology.

Steiner spent most of his exile years attached to the Oxford Institute of Social Anthropology, eventually becoming a member of teaching staff for the less than three years between submission of his D. Phil. and his young death. He had met Evans-Pritchard in London before the war, and the two were close for the half dozen years between Evans-Pritchard taking up the Oxford chair and Steiner's death. In the following sections I want to look in general terms at the bearing of religious and war experiences on their anthropologies (in both narrow and broad senses): Evans-Pritchard, whose formal conversion to Roman Catholicism occurred during his war service in Africa, and Franz Steiner, whose Jewish religiosity intensified during the late years of his exile as the evidence for the Shoah in Europe became apparent.

EVANS-PRITCHARD'S SLOW CONVERSION[6]

The facts, such as they are, of Evans-Pritchard's conversion to Roman Catholicism seem not to be in doubt; but the facts are precious few. How far the changes in Evans-Pritchard's post-war anthropology should be construed as consequential on his religious beliefs has been a matter of surmise.

Born the second son of an Anglican vicar in 1902, Evans-Pritchard was privately educated at Winchester and then at Exeter College Oxford where he graduated in Modern History in 1924. He directly moved to the London School of Economics to study under C. G. Seligman, the ethnographer of Sudan, arriving there in the same year as Malinowski, and attending Malinowski's first seminar. Evans-Pritchard's doctorate was soon completed on the basis of Zande fieldwork in 1927 (when he was twenty-five), after which he taught intermittently at the LSE until 1932 then occupying a chair for a couple of years at the Fuad I University in Cairo. After he left Cairo (following a dispute over sociology losing status because of fears about its potentially subversive effects on young Egyptians), he took up a research lectureship in African Sociology at the University of Oxford where he remained until his war service.

Witchcraft, Oracles and Magic among the Azande (1937) and *The Nuer* (1940) were both completed in pre-war Oxford. They overlapped as ethnographic and writing projects; the first, Azande, book has clear relation to lectures Evans-Pritchard wrote when in Cairo, most especially a critical essay on Lévy-Bruhl's theory that primitive and Western thought employed differing logics.

---

[6] Biographical details about Evans-Pritchard are mostly from John W. Burton's invaluable account, *An Introduction to Evans-Pritchard*, Studia Instituti Anthropos 45 (Fribourg: University Press, 1992).

The Azande book's tone and argument is not all that dissimilar to what he would later castigate in others as thoroughly rationalist; nowhere in that book does Evans-Pritchard claim to have done more than suspend disbelief in witchcraft in order to understand how the Azande thought. Several chapters of the second book, that on the Nuer, were first published as journal articles; however, the book shows some biblical influence in its final framing. Its fore-word quotation is from Isaiah (xviii, 1–2):

> Ah, the land of the rustling of wings, which is beyond the rivers of Ethiopia: that sendeth ambassadors by the sea, even in vessels of papyrus upon the waters (saying) Go ye swift messengers, to a nation tall and smooth, to a people terrible from their beginning onward; a nation that meteth out and treadeth down, whose land the rivers divide.

The passage serves to historicize and localize the Nuer, but it cannot be said to set them into a relation of biblical intertextuality in religious terms. *The Nuer* was a (temporary as it happened) valediction to anthropology and an indication that Evans-Pritchard might have been revisiting the religious resources of his upbringing. But its author was, on the face of it, less concerned with religious issues than he had been in *Witchcraft, Oracles and Magic among the Azande*. We know that Evans-Pritchard reacted differently to the courtly Azande and the egalitarian Nuer, and that his Nuer fieldwork had been carried out under difficult conditions towards the end of the period (1926–36) when he was able to devote much of his time to African research. The war years – also spent in Africa – included stints with Anuak irregulars harrassing the Italians (Evans-Pritchard's brief and gungho account of which became well known thanks to the impression it made on Clifford Geertz[7]), and two years as a liaison officer with the Bedouin (which gave rise to a history book on the Bedouin of Cyrenaica). Evans-Pritchard was to return to Oxford to take up Radcliffe-Brown's chair only in 1946 – having first spent a year in Cambridge. Radcliffe-Brown had been Evans-Pritchard's Oxford sponsor before the war, but Evans-Pritchard was not long in banishing the older man's influence from the place.

Little studied nowadays I fancy, the programmatic writings of Evans-Pritchard's early tenure of the Oxford chair used to be well known. In my undergraduate days thirty years ago, they were reading list staples which were supposed to demonstrate British anthropology's move from structural functionalism's scientific aspirations in the direction of a more interpretative anthropology that was closely related to history. Evans-Pritchard's own conversion to Catholicism was usually held – in a rather unspecific fashion – to be a

---

[7] Geertz, *Works and Lives: the Anthropologist as Author* (Cambridge: Polity, 1988)

contributory factor in this change, both of paradigm and mood. It was only recently, however, that I looked up what must have been one of Evans-Pritchard's earliest post-war statements: a broadcast talk published in *The Listener*, a magazine that used to carry transcripts of selected BBC wireless transmissions (in this case from the 'Home Service' – domestic counterpart of BBC's external service – nowadays Radio 4). This is from 1947, the year after Evans-Pritchard took up his chair, and addresses us under the title 'Does anthropology undermine faith?';[8] it is not gripping radio drama, but here is how it starts:

> Social anthropology is the study of human societies and their development. It treats particularly of primitive societies. The question I have been asked is whether this study affects the religious faith of those who engage in it or read its literature. I take the question to mean: does it often happen that a man holding a religious faith loses it as a result of his studies in social anthropology? (p. 714)

Read over a half century since its transmission, much about this mode of address to a popular audience now seems dated: a study which '*treats of … primitive* societies', the worrying over corruption of a 'man's' 'religious faith' perhaps by no more than reading about other peoples. The question itself seems uninteresting: as readers of ethnography would we not be more interested how far 'a man's' (if we must) religious faith affects his social anthropology? Evans-Pritchard's hardly riveting answer to the scarcely riveting question posed him is more or less to say that the study of social anthropology by itself is not likely to sway a man's belief one way or the other. If a man were looking for reasons not to believe then anthropology (having been practised predominantly by rationalists and agnostics) might furnish some arguments for the decision. However, there have been distinguished anthropologists who were believers. Evans-Pritchard's pose of slightly wearied dismissal of the topic put to him slips only once:

> The agnosticism or indifference of most anthropologists has nothing to do with social anthropology as such but is part of a general agnosticism and indifference to religion common to those intellectual circles anthropologists mostly come from and mostly frequent. They are symptoms of a widespread disease which, among its other effects, makes its victims blind to whatever lies outside their partial experience of a patch of reality. (p. 715)

Here is some intimation of an answer to the unposed question: does religious belief affect anthropologists' experience? I do not recall Evans-Pritchard again

---

[8] E. Evans-Pritchard, 'Does Anthropology undermine Faith?', *The Listener*, 8 May (1937): 714–715.

describing lack of belief as symptomatic of a disease. And if agnosticism is the symptom, what are we to understand as the disease? One wonders what was so awful about a world in which a murderous fascism had recently been defeated, peace restored, and the nuclear-fuelled stalemate of the Cold War not yet become apparent. Was it just the election of Attlee's Labour government? (I hear echoes of this embattled tone in Mary Douglas's opening to her lectures on 'The Contempt of Ritual' in 1968 and in her 1970 *Natural Symbols* which developed their arguments.[9]) But if nothing else the passage I have quoted strongly supports those who have related Evans-Pritchard's faith and intellectual beliefs. This change in Evans-Pritchard's views was also reflected in his deteriorating relations with his predecessor, A. R. Radcliffe-Brown, a notoriously godless social scientist. Despite apparently endorsing Radcliffe-Brown's 'Oxford School' of structural functionalism in his unpublished Inaugural Lecture,[10] by 1950 Evans-Pritchard had written the first of several lectures declaring an antipathy to Radcliffe-Brown's natural science of society and advocating that anthropology was a humanity and closely related to some types of history. Evans-Pritchard had also egged on Franz Steiner to (twice) deliver the series of lectures that would posthumously be published as *Taboo* (1956): 'taboo' was a subject closely associated with Radcliffe-Brown, and Steiner would not simply dispute but ridicule Radcliffe-Brown's theory relating taboo to social value (to say that a particular avoidance expressed social value, Steiner asserted, belonged to the same order of explanation as the claim a mountain was big because it was 'magnus', mere word substitution [SWI: 194]). In 1956, Evans-Pritchard collected essays he had been writing since the war and published *Nuer Religion*, an, in parts, phenomenological account of Nuer religious ideas, and especially their ideas of the unity and refractions of a supreme spirit; and on 7 March 1959 Evans-Pritchard delivered the Aquinas Lecture at Hawkesyard Priory under the title I have borrowed for this chapter: 'Religion and the anthropologists'. His subject was the 'bleak hostility' of sociologists and anthropologists towards religion. (Again, there is an after-echo in Mary Douglas's work since 'The Contempt of Ritual', delivered as Aquinas Lectures and precursor to *Natural Symbols*, took as their initial subject the resurgence of 'anti-ritualism' among reforming priests and the British middle classes.)

Although on this occasion he reversed his question a dozen years earlier and asked what effects their own religious beliefs might have on social think-

---

[9] Fardon, *Mary Douglas: an Intellectual Biography* (London: Routledge, 1999), Chapter 5.
[10] Although the term 'Oxford School' was disowned by some of its post-war members, it is commonly used to refer to Evans-Pritchard and the members of his Institute. However, Steiner uses the phrase in a 1944 public lecture on 'How to define superstition?' to refer to Radcliffe-Brown's views (this during Radcliffe-Brown's war-time absence in Brazil) (SWI: 227).

ers, Evans-Pritchard's 1959 address, 'Religion and the anthropologists', remains largely evasive about contemporary anthropology, consisting instead of a historical review of the differing sources of antipathy to religion in French and British schools of sociology from the Enlightenment to the early twentieth century. Evans-Pritchard's French lineage transmits a long argument that recognizes religion as fundamental to society but rejects any (other than social) transcendent grounds for it. It has three major figures. Montesquieu's *Spirit of the Laws* (1748) sought law-like conditionalities in human affairs including religion, though Evans-Pritchard feels Montesquieu was really a Deist rather than atheist. Montesquieu's intellectual descendants included both economists (who are not closely examined) and Henri de Saint Simon, whom Evans-Pritchard presents as a second foundational figure on the (at first sight odd) grounds that his beliefs in social law, planning, and progress also recognized the necessity for a religion-like set of ethics – which he set about supplying. Comte, treated by Evans-Pritchard as a pendant to Saint Simon, was a 'strange' and 'paranoiac' figure (p. 31) who systematized Saint Simonian ideas, admired the Catholic church, and suggested the need for a Secular church (to which Evans-Pritchard's sometime moral tutor – R. R. Marrett – had belonged). The third founder of French sociology was Durkheim who, in producing an argument for the universality of religion, also supplied a case for a secular religion (in his case one of moral individualism). In short, this French tradition, as Evans-Pritchard interpreted it, recognized the social need, rather than transcendent grounds, for a churchly function. It was, not accidentally one supposes, the tradition to which his Oxford predecessor had belonged.

The British tradition's more uncompromising rejection of religion is traced to a utilitarian and empiricist legacy. Tylor, McLennan, Frazer, and other late nineteenth-century anthropologists were, to Evans-Pritchard's mind, all agnostics.[11] Subsequently, all leading anthropologists whether in Britain or America have been positivists and agnostics. Evans-Pritchard concludes this section of his argument on the interesting note that Catholic, Protestant, and Jewish agnosticisms have involved different forms of hostility or indifference towards religion. (This conclusion presumably follows from the contrast between the Catholic and Jewish agnosticism of the French – which sees a future for the social functions of a religious practice not unlike that of the past – and the Protestant agnosticism of the British which does not. I am guessing since Evans-Pritchard does not develop this line of argument.)

---

[11] In his 1947 essay Evans-Pritchard had recalled Tylor's Quaker parentage but claimed that he became agnostic; George Stocking, *Victorian Anthropology* (London: Athlone, 1987), corrects that the founder of Oxford anthropology retained his Quaker principles (156–158).

Evans-Pritchard is willing to concede to the critics of nineteenth-century church dogma on two grounds: those who insisted on a historical approach to the Bible were justified and, as to the scientists, 'It was monstrous that men of science should be attacked, even vilified, for expressing opinions on matters within their own province by men ignorant of these matters' (p. 39). However, a 'counter-attack' to churchly dogma that rested on the socially useful function of religion through the ages was tantamount to

> an avowal of the irrelevance of the truth or otherwise of theology; and no one is going to accept a religious faith simply because a sociologist says it is socially useful. An even greater embarrassment were the desperate attempts to save the ship by jettisoning its entire cargo. Overboard went prophecies, miracles, dogma, theology, ritual, tradition, clericalism, and the supernatural [...]. (p. 41)

From the perspective of the (mid-twentieth-century) present, says Evans-Pritchard, 'Looking back we may wonder what all the fuss was about' (p. 42). Who now cares about the resemblances between Christian and non-Christian rites, or the literal truth of Biblical stories?

> [F]undamentally there never were any real grounds for dispute between what natural science teaches about the nature of the physical world and what the Churches teach about faith and morals. After all, there cannot be a stronger assertion of natural law than belief in miracles. (p. 43)

Here, one wants to interject 'yes and no': belief in miracles is not the *strongest* assertion of natural law I can think of since miracles do not simply underwrite natural regularities but supernatural regularities too, even if the latter are far less frequent. And if Evans-Pritchard still thought, as he had in 1947, that the non-religious experienced only a patch of reality then it would be difficult to argue that the church had no axe to grind with a natural scientific understanding of the physical world. But we shall let this pass, because Evans-Pritchard continues,

> But this [absence of grounds for dispute] is not the case between the claims of social scientists, or very many of them, and those of the Churches. (p. 43)

Most thinkers continued to assume that where religion had been ousted from natural science so it would be ousted also from the social sciences in their turn:

> [...] I believe we shall not hear much more of sociological laws ... [but] this would prove nothing with regard to any religion except that it is not contradicted by the conclusions of [sociology and anthropology]. (pp. 43–44)

This is a surprisingly tame conclusion for Evans-Pritchard to draw: social anthropology will refrain from law-like generalizations (although on grounds other than their incompatibility with religion); thus religion will not have to cede 'faith and morals' to social science in the same way as it must bow before natural science's understanding of the physical world or before historical understanding of its sacred texts.

As in 1947, Evans-Pritchard's parting salvo has little to do with his preceding arguments: anthropologists are still 'atheists, agnostics or just nothing', except for a Christian minority, who are predominantly Catholics, the result, he concludes, of their choice being between all ('a [Catholic] Church which has stood its ground and made no concessions') and nothing (including Protestantism which 'shades' into Deism and agnosticism) (p. 45).

Its obvious biases apart, Evans-Pritchard's argument is most interesting for what it omits and avoids. For instance, although he refers to different styles of agnosticism earlier on, in conclusion he speaks only of Protestantism (and he probably has in mind Anglicanism, the state religion, which in the recently past war had been the fallback entry under religion for all servicemen; the jibe works less well say of Quakers, who had died for their religion as stretcher bearers; or for secular Jews who had died on account of others' state religion). British anthropology had numerous prominent Jewish members (many of them South Africans) whether atheists (like Gluckman or the younger Fortes) or believers (like Evans-Pritchard's late colleague Steiner). They – let alone members of other religions represented at Oxford – are not included in the account, which turns out to be parochially concerned with Anglicanism and Catholicism. As in 1947, Evans-Pritchard concludes that studying anthropology 'probably affects faith little either one way or the other'; although he does not tell us so, presumably this must be because the choice of religion to which he avers above is an entirely personal one.

In his antipathy to social scientific reasoning about religion, Evans-Pritchard has effectively (at least in these accounts) denied religion's public role. While concerning himself again with anthropologists' attitudes towards religion, Evans-Pritchard has left unconsidered the influence of religion on anthropology, and this is odd if we are to believe that faith and morals are contested between religious and sociological understandings. Coming in the wake of the moral disintegration of a large part of European civilization on what must be construed as at least quasi-religious grounds, this disavowal of the public significance of religion is extraordinary and, at least with such implications, probably unintended.

By accommodating his Catholic faith alongside rejection of a social scientific conception of anthropology, and conjoining this with an emphasis on the

translation of moralities and beliefs, Evans-Pritchard made an awkward relationship more comfortable. He believed – as he put it in 1950 – that,

[…] Social anthropology is a kind of historiography [that] studies societies
as moral systems and not as natural systems, that it is interested in design
rather than in process, and that it therefore seeks patterns and not scientific
laws, and interprets rather than explains […] as the history of anthropology
shows, positivism leads very easily to a misguided ethics, anaemic scientific humanism or – Saint Simon and Comte are cases in point – *ersatz* religion.[12]

It is unclear how the second of these propositions can be derived from the
nature of the enquiry outlined in the first but, leaving this aside, taken at face
value (rather than with reference to Evans-Pritchard's own practice) this conclusion would render religion an entirely private matter and deprive anthropology of any role in understanding the public and political significance of
religious affiliations. Evans-Pritchard's horizons in the post-war period seem
on this evidence to be bounded by personal experience in Africa of the recent
war, antipathy to his Oxford predecessor's structural functional anthropology
(and to many of the ancestors of this approach), and preoccupation with an
Anglican-Catholic divide in British society. By contrast Steiner's apprehen-
sions about the relations between religious values and political life were
rooted in his experience of central European genocide and his hopes for a Jewish state – whatever else, unarguably public matters.

THE ANTINOMIES OF FRANZ BAERMANN STEINER

Franz Baermann Steiner's attempt to relate religion and sociology was not just
more systematic than Evans-Pritchard's but more fraught: rather than dividing up the turf between the contesting powers (the hard sciences get the physical world, religion gets to adjudicate moral questions, and anthropology to
translate moral systems) as Evans-Pritchard did, Steiner envisaged religious
and sociological understandings contesting a single terrain in terms of incommensurable standards. Although 'antinomies' is the word I have used in the
title of this section, it is only partly appropriate: there are indeed contradictions between two valid ways of envisaging the world (as the term suggests)
but in terms of absolute value there is no doubting the precedence that the
religious understanding must take. One way to construe Franz Baermann

---

[12] E. Evans-Pritchard, 'Social anthropology: past and present (The Marett Lecture 1950)', in
Essays in Social Anthropology, pp. 13–28 (pp. 26–27).

Steiner's anthropology is as an anthropology of value: how value is created, what different forms it takes, and how any one of these forms is transvalued into another. These questions are pursued with sociological rigour, but their framing is religious or metaphysical: Steiner envisages humans as suffering creatures in a world suffused with dangers. Of enduring value – transcending truck, barter, and worldly achievement – is whatever mitigates those sufferings. Anthropology is a comparative enquiry into the mortal answers to moral questions.

Steiner's best known work, the posthumous *Taboo* edited by Laura Bohannan from a lecture series he delivered twice,[13] may be the most familiar place to start. Its summative concluding quotation concerns danger and other values:

> [...] it is a major fact of human existence that we are not able, and never were able, to express our relation to values in terms other than those of danger behaviour. (SWI: 214)

Thus Polynesian *tabu* is an instance of a universal and necessary phenomenon – not some primitive oddity as Victorian scholars had believed. Implicit in *Taboo*, but clearly stated in Steiner's significant short essay 'On the Process of Civilization' (SWII: 123–128), is a pan-historical vision of the way human societies relocalize danger as a result of expansion of their technological capacities – capacities that extend not just over the physical world but also inhere in powers of governance and domination. As external dangers (the demons as Steiner tellingly calls them) are conquered, so the locus of danger moves into the heart of society and into the person. The introverted gaze of psychoanalysis, the dependence of bourgeois society upon the market, and the increasing virulence of anti-Semitism, all relate to one another in the collapse of the Weimar Republic when seen in these terms. This branch of knowledge (whether of Arctic hunters or Europeans) Steiner characterizes as the study of 'political demonology and cosmology' (SWII: 126). This vision is more readily comparable to the projects of a Spengler, a Norbert Elias, or an Elias Canetti than with anything that comes to mind in post-war British social anthropology.

Leaving aside for a moment its grander historical narrative, Steiner's mature anthropology, I am suggesting, can be construed as a project predominantly focused on values: particularly of the way social forms correlate with regimes for creating and circulating values. Although Steiner usually avoids a general definition of value, a definition does occur in an aphoristic statement, and it is closely related to his sense that danger is symptomatic of value:

---

[13] Franz Baermann Steiner, *Taboo*, with a Preface by E. E. Evans-Pritchard, ed. by Laura Bohannan (London: Cohen and West, 1956).

[...] Value is organized anxiety. It is also organized love. That is the mystery of value. And that is the mystery of sociology. It lies behind every sociological antinomy [...]
Sociology is only meaningful for someone who treats the polarity of value between anxiety and love as a sociological polarity and not a psychological one. As soon as this polarity is regarded as lying outside the area of social regularities, social regularities simply cease to exist. (SWII: 244–245)

The lectures published as *Taboo* dealt with that side of value defined by danger and anxiety. However, Steiner also theorizes value positively, as organized desire, in ways that are strikingly reminiscent of Lévi-Strauss's levels of social exchange: of things, words, and peoples:

Exchange of things: Steiner was fascinated by the narrowly economic aspects of value creation, and he left a detailed lecture series on labour organization and a book fragment concerning the circulation of values and especially their partibility (for the expression of which he devised a set of symbols [SWII: 160–173]). For Steiner, the values of things human beings create are related to the values they invest in one another and in their social projects. This is particularly apparent in his analysis of treasures – items which derive their special value from the memorably intensive labour they objectify. When a regime of value is subjected to perturbation (as in Weimar, but also in societies to which market forms are introduced for a first time, or within which market functions expand beyond their accustomed circuits) there may follow disintegration of broader moral values too. Paul Bohannan was to formalize anthropological notions of spheres of exchange drawing upon ideas in Steiner's writings which he had edited for posthumous publication.[14]

Exchange of words: Steiner, the speaker of a dozen languages, was preoccupied by problems of translatability. Were it not for his more alert appreciation of the politics involved in representing other people's cosmologies, it might be argued that Steiner hardly differed from Evans-Pritchard who redefined anthropology as a translational discipline. But the edge to Steiner's interest came from aligning himself with the subjects of anthropology: the primitive or the Oriental. The sources of his identification were various: his understanding of Judaism as an Eastern religion, his lifelong immersion in the philosophy and literature of India and China, and his enduring fascination with the ethnology of the Arctic. Translation between unequally em-

---

[14] Paul Bohannan's notions of conveyance (within spheres of exchange) and conversion (between them) are similar to Steiner's distinction between trade and barter, on the one hand, and, on the other, translation which especially involved the exchange of a useful for a ritual object. See P. Bohannan, 'Some principles of exchange and investment among the Tiv', *American Anthropologist*, 57 (1955), 60–69, and SWII: 163.

powered languages always finds Steiner's nervous reactions at their most exposed.

Exchange of rights in people: Steiner analysed the values exchanged in people with similar empathy. His major – if fragmentary – work in this respect is his D. Phil. on forms of slavery, a labour undertaken as a duty in the light of the captivity of Jews in Europe and the ongoing attempt at their annihilation. Recall that under Steiner's own definition, treasures are the product of memorably intensive labour. The part of his uncompleted project which constituted Steiner's doctorate in fact only treated societies in which servile institutions fell short of slavery: Steiner saw clearly that an account of slavery would need to look at all transactions in people (including marriage, pawnship, the adoption of orphans, symbiotic relations between hunters and agriculturalists, and so forth). I do not know whether there was a direct influence on Igor Kopytoff (perhaps through Paul Bohannan's careful editorship of Steiner's doctorate for a publication that never eventuated) however Steiner certainly prefigures Kopytoff's later formulation of an antithesis between kinship and slavery.[15] Universally, slavery is the denial of kinship. However, in twentieth-century Europe the Jews were denied any role in their societies of birth except as raw material: one of Steiner's bitterest aphorisms states with horrifying simplicity – 'Among the *Naturvölker* who engage in head-hunting, at least the trophy head is a valuable object.' (SWII: 232) Trophy heads also would be treasures in the terms of Steiner's classification of exchanges, but the extermination camps went beyond the commodification of slaves to the commodification of body parts.

Steiner's ideas may fall into a schema comparable to Lévi-Strauss's levels of exchange. However, making the comparison also points up the differences. Steiner addresses his analysis to contemporary, mid-twentieth-century society, especially European society, as well as to the forms of society on which his ethnological training in Central Europe had made him expert. The image fundamental to his conception of social functioning involves the values that human beings put into circulation through their labour, their anxieties, and their desires; Lévi-Strauss's communicational model of society seems abstracted and passionless by comparison.

Nonetheless, I feel another partial parallel worth pursuing, although I have to confess the possibility of serendipity in making it. When I was a student Steiner's *Taboo* (originally 1956; Pelican 1967) and Lévi-Strauss's *Totemism* (1962, translated 1963; Pelican 1969) were available as inexpensive, slim vol-

---

[15] Kopytoff & S. Miers, 'African "slavery" as an institution of marginality', in *Slavery in Africa: Historical and Anthropological Perspectives* ed. by Igor Kopytoff and Suzanne Miers (Madison: University of Wisconsin Press, 1977).

umes in the same blue backed Pelican library of anthropology. I bought the copies of both that I still use during my undergraduate years at University College, by which time Mary Douglas's *Purity and Danger* (1966; Pelican 1970) had been published in the same series. But I hope there is more than this to the habit I have had since of bringing them to mind together. *Taboo* and *Totemism* are both deconstructive texts, and what each deconstructs is the entity in its title. *Totemism* paves the way for the study of bricolage and the science of the concrete in Lévi-Strauss's *The Savage Mind* (1963); *Taboo* opens the way to a comparative and historical study of the formation of regimes of value; its project of comparative moralities was not developed by Steiner but – at least in some respects – by Mary Douglas who acknowledges Steiner's influence both in *Purity and Danger* and more extensively in a 1962 precursor article under the title 'Taboo'.[16]

These resemblances between Steiner's ideas and those of Lévi-Strauss and Douglas are not surprising given that they broadly shared sources and an intellectual milieu. However, the ways that, unlike either Lévi-Strauss or Douglas, Steiner's mid-twentieth-century project foreshadows later twentieth-century post-colonial and subaltern studies must derive from structural circumstances he shared with post-colonial writers, since no direct influence is demonstrable. Steiner's complex interstitiality is reminiscent of a positionality attributed to many post-colonial critics: origination from once colonized societies, Western education (perhaps in a Western language) which implies at least relatively elite family background, and a likelihood that they ply their trade in (often elite) academic institutions in the West, particularly in the USA where hyphenated American ethnic identities are vital to contests of political economy. With suitable modification much of this could apply to Steiner also. Reflecting partly their own positionality (as we all must), post-colonial critics have, as a rule, either concentrated their attentions on the complexity, hybridity, or general fuzziness of post-coloniality, or else/or also they have proposed that there are fundamental differences between incommensurable and unequally empowered cultures. Steiner's intellectual trajectory drove him increasingly towards an argument about the incommensurabilities of (particularly Oriental and Western) cultures, and to a concentration on the unequal politics of representation between them (Adler and Fardon, SWII: 11–104). However, his tools in this analysis were those of the Western academy, and this led to the kinds of internal tensions (for instance about the nature of truth in relation to representation) with which later scholarship has made us familiar.

---

[16] Douglas, 'Taboo', *New Society*, 12 March (1962), 24–25; *Purity and Danger: an Analysis of Concepts of Pollution and Taboo* (London: Routledge and Kegan Paul, 1966).

Steiner's sense of marginality was both personal and political. Temperamental outsiderhood was reinforced by his experience of exclusive nationalisms and the internal colonization, as he saw it, of Jews in Europe. Born a Jew into the tail end of the Catholic Austro-Hungarian Empire, he grew up a Czech of German expression[17] in a modernizing Czechoslovak Republic undergoing a Czech language cultural renaissance. Returned from his Palestinian sojourn, he redefined himself as an 'Oriental in Europe', an exile, albeit an exile still at home, with a family, in Prague. When his researches took him to London, it proved to be (a brief return aside) a one-way trip: Steiner found himself in exile from his language, homes (both Prague[18] and Jerusalem), even from London which could seem like home when seen from Oxford![19] In Britain he was certainly at the heart of mid-twentieth-century colonial power (albeit one in decline – as he saw more clearly than most of the locals). So Steiner meets the conditions of dislocation that have tended to characterize the positionality of Western-engaged, post-colonial intellectuals.

Three broad phases may be discerned in Steiner's political trajectory. In his early youth he was attracted by a romanticized communism which he allied with pastoral interests. From this he soon developed into a young man of progressive liberal sympathies concerned with co-modernizing peoples (German and Czech speakers in Prague; Arabs and Jews in Palestine; Gypsies and Ukrainians in Ruthenia during the period of the Czechoslovak Republic). As a prematurely middle-aged man, Steiner adopted an anti-colonial and pro-Zionist position founded in the fundamental antinomies between European and Asian types of society. This second turning point arose with the personal deepening of the war years and is particularly evident in two papers related in their arguments: the trial ('Der Prozess', perhaps a nod in the direction of another son of Prague: Kafka) to which he subjects Western civilization (seen as inherently expansionary since Roman times and encompassing the demonic which surrounded it – and internally colonizing the Jews as a result), and the defence of the Zionist project against

---

[17] Steiner did speak Czech but German remained his medium of private expression even after his professional life came to be conducted in English: his poems, aphoristic remarks, diary, and his most personal letters continued to be written in German (a stark difference from, say, Kurt Weill and Lotte Lenya who conducted even their intimate correspondence in English on moving to the USA).

[18] In *The Flight from the Enchanter*, written soon after Steiner's death, Iris Murdoch closes her account of Peter Saward (a projection of elements of Steiner) with a glimpse of him studying a book of photographs of a city that seems to be Prague. Steiner's intimate relation to Jerusalem included his poetic belief that he had lived there in a previous incarnation.

[19] Steiner kept a London flat and a circle of London friends who knew little of his Oxford life. This marked tendency to keep his social circles distinct increased in Steiner's later years.

Gandhi's accusations of the state of Israel being just another element of Western hegemonization (SWII: 123–146). Countering Gandhi's allegation of Jewish colonization of Palestine, Steiner argues that the Jews were themselves the first and most decisively colonized of Oriental peoples, deprived of any land to call their own and subjected to centuries of representation and persecution by Europeans.

Steiner's later arguments and positionality required him to articulate antinomies between Western and Oriental peoples, and he attempted this in a fashion reminiscent in some respects of his friend Louis Dumont – though here again direct influence is not demonstrable. In expressing these differences we might now feel that Steiner fell into a series of 'Orientalizing' traps: collective versus individual; unreflective versus reflective; fatherly versus husbandly pride; contemplative versus active:

> Sociology is a western discipline. Of all the Eastern peoples only the Chinese have a leaning towards sociology. The philosophy of history is barely understood in the West. The Western peoples are very aware of making history. For the Eastern peoples, the means of socialization are so very real, so unquestionable, that they can never develop into scientific systems.[20] (Nr. 218)

> When you hear: 'And he saw their proud wives' – don't you just know this describes a European people? And: 'Their proud daughters' – isn't it now an Oriental people? (Nr. 223)

> The sociology of religion is surely the oddest development of our time. How distanced did people have to become from their inner lives and cultic communities to be able to properly discover that religious totalities influence the means of socialization. Will anyone be able to understand this [discovery] at all in later years? One will surely have to ask oneself how it can be, that, over a long period of time, different kinds of 'You should', 'You cannot', and 'We want' were proclaimed, and that a precise apparatus of knowledge was required in order to realize that all of this was not without consequence. This is surely just as alien to the Eastern, collective peoples, as the notion that philosophers and artists really possessed the ability to think and influence would be to an individualist. (Nr. 222)

The oddity of Western society that these examples pick up on, can be a source of humour, especially at the expense of the middle classes:

---

[20] The following aphorisms were translated by the author and Carol Tully from Franz Baermann Steiner, *Fluchvergnüglichkeit. Feststellungen und Versuche*, ed. by M. Hermann-Röttgen (Stuttgart: Flugasche, 1988).

Evolutionism falls into disrepute once the bourgeois realizes he hasn't come far! (SWII: 229 modified)

Europeans have learned from the Bible that the sea was created. Otherwise they would have worked out that it had been filled by the rivers. For what purpose would the most restless of all activities have, if not to form the greatest store, the greatest known quantity? (SWII: 230)

It would be easy to continue collecting Steiner's derogatory comments about the West and counterposing them to more flattering assessments of the East. How seriously these are to be taken is debatable since so many of them appear in what, rather than aphorisms, Steiner preferred to call 'Essays and Discoveries' – actively denying them any finality as propositions. However, similar ideas do underlie avowedly more sober projects – such as the 'Letter to Mr Gandhi' discussed above.

Steiner deploys Western standards of academic discourse while simultaneously subjecting them to nagging critique from the standpoint of the kinds of knowledge the West seeks to subordinate. If this critique cannot serve to displace European thought from its position of power, it does disrupt its claim to be beyond dispute. In biographical terms, this strategy becomes increasingly evident along with Steiner's (if not abandonment then at least) diminished advocacy of liberal, modernizing policies, his realization of the conjunctural complexities involved in co-modernizing popular projects, and his espousal of more intransigent anti-colonialism. Simultaneously he comes to advocate transcendent non-Western values rooted in a particular (collective) social formation, one expression of which is his distrust of nationalism and his support for the radical alterity that would have followed from creation of a theocratic state in Israel.

I do not want to suggest that Steiner's project entirely coheres – although I have tried to select its most coherent elements. Steiner would have abhorred the notion of his having a project since he avoided totalizations (or even such mundane matters as getting things finished). '"Why are you building a net?" someone asked the spider, "To organise the flies", he replied.' (SWII: 240) Steiner knew too much about totalizing schemes not to avoid them – even in such slight matters as titling his aphorisms 'experiments'. This – albeit inconstant – refusal to totalize strikes me as another unsettlingly contemporary feature of Steiner read at the end of his century. Only forty-three when he died, he left unfinished poems, essays, lecture series, collections of aphorisms, books ... No really substantial publication occurred in his lifetime (though a few poems and review-type essays appeared). Even his submitted D. Phil. was a fragment of a lost project. A life left unfinished by intention one almost feels.

RELIGION AND THE ANTHROPOLOGISTS

The reticence and British provinciality of Evans-Pritchard's writings on an-thropologists' religious beliefs become more striking when compared to those of his contemporary and friend Steiner (or indeed to Evans-Pritchard's own ethnographic writings on religion). Although we may assume no-one forced him to write them, a curious air of reluctance and evasion hangs about Evans-Pritchard's remarks. I have suggested that this is symptomatic of Evans-Pritchard's unresolved equivocation between the intensely private nature of religious experience, on the one hand, and the conviction that religious belief must impinge on the capacity of an ethnographer to report other religions sympathetically on the other. His description of anthropologists' attitudes to religion as varying between hostility and indifference suggests that the posi-tive absence of personal religious beliefs must prejudice an ethnographer's capacity to appreciate other people's religions. Evans-Pritchard does not pur-sue his own interesting observation that there are denominational styles of agnosticism (presumably more or less equated with 'indifference' in this con-text), and he is dismissive about any influence anthropological theorizing might have on religious faith. Yet his delineation of distinct British and French traditions of social thought argues for there having been an influence of reli-gious faith upon past anthropological theorizing. So the same should presum-ably hold good for the present.

Explicitly, Evans-Pritchard seems to express hardly more than regret that some anthropologists are unable to benefit from religious experience them-selves (rather as we might extend sympathies to a tone deaf friend at the op-era).

These evasions and unposed questions strike me as evidence that discus-sion has strayed into a properly private realm (akin to people's emotional in-volvements); something a person was entitled not to be asked about. Appar-ently, Evans-Pritchard averred that a good English anthropologist was a con-tradiction in terms, and he chose to define himself as Welsh. That was far as he had to go in making his ethnic or religious affiliations a matter of public con-cern or political accountability. The unspoken backdrop to all this is, of course, the fact of living in a more or less secular state; one that may have had a state religion (Anglicanism) but from which hardly any implications of conse-quence still followed. Religion could indeed be a private affair, and being a Welsh Catholic – as well as Fellow of All Souls College – was not a politically costly identity. Contrast Steiner's case.

Born a German-speaking Czech Jew, the young Steiner grew up in a mod-ernizing Czechoslovak state with strong nationalistic reawakenings. He be-longed to a people whose historic persecution was about to enter the horrors

41

of the Shoah which would see his parents killed, his friends interned, and his home confiscated. Living as a refugee in a colonial nation, he became involved in the movement for establishment of a Zionist state. Steiner's writings on Zionism are not extensive, but there is sufficient to demonstrate that he was well aware of the contradiction that would be involved in opposing colonialism through the creation of a nation state with a reinvented history. Hence Steiner's sense (perhaps philosophical more than practical) of the need for the radical alterity of the theocratic state as means of expunging the internalization of Western values by Eastern people.

The point of my comparison made, it is not to disparage Evans-Pritchard to say that he was spared his religion, ethnicity, and communal affiliation becoming a matter of life and death in the same sense as it did for Steiner. Evans-Pritchard fought with bravery in the Second World War, but his was a campaign in the colonies not a desperate attempt to avert systematic genocide. Looked at this way, Evans-Pritchard's avoidance relation with his avowed subject matter of 'Religion and the anthropologists' was not just a matter of personal taste but of personal taste felt and followed in the conducive environment of the secular state. So conducive, in fact, that its presence as context may have gone undetected.

Half a century on from his death, the world may seem to share Steiner's preoccupations more than Evans-Pritchard's. Ethnicity, identity, and religion have overwhelmed class and political creed as the proclaimed grounds of positioning and action. Steiner's concerns come to seem more contemporary than those of the man who outlived him by two decades. But this is a mere chronological paradox; Steiner's uncomfortably dislocated subjectivity make his ancestorhood of these concerns both comprehensible and tragic.

TRANSFORMATION AND IDENTIFICATION

Franz Baermann Steiner's 'chief sociological principle'

Erhard Schüttpelz

For Thomas Hauschild

Initially, Franz Baermann Steiner's work of the 1940s was dominated by two major projects: the poetic cycle *Eroberungen* (Conquests), and the dissertation on the institutions of slavery and bondage from which his later anthropological lectures and articles were derived. Each of these remained a torso. Completion of *Eroberungen* was postponed, and work on the dissertation was terminated in 1949 when Steiner handed in only the first three of eight parts of his projected outline. Since the early 1940s, alongside the lyrical writings and the anthropological drafts, a completely different category of texts had appeared in Steiner's notebooks which he called *Feststellungen und Versuche* (Essays and Discoveries): short texts with no restriction as to genre – aphorisms, essays, single lyrical and anthropological thoughts, and musings on language philosophy, comments on German literary history and on single words from different languages and dictionaries, personal and intimate experiences of alienation, religious reflections, short satires, and polemics, drafts and statements of every kind.

Around 1948 Steiner himself started several attempts at arranging these notes, for which he created numerous headings, including the rubric *An den Rand der Sozialwissenschaften* (On the margins of the social sciences). However, the writings burgeoning in the notebooks outstripped all the rubrics Steiner created to contain them; a strange atmosphere of 'distracted concentration' reigns, which only occasionally breaks out of the lyrical, religious or scientific framework of exercises and commentaries, but nonetheless transforms their constraints into something playful and speculative.

In what follows I track one train of thought in Franz Baermann Steiner's socio-anthropological writings and unpublished notes: 'Transformation and Identification'.[1] The trail leads from a socio-anthropological principle to dif-

---

[1] Steiner's unpublished notations in his original loose-leaf binders are kept at the Deutsches Literaturarchiv in Marbach, Germany. I have followed the (varied) numbering he used in his notebooks (year–month–number), but have not hesitated to resolve some of his abbreviations.

ferent and irreconcilable genealogies of European anthropological theories and of being a 'privileged outsider'; it drops in on a memorial to a friendship and visits the ruins and building plans of Steiner's methodological reflection. And every passage – from one place to the next, from one text to another – will contain something speculative and aberrant that competes with the speculation and aberrance of Steiner's thought. In short, at issue are genuine *disiecta membra poetae* that can be spelled out and pieced together only in terms of such an improbable, if not impossible journey.

I.

During the decisive phase in his work which led to his dissertation, and after his visit to the International Congress of Ethnology in Brussels in August 1948, Steiner composed the following note that was indubitably written 'on the margins of the social sciences', since it claims to formulate neither more nor less than the 'chief sociological principle':

> The chief sociological principle is probably this: that no individual can have a position *(eine Stelle)* without identifying him/herself with something and that there is no identification without transformation. The need for identification is primary. This is the chief difference between human and animal social forms of association. The 'I' of human society is at the apex of a triangle whose other points are called 'communication' and 'identification'. The sides adjacent to the I-point are called 'language' and 'transformation'. The circle surrounding the triangle is 'society' – in its metaphysical sense. (48 IX 19)

The notation is divided into two parts.[2] It situates the 'chief sociological principle' between transformation and identification, and then draws a triangle into one 'side' of which it incorporates this principle. The 'chief principle' is itself characterized by a strange tension that might even be considered as an-

---

[2] A brief comment on the edition of 48 IX 19 and a correction of the English version in volume II of Steiner's *Selected Writings* (p. 240). The notation 48 IX 19 has the peculiarity of merging two parts. One '48 IX 19' sheet of paper notes: 'The chief sociolog. principle is probably this: that no individual can have a position without identifying him/herself with something and that there is no identification without transformation. The need for identific. is primary. This is the chief difference betw. human and animal social forms of association. The 'I' of human society is one point of a triangle whose other points are called 'communication' and 'identification'. The circle surrounding the triangle is 'society' – in its metaphysical sense.' On the reverse side of the preceding sheet (on the left) is written 'for 48 IX 19': 'whose other points are called communication and identification. The sides adjacent to the I-point are language and transformation. The circle surrounding the triangle is ...' This (in all probability) is a correction via the insertion of 'for 48 IX 19' into the relevant sentences of '48 IX 19'.

tinomy. Steiner writes that in order to have 'a position' or a 'status' (*eine Stelle*), the need for identification is primary; but it is also the case that 'there is no identification without transformation'. Which then is 'primary'? And are they identical? Similar questions are raised by the diagram Steiner describes. Jeremy Adler and Richard Fardon have pointed out that such a triangle within a circle, which draws a microcosm in a macrocosm, has its origins in the cabbalist literature of the Renaissance (SWII: 87). And when you draw the triangle with three sides, the two sides from I to Communication and from I to Identification are depicted as paths towards (social) goals at two of the triangle's corners, without their being determinable via these points. Elementary geometry turns into allegory, and geometrical-allegorical questions arise that call for an answer. A further notation – following immediately after this draft – tries to spell out some of these questions:

No transformation is conceivable without prior identification. The goal of transformation is thus communicable, lies within language. The process of transformation is only indirectly language-related – via the goal that it points to (*das er meint*), but that goal does not interpret this process (*das ihn aber nicht deutet*). The mythical occurrence is a transformation completely expressible through identifications, that is, it may be conjured through language. As such it is not irrational, but the series of mythic transformations are the quasi-rational organizing principles of all non-communicable series, i. e., of the entire chaotic transformative potential of the human universe. (48 IX 20)

We could read the beginning of this notation as reinforcing the wish to prove identification is 'primary' and thus resolve the antinomy between identification and transformation, were it not that, in the attempt to extract maximal coherence from the geometrical-allegorical reading of the triangle, transformation returns through the back door as something even more 'primary'. The side of the triangle described in the first notation as Transformation may be drawn (geometrically), indirectly but completely, via the two other sides, as well as through their three corners/end points: I, Communication, and Identification. In this way Steiner gains a new dimension, 'mythical occurrence', a counterpart of this indirect but complete designation: 'The process of transformation is only indirectly language-related – via the goal that it points to (*das er meint*), but the goal does not interpret this process (*das ihn aber nicht deutet*). The mythical occurrence is a transformation completely expressible through identifications, that is, it may be conjured through language.'

It is precisely the 'communicability' of the mythic occurrence, however, that allows it to appear merely as a figure against the background of the non-communicable: 'the entire chaotic transformative potential of the human universe'. (Other notations indicate that this 'transformative potential' also entails the potential for metamorphosis portrayed in myths.) Here too, transformation is not completely subsumed under identification and the communicability of identities; the goal of the transformation process 'does not interpret it'. Therefore the question still remains: in what does the 'prior identification' of every transformation consist? On the formulations of both notations, the relationship between 'transformation' and 'identification' has a certain fragility if not to say antinomy.

It is notable that the second notation may be deciphered – as I have here – with the help of the diagram depicted in the first notation, however this triangle is not even mentioned in the second notation. We may assume that some of Franz Baermann Steiner's most exciting and mysterious aphorisms and drafts were written exactly like this: stemming from a playful 'axiomatics' and its conscious blurring.

II.

'Transformation' is one of the keywords in this notation, and initially it presents a riddle. How can the relationship between 'transformation' and 'identification' lead to a *sociological* principle? Some clarification of this question may be found – not in Steiner's notations where, so far as I can tell, 'transformation' is never subjected to a definition or clarification, but from his lectures on 'taboo', published posthumously by Laura Bohannan (1956), where Steiner states of Arnold van Gennep:

> He concerns himself with ritual behaviour occasioned by passing from one social status to another and from one age or relationship to another. He shows us the eternal pattern of transformation, of becoming, in which the stage *before* transformation and the one *after* are socially recognised, safeguarded, and protected. The passage over the border itself, however, is unrelated to such safeguards and lies in a sphere of danger. In passing through, and even in enacting, these dangers, various ritual abstentions are observed, and in this context one suddenly discovers that the greater number of taboos are indeed concerned with the various delimitations of our spheres and boundaries, our time spans and our experiences. Taboos are concerned with the passing of things into the body and out of it; they guard the body's orifices. Taboos control such changes as the passage to a strange or alien setting from a familiar one. One aspect of taboo undoubtedly consists in providing an idiom for the description of everything that matters in terms, quite literally, of transgression; of passing, that is, from inside-outside the individual's rights or competence. (SWI: 189)

The theory of taboo that Steiner outlines here, following van Gennep (*Rites de Passage*, 1909), places transformation in a framework that is as well-known as it is infinitely refinable: that of the *rites de passage* which ritually shape initiation. 'He shows us the eternal pattern of transformation.' Van Gennep gave Steiner a cogent explanation why transformation itself – or, at least, its central stage (*'marge'*) – must make do without the safeguards of social 'identification', which classify and protect those undergoing initiation both before and after their change of status. The protection furnished persons exposed to danger during the process of initiation consists in ritual abstentions, such as prohibitions on eating, looking, touching, speaking, and communication.

Steiner's lecture offered only a short exegesis of van Gennep's key work; however, Steiner subsequently transfers van Gennep's theory to all abstentions and taboos, stating that most taboos have to do 'with an analogous passage': that they create 'delimitations' insofar as they devise, in the form of abstentions, the means by which delimitations may be overcome. The theory of 'transformation' and the theory of 'taboo' are conjoined at this point, and out of this conjunction another term emerges that is meant to deal with both aspects: 'transgression', a word that Steiner will take up once more near the end of his lectures.

In using van Gennep's phrase *rites de passage*, Steiner both refers us back to the entire history of ethnology leading to Lafitau's origination of the comparative term of 'initiation', and also points towards the future importance of the idea of the threshold, or *'marge'*, as a zone of danger for anyone undergoing initiation. This is the notion Victor Turner was to take up in his later coinage as 'liminality';[3] and in Turner's version liminality might well encompass what Steiner described as 'the entire chaotic transformative potential of the human universe'. If Steiner here subscribes to van Gennep's own claim – 'He shows us the eternal pattern of transformation' – we should neither forget Frazer's question concerning the setting up of death experiences during initiation,[4] nor Robert Hertz's study of the 'double burial',[5] in depiction of which, he already employed the concept and term 'passage' in a way that van Gennep was able to adopt. If we choose to read such over-determination by the history of ethnological terminology into Steiner's notations – and to do so is questionable,

[3] Victor Turner, *Ritual Process: Structure and anti-structure* (Ithaca, New York: Cornell University Press, 1969).
[4] James Frazer, *The Golden Bough*, abridged version in one volume (London: Macmillan, 1922), pp. 694–701.
[5] Robert Hertz, 'A contribution to the study of the collective representation of death', in *Death and the Right Hand*, ed. by R. Hertz (Aberdeen: Cohen and West, 1960 [1907]), pp. 27–86.

because it reduces their polyphony to a single melody – we will find others of Steiner's sentences in which 'transformation' seems to correspond to van Gennep's 'passage', such as the following:

> Dying is the greatest transformation. Whoever has experienced it, must think of death at every transformation. (48 V 6)

> To know yourself, you must first be introduced to yourself. This is either a very ceremonial or a very painful affair. (47 XI 111)

III.

Steiner's 'taboo' lectures served to examine the history of ethnological theory, but above all they prepared a way for his own sociological 'theory of danger'. The short commentary on van Gennep made explicit where theoretical consideration of 'transformation' and 'danger' must converge: in the *'marge'*, in those intervals and thresholds of all passages when social safeguards are (necessarily) suspended. At this point, the theory of danger comprises a theory of 'transformation'; and the question still to be asked is how far the characterization of *'marge'* spills over into the total constitution of Steiner's theory of danger. At the same time, we can (if we bring the 'chief principle' from 1948 together with the commentary on van Gennep) make a plausible case that the issue concerning an individual's 'position' is 'status', and 'that there is no identification without transformation' because every conferment of a position, every 'awarding of status' requires an initiation process (by a group or by a group's self-recruitment). Such a reading makes more credible the assertion that what was and is at issue in the relationship between 'transformation and identification' is indeed a 'sociological principle'. But can Steiner's wish for such a link between anthropology and sociology be realized at all other than within the unsorted series of his notations? How did his wish become scientifically fruitful? And can the 'chief sociological principle' (48 IX 19) be applied to the analysis of social phenomena?

The key to these questions, it seems to me, lies hidden in the project of his second main work, in the unrealized complete dissertation on slavery of which he left only a torso. As Adler and Fardon have stated, Steiner gave up his original plan of a worldwide comparative exposition of the institutions of slavery at the end of the 1940s (SWII: 28–38). What replaced it was largely an analysis that one could call *ex negativo*: the attempt to end the impossible task of a worldwide comparison by a trick – at once a shortcut and a detour. In place of the 'servile institutions' that he had originally wanted to (and would have) set at the centre of his thesis, Steiner placed the depiction of institutions

that he called 'pre-servile'. The point of this manoeuvre was to reveal the social difference, the criterion, that distinguishes institutions of slavery from institutions of non-slavery ('the difference that makes a difference'):

> By investigating 'pre-servile' institutions, Steiner develops his analysis of
> the social conditions under which enduringly servile relations might, or
> might not, be institutionalised. [...] In purely typological terms, pre-servile
> institutions are anterior because the inequalities on which they rest are rou-
> tinely overturned; servile institutions surmount these subversions with the
> effect that inequalities are permanently entrenched. (Adler and Fardon,
> SWII, 32)

This procedure *ex negativo* was oriented especially towards the following
problem. In societies that define their elementary units by family membership,
'The slave is a kinless person'.[6] How does it happen in such societies that individuals *without* family membership may be so integrated that slavery does
not ensue and a form of dependency analogous to slavery is recurrently
averted? The second (and thus central) part of Steiner's dissertation is dedicated solely to this problem: 'The Apportionment of Detached Persons in Pre-
Servile Relationships and Institutions'. The issue addressed here concerns elementary processes of the social: the 'detachment' and 'attachment' of the kinless, of widows, orphans, outcasts, prisoners of war, the shipwrecked, the exiled, and seekers after sanctuary, in short the internal and external borders of
a society that defines itself through kinship. More precisely, the thresholds of
these statuses may be mapped only through the re-enactment of processes:
'the processes inherent in the societies by which people become detached from
their kinship groups and attached, on different terms, to others' (p. 76).

How does someone become kinless within their own society, or ensnared
into another society where they have no kin? What status are they then given,
and how does this occur? The mechanisms of 'status change' appear here as
prior to status itself, and so it is not coincidental that Steiner's terminology
might serve as a translation of van Gennep's: 'detachment' for *'séparation'*, 'attachment' for *'agrégation'*. On one occasion, Steiner characterizes *'marge'* as
just that no-man's-land with which Gennep's *rites de passage* also begins: 'As
soon as the man finds himself severed from his clan, he is situated in a social
no-man's-land, a space which is not structured by clan life and by clan
spheres' (p. 263). While van Gennep's book concentrated on the ritual composition of passage, Steiner is interested in the total social process by which an

---

[6] Franz Baermann Steiner, 'A Comparative Study of the Forms of Slavery' (D. Phil thesis,
Magdalen College, University of Oxford, 1949), p. 76. Here quoted from the examiners'
copy held in the Deutsches Literaturarchiv, Marbach; further references appear in the text.

elementary social 'alienation' (i. e., kinlessness) arises and is either resolved or maintained. Appropriate *rites de passage* would constitute one part of these processes, and in fact some of the mechanisms Steiner describes are nothing but elaborated *rites de passage*.

The second part of Steiner's dissertation – read in this way – explores the putting into effect of the axiom 'that no individual can have a status without identifying him/herself with something and that there is no identification without transformation'. In a society that defines itself in terms of kinship units, the individual without kinship has no status, cannot identify him/herself with anything (cannot be identified, indeed has become unidentifiable), and therefore stands in need of social and ritual transformation. I cannot claim that this way of reading Steiner resolves the entire thesis, which is a rabbit warren with several entrances and variously interlocked main and subordinate themes. Of these, without doubt the most important remains the whole question of the 'structure' of inequality which, even in so fragmentary a state, offers a persuasive complement to the social anthropological theory of institutions of equality and mutuality in segmentary societies. The four institutions of inequality Steiner called Class, Caste, Rank, and Servile Institutions (including Slavery proper). The proposed (never completed) thesis would scrutinize all their essential compatibilities and incompatibilities (Adler and Fardon, SWII: 37).

However, in another tunnel of this warren, where a programmatic debate is carried on with Steiner's teacher Radcliffe-Brown, it becomes apparent how important to the dissertation are questions of status change.[7] Steiner argues for a distinction between the question of 'status relationships' arfd questions of economic inequality (p. 137), but he also holds that status relationships are not simply identifiable with 'jural relationships as connoting rights and duties'. He reasons that,

> We have to deal with persons changing their status according to rules which would be difficult to define in terms of rights and duties. Society can be perceived as a static system and then the relations between the individuals can be seen in such jural terms. The most uncompromising statement of such an approach is given by Radcliffe-Brown where he proposes to deal

---

[7] As is well-known, a rift occurred within Oxford's Institute of Social Anthropology at the end of the 1940s between the two main protagonists Radcliffe-Brown and Evans-Pritchard; Adler and Fardon rightly indicate that the public debate, at least, was conducted below the scholarly standards of both sides (SWII: 38–46). It is therefore helpful to look at Steiner's dissertation for a scholarly explanation of this break, in a manuscript that was forced to address both opponents as readers and reviewers. Since the Radcliffe-Brown discussion in the dissertation – contrary to that in the 'taboo' lectures – has remained mostly unknown, I will quote it in greater detail.

with the most general principles conceivable – he calls them sociological laws – in terms of rights and duties.
The sociological laws (he says) i. e. the necessary conditions of existence of a society [...] are:

1. The need for a formulation of rights over persons and things sufficiently precise in their general recognition as to avoid as far as possible unresolvable conflicts,
2. The need for continuity of the social structure as a system of relations between persons, such relations being definable in terms of rights and duties.

But we may very soon find ourselves investigating kinds of rights that can be exercised over a person while other rights are active, and we may find that the question of compatibility of rights is answered differently in various social structures. General propositions about these types of compatibility cannot be made in terms of rights and duties, though they are undoubtedly relevant to the study of social structure.
To this could be answered that Radcliffe-Brown's definition does not imply that there is only one type of social structure in existence, and that in my remark I merely maintained that there are several types.
This could be accepted as relevant if

1. it can be shown that variations of the compatibility of rights are variations of the same structural principle, and
2. that the range of these variations can be deduced from the nature of the jural relationships.

I intend to make it plausible that this may not be the case, and that, to speak on the same level of abstraction, there may be a relation between the kinds of status mobility and the kinds of compatibility of jural relationships. (pp. 139–140.)

This is a case of one claim against a counter-claim, of a Euclidean versus a non-Euclidean version of 'social structure': Radcliffe-Brown's sociological principle (or 'law') that assumes the priority of one single 'jural' structure and derives social variations from it, versus another 'chief sociological principle', as outlined by Steiner, that recommends the priority of a systematic 'correlation', namely a 'relation between the kinds of status mobility and the kinds of compatibility of jural relationships', still in need of a plausible explanation. This correlation is what first constitutes the 'status relations' and also allows the diversity of jural terminology itself to be evaluated.

What might serve as the touchstone of such a criticism of Radcliffe-Brown's axiom? Steiner takes Radcliffe-Brown's own formulation as the most important touchstone: 'The need for a formulation of rights over persons and things sufficiently precise in their *general recognition* as to avoid as far as possible un-resolvable conflicts.' Instead of postulating general recognition of particular jural statuses (defined in terms of rights and duties) in a given society, Steiner starts out from the assumption that there remain 'possible unresolvable conflicts' in every attribution of social status. This assumption disrupts Radcliffe-Brown's static, jural social picture by making processes of 'status mobility' central to the analysis, for only when these are studied does it become clear in dynamic terms how compatible or incompatible are jural relations.

Thus, several sections of the thesis are devoted to the presentation of evidence that even where a 'status' within a society is generally recognized (that is to say is attributed to a person by members of all social units and, therefore, has what Steiner calls, a 'total social range') that status may nonetheless be split: a duality that no purely jural terminology can encompass but which becomes understandable only when a person's integration ('attachment') is simultaneously taken into account.

Furthermore, Steiner devotes attention throughout his dissertation to 'jural pluralism' in non-European societies which is not amenable to depiction in terms of a 'general recognition' of a well-defined 'status of rights': 'it is an erroneous presupposition that jural relationships *throughout* the society must be consistent; they may be as inconsistent as religious attitudes' (158). The 'totalitarian' picture of a 'primitive society' throughout which a single jural terminology is applied, as Durkheim's school and others had suggested, is in Steiner's view outmoded. That view is to be replaced by observation of the processes of 'status mobility' and of the degrees of consistency and inconsistency amongst the different statuses that may apply to the same person. For Steiner, observations of status mobility and of personal status sets were, as my earlier quotation suggested, aspects of the same phenomenon, namely a correlation of relationships or, we could say, the 'structure' of status relationships. The clearest proof of any priority within this correlation (between 'status mobility' and 'compatibility of status') appears to Steiner in the evidence that a single process of 'attachment', a single 'passage', can eventuate in a dual status. The absence of 'total social range' of a status attribution also means the splitting of the person.

I quote two of these processes at some length because they reveal a theorist convinced that he had identified a whole category of phenomena (and this within elementary 'institutions of alienation', of hospitality and slavery, of asylum and the integration of foreigners) which had previously remained inaccessible to convincing sociological (and non-jural) inquiry.

According to Steiner's definition, a status has 'total social range' if, and only if, it is recognized in all social units (from the individual household to the society), and 'total social range' is a necessary element of the definition of slavery proper (pp. 74–79). If a status produces subordination within the household but has, for instance, no effect upon the marriageability of a woman, then we must 'speak of two statuses, one referring to society as a whole, the other to the rank order within her home group'; the subordination in question lacks 'total social range' (p. 79). This doubling of statuses potentially puts the slave in a complex position: his 'attachment' to the household lends him a familiar status in terms of which an outsider referring to him as 'slave' risks insulting the household group:

The conception of the range of inequality viz. that of the two statuses, is relevant to our inquiry for yet another reason. The authority structure of a household, or what we call the smallest territorial unit, has to follow a different logical model from those underlying the rank order in a society. In the first case the rank order does not allow for duplication of status and the concomitant structural opposition, which is all important in a larger social framework. The family which identifies itself with a household ranges its members according to sex and seniority; if the unit is polygamous, the seniority of the various wives is taken into account. The relation of the members is such that it can be recognised in terms of a single scale of authority or gradation. This can be expressed by two axioms:
1. The gradation is identified within the group, the associated persons referring to each other and to their association in terms of the gradation.
2. Contacts of certain kinds between the graded group and other individuals take place in terms of that gradation or scale of internal authority.
The latter point is decisive when a person who is not a member of the family pays them a formal visit, or when a person is attached to the household without being a member of the family. Then the relationship is established in such a way that the cohesion of the scale remains unbroken. The new person cannot be treated as ranking, say, between father and elder brother, or elder and younger brother; nor can he remain, strictly speaking, outside the scale. The rank is given in terms of the projection of the scale; the newcomer ranges either above the pater, which is the formal treatment of the 'honoured guest', or below the youngest child, when he is attached to the household as a servile member. The stricter the rank order is observed in the family, the less it is possible to place the honoured guest otherwise than above the family rank.
Servile persons attached to a household very often have a dual status. The degree of intimacy they enjoy in the household and the fixed place they accordingly hold in the authority structure of the household group cannot be reconciled with their status in the society as a whole. In a study of this kind, our interest lies not in effecting a reconciliation, but rather in showing

the divergent principles involved. The quick advancement of a slave to leading roles in the family to which he is attached, unrelated to his low social status, is a feature which often has been remarked. Another is the resentment shown by servile persons (and even by their masters) when they are addressed to their social rank. 'Slave' then is a word of insult – to the slave when he appreciates his position in terms of the household to which he belongs. (pp. 81–82)

This line of argument is quite paradoxical; a society contains paradoxes, irreconcilable contradictions, but 'our interest lies not in effecting this reconciliation'. The greater the likelihood that the structure of authority internal to the family cannot provide a dual status (the less it allows anything but higher or lower ranking), the easier it is for a 'dual status' to arise *between* the household and the general society, through the integration of a stranger (in his/her 'attachment' or 'passage').

The 'law of hospitality' generates 'privileged outsiders' by means of a logic Steiner illustrates with his own diagrams at the quoted place (p. 80a). These 'privileged outsiders' are the focus of other passages in the thesis that deal with 'dual status' or status split. Elsewhere the study of such a duality turns into a regular literary ethnology, a social anthropology, that is mirrored in an epic of attachment and detachment. Whereas the marginal/pivotal figure of the kinless slave raises his status within the household, the marginal/pivotal figure of the raised kinless hero leads to his constantly threatened fall from his irreconcilable statuses:

There may be a great discrepancy between a person's status in regard to a specific action in which he takes a dominant part, and the status he enjoys as a member of the respective society in terms of the solidarity which groups of that society are or should be obliged to extend to him. As in simpler societies these solidarity groups are secured by an individual's kinship ties; we find in many a myth or tale of oral literature the theme developed of the man who is esteemed for his personal prowess but at the same time, being a stranger, a person without kin in that society, is unable to overcome his isolation; the honours heaped on him by the king or paramount chief cannot make up for the lack of that solidarity which only kinship can command.

This discrepancy is shown perhaps most poignantly in the terrible climax of Er Taghyn, a Kirgis epic, that jewel of oral literature which Radloff has preserved for us. Er Taghyn, a hero in the truly epic fashion who slays whole armies single-handed, has lost touch with his tribe and serves as war leader under foreign chieftains. He is a great man as long as he is in charge of his warriors, or more precisely, as long as the warriors are in action.

Once, after a great battle in which his leadership and bravery again had saved the tribe, he climbs a tree to make sure how many of the hostile force have managed to escape. While his victorious men are dispersing he falls from the tree. He has injured only the muscles of his back, but this makes it impossible for him to get up unaided. He calls for help but after the battle his authority over the men is ended, and nobody turns back; nobody is obliged to listen to his call, only his horse remains obedient. Thus he has to resign himself to impotence and death, and at the same time the hero of the day and the underdog of tribal society, he starts that terrifying monologue, cursing human society and futile ambitions. (pp. 144–145)[8]

IV.

How does Steiner explain this equally sociological and literary theme of dual status? One answer to this question leads to a more exact evaluation of the sociological method Steiner had advocated since the conception of his thesis (but, as I see it, not before this conception in 1948) and which he repeatedly demonstrates both in the thesis and in his later lectures and drafts.

The remarks on dual status have one principle in common, which Steiner defines, shortly after Er Taghyn's monologue:

In all structures which are based on or evolved from the familial pattern, the person wielding authority and the persons committed to actions of solidarity are not necessarily the same. (p. 149)

It is thus in the course of the elementary processes of social integration of strangers, of the attachment of the kinless, that duality arises, for instance when the issue involved is the integration of orphans or of those rescued from fatal danger.

On the whole, authority structure and solidarity groups which are involved in one relationship of the above two types, are never identical, or completely overlapping, but interdependent. (p. 149)

---

[8] Steiner here follows: W. Radloff, *Proben aus der Volksliteratur der türkischen Stämme Süd-Sibiriens, Teil III: Kirgische Mundarten* (St. Petersburg: [n. publ.], 1870), pp. 153–154. And he ends this paragraph with a comment: 'Thinking of Aristotle's famous words: "The man who is isolated – who is unable to share in the benefits of political association, or has no need to share because he is already self-sufficient – is no part of the *polis*, and must therefore be either a beast or a god." – we may say that the epic negates the alternative: the hero is both, beast and god ...' Steiner's friend Julian Pitt-Rivers later continued work on the 'paradoxes of the stranger', especially in his *The Fate of Shechem* (Cambridge: Cambridge University Press, 1977), pp. 94–112 ('The Law of Hospitality').

This distinction between the 'authority structure' and 'solidarity group' prevailing among people who nonetheless belong to a single group (especially a household group) is a general theme of Steiner's social anthropology. Shortly after completing his thesis, Steiner made a notation that generalizes this question: 'Probably the chief problem of sociology would consist of explaining why authority structures and solidarity groups never completely tally' (49 V 19). And later, in his lectures on kinship, Steiner asserts that these two must coincide in a household, and then concludes by returning to the theme of hospitality (already familiar to us from his thesis):

> The domestic group combines the authority structure of the family and the institutionalised regulations concerning the division of labour, and a discrepancy between the two is impossible. Thus when people are added (as inmates) to the household, this is done in terms of the existing authority structure of the family group dominant in that household (whether as co-familiar, honoured guest or servant). Established servants may be 'treated as members of the family'. (SWII: 199–200)

The thesis's other reflections on dual status also touch on this dual principle of a 'distinction/overlapping' between authority structure and solidarity group. Er Taghyn falls through a momentary, but necessary, crack in the overlap between the two; the slave experiences potential solidarity in the household precisely because he cannot belong to the family, and only then is he 'treated like a member of the family'. Put differently, a social unit is broken down into two groups of relations (in this case, the relations of the authority structure and those of the solidarity group), and by means of this break-up it is made clear both that these two groups of relationships must coincide and that they nonetheless contain irreconcilable (mutually incompatible) principles which, through a single process of integration (that of attachment) can and must lead to particular splits (that stem, however, not from a psychological, but from a social, basis). Such an analysis proposes exactly what Steiner maintained against Radcliffe-Brown: the priority of 'a relation between the kinds of status mobility and the kinds of compatibility of jural relationships'.

Steiner found precedents for his analysis not so much in contemporary sociologists or ethnologists but in Aristotle. It remains doubly remarkable that during work on his thesis Steiner rediscovered Aristotle as a sociologist and, from his reading of Aristotle, adopted not only a basic theory of the ancient 'household', but also what could be called his method. Aristotle writes in the first book of *Politics*: 'every subject of inquiry should first be examined in its simplest elements; and the primary and simplest elements of the household are the connection of master and slave, that of the husband and wife, and that of parents and children.'[9] Steiner takes over and refines this resolution (*analysis*) of the ancient term *oikos* into its elementary relations and develops from this a basic reflection on 'potestal change', that is to say on the attachment of the kinless and on the consistency and inconsistency of these integration processes, but also – somewhat aphoristically – on the worldwide comparison of types of slavery. His later lecture on 'Aristotle's Sociology' characterizes the method of this part of the text as follows:

> And this seems to have been Aristotle's concern: to distinguish kinds of social relationships and to explain social units and institutions as combinations of relationships. The isolating of kinds of relationships is the work of abstract reasoning which, however, does not involve motives or other psychological constructs; the interrelating of various kinds of social units is a straightforward affair of everyday observation and commonsensical generalisations. (SWII: 202)

This characterization strikes me as also applicable to the method Steiner followed from his thesis onwards: to break down social units and institutions into combinations of relations and then to put them together again. The essential step taken here is not an inductive one and is not oriented towards specific phenomena: 'The isolating of kinds of relationships is the work of abstract reasoning.' This step does not immediately stem from a comparative viewpoint, at least it does not compare societies. Steiner differentiates accordingly (in his review of George Murdock's *Social Structure* [1949]) between four fields of sociology and, *en passant*, dissolves social anthropology in terms of a more subtle distinction: 'Instead of talking of Social Anthropology, a simple distinction could be made between analytical and descriptive sociology on the one hand and comparative and general sociology on the other' (Adler and Fardon, SWII: 45). A notation explains this distinction according to a division of tasks: 'Descriptive sociology treats societies. Analytical sociology treats structures. Comparative sociology treats systems' (50 III 106; SWII: 242).

I am tempted to generalize that the entirety of Steiner's socio-anthropological writings, theoretical drafts, or theorems from the time of his thesis – whether fragmentary or comprehensive – ask first about structure and are pre-eminently therefore analytical sociology. Steiner ranges comparatively and descriptively only after putting in place the prerequisite of a structural analysis that enables him to compare systems and describe societies. The method

---

[9] The 'Discourse on the Aristotelian theory of slavery' is quoted here (based on a copy in the Deutsches Literaturarchiv, Marbach) from an unpublished abridgement of the thesis by Paul Bohannan: 'A Prolegomena to a Comparative Study of the Forms of Slavery' (1957): pp. 177–194, (p. 178). In the original thesis, this digression is found at the end of the second of three parts, in Bohannan's version at the end.

remains the same whether it is applied to taboo (or social 'danger'), or truth in general and 'Chagga truth' (SWI: 244–250) particularly, or economic transactions and work, or (in the dissertation) servility and the status of a caste. A unit or institution is broken down into two or more groups of relationships that coincide within it. Description then shows – by analysing processes of attachment and detachment – both the consistencies and irreconcilable contradictions within the unit, which only then can be understood as a social structure, that is in terms of relationships, and not in psychological terms.

The significance of Steiner's use of the term 'structure' is not readily understandable today, now that structuralism and post-structuralism lie between his drafts and the present, with the widespread acceptance, on the precedent of linguistics, of the priority of 'structure' (the invariant relation of relationships) over variations in single relations (and any of their respective interchangeable elements). Steiner's structure also deals with the relation of relationships; there is no contradiction here with either structuralism that was contemporary to him or to later structuralist argument. However, Steiner's 'structure' remains an entirely hermeneutic structure, that is a structure which does not claim the existence of 'something' prior to its own analysis: Aristotle only explains 'relationships in the case of which he is aware of his dealing with abstractions he created' (SWII: 203). And the whole point of Steiner's 'structure' is exactly the fact (and this would seem completely absurd to a later structuralist in search of 'invariant structures') that the 'same structure' can *never* be proved, and would contradict the goals of his analytical method. Thus a kind of writing on the wall for the entire terminology of 'structure and system' is found in his notations:

> The words 'structure' and 'system' should be used in sociology in such a way that one can speak of two very similar structures, but not of the same structure in two different societies. To the extent that a society is unique, its structure is also unique; the nature of the process – of generalisations, abbreviations, simplifications and abstractions – produces the structure of a social entity from the states of affairs prevailing within it. A structure never arises from comparison between phenomena. In 'structural sociology' we compare structures, not societies. The similarities may prove to be traits, or they may appear as systematically connected amongst themselves, so as to form a 'system'. Seen thus, various capitalist economies are particular instances of the capitalist system. A 'system' is at the same time a category (of structures) and the analytic symbol characteristic of that category, i.e. something which goes beyond the definition of the category itself. (50 III 17; SWII: 241)

V.

I have tried to make a plausible case that some – if not all – of Steiner's social anthropology subsequent to his thesis was dedicated to demonstrating relations between status changes and the consistency/inconsistency of a social system – 'a relation between the kinds of status mobility and the kinds of compatibility of jural relationships' – and that Steiner saw in this relation (of relationships) what we can and should call the unique 'structure' of a society. I cannot yet address Steiner's questioning of this 'structure' with all its idiosyncratic consequences and fragmentary reflections; here too Steiner's *mathesis universalis* remains unwritten and unexplained. But I would like at least to sketch how it was developed further in four of his manuscripts.

With help from the Aristotelian dissection of *oikos* (and ancient patriarchal authority) into its three social relations (master/slave, husband/wife, father/children), Steiner's thesis distinguished three corresponding forms of *potestas* (of the man as master, husband, father). Steiner confirmed the capacity of the *potestas* of the slaveholder to assimilate other forms of *potestas* in Greek-Roman antiquity, which was the model society for later occidental 'empires'. Proof for this conceptual and practical assimilation is not sought only under jural terminology, but in a 'relation between the kinds of status mobility and the kinds of compatibility of jural relationships'. Amongst other things, Steiner inquires of Roman antiquity, how is a slave set free? He is integrated into the clientage system of his former master as a kind of son.[10] A Roman soldier was not allowed to marry; how then did he become a father and a family head? Put otherwise, how was the incompatibility between being the 'son' (of the military) and his later marriage resolved? In this way Steiner examines the compatibilities and incompatibilities between the three forms of ancient *potestas*. By interrogating the relationship between the forms of status change particular to each form of *potestas* and the integrative capability of each jural status, he generalizes – rightly or wrongly – that within the Roman social system, which was the social system of the Empire, the patriarchal slave status served as a model for other social relationships or, in Steiner's terminology, the *potestas* of a master over his slave could 'assimilate' other relationships.[11]

---

[10] 'A Prolegomena', p. 184.
[11] 'From this we see that, not in the terms of a legal system but in practice, the case of the slave who could not conclude a legally valid marriage was one instance of a type,' and 'which of the three kinds is sufficiently dominant to assimilate others. In Greco-Roman society we saw this was the *potestas* exercised over the slave' ('A Prolegomena', p 190). 'The slave's inability to control and own is of the same kind as the inability of the Roman soldier to marry.' (p. 192)

As a kind of exercise, the dissertation was preceded by a philological, ethno-historical conjecture, which even more radically postulated the existence of a whole jural terminology from a single documented *rite de passage*. While within the thesis the passages of the freed slave, of the former vestal virgin, and of the demobilized Roman soldier were meant to demonstrate which forms of potestal change were at the base of their jural definition (so as to undermine and side-step the excessive Roman jurist vocabulary), Steiner's lecture on the 'Early Hebrew Lineage System' (SWI: 230–233) asks what specific jural terminology must be presupposed to have existed so that the rite of passage described in Genesis 47: 29–31 and 48: 1–16 with its legally binding symbolic operations can make sense. Here too, the train of argument proceeds from a 'relation between the kinds of status mobility and the kinds of compatibility of jural relationships' to the conjectured jural status of the participants before and after the jural rite (Jacob, Joseph, and their children and grandchildren). Only the plausible reconstruction of the specific rite of passage involved in the detachment and attachment of the children of a slave can provide convincing evidence both of Joseph's real status – as multiple split 'privileged outsider' – and of the entire 'structure' of the early Hebrew lineage system, its kinship, and lack of kinship.

These two interpretations inquire (comparatively) of specific systems and (descriptively) of specific societies of the past that – in the sense of the aphorism noted (50 III 17) – can be made accessible to interpretation only through the analysis of their unique structures. In the 'taboo' lectures, on the other hand, the accent lies on an extremely general 'structure' of social danger, on a structure that is so generally formulated that we must almost specify it as general sociology, even if – with the help of the single lectures – it does demonstrate local and unique structures (especially in chapters I-III, as well as IV-VII). Undoubtedly this ambition (setting an example of general sociology, understood as such by Mary Douglas) had to conflict with Steiner's obligation as a 'Lecturer' to present and comment on the texts of others.

So what does Steiner's general sociology consist of? A notation from 1950, following almost immediately after his division of four sociologies, contains the memorable distinction:

Social structure:
1. As an objective norm of typical social relations.
2. As an organic principle of linking and layering situations. (50 III 118; SWII: 242)

This distinction – another typical Steiner determination of structure involving the dismantling into different social relations that must be 'interlaced' even where they lead to irreconcilable consequences – is pretty opaque; it may seem impenetrable. However it is striking that the 'taboo' lectures distinguish quite analogously two functions or types of social relations that in the sociology of danger must also coincide:

> Social relations are describable in terms of danger; through contagion there is social participation in danger. And we find expressed in the same term[s], those of taboo, two quite separate social functions: (1) the classification and identification of transgressions (which is associated with, though it can be studied apart from, processes of social learning), and (2) the institutional localisation of danger, both by the specification of the dangerous and by the protection of society from endangered, and hence dangerous, persons. (SWI: 214; see also SWI: 188)

It is striking that this twofold division corresponds to what the notation distinguished as the (1) 'norm of typical relations' and the (2) 'principle of linking and layering situations', in other words the general division of social structure into (the relation of) two relationships. The 'norm of relations lies' (1) in the classification and identification of transgressions (e. g., ritual and/or illicit transgressions of the body's bounds in birth, menstruation, marriage, death). The 'principle of linking and layering situations' consists here (2) in the institutional localization of danger, such as the danger of 'infection' or 'pollution' by which an endangered person becomes dangerous for others, as Steiner repeatedly stresses, a constant danger that defines and links situations. Both parts of the social structure of danger – if we decide to call it such – can be depicted only through processes, namely those of the detachment and attachment of a person. The norm of typical social relations establishes which socially defined transgressions are within and which outside the norm and, among other things, this norm prescribes certain *rites de passage*. However, since Steiner endorses van Gennep's categorization, we must also claim the very opposite that each within-norm transgression must take the form of a *rite de passage*. And for (2) the principle of linking and layering situations, Steiner notes (and does so in line with William Robertson Smith) exactly that process of an 'infection' by which the endangered become dangerous, that is their attachment within a localization of danger results in the need to isolate them from the group and keep them under control, entailing their detachment. And this procedure too can hardly be characterized otherwise than the practical realization of a 'transformation and identification'.

To Steiner, these two functions of taboo relationships – (1) the norm of relations, and (2) the principle of situation formation – were not at all identical. Yet he maintained, 'We are dealing with two separate social functions; but as no society can afford to keep them separate, we find them expressed in the same terms' (SWI: 188). Why then Steiner's strange, even annoying insistence on separating them, at least for the purpose of analysing their structure? I can only speculate: what remains striking is that Steiner's theories subsequent to his dissertation were divided into a whole series of subdivisions/overlappings that we could just as well interpret – following good structuralist reasoning – as variations on a single duality: norm of relations versus principle of situation formation (of the social structure), classification of transgressions versus localization of danger (taboo customs), (household) authority structure versus (household) solidarity group, identification processes versus affirmation processes (of truth), or truth versus verification (of truth), 'the kinds of compatibility of jural relationships' versus 'the kinds of status mobility' (counter to Radcliffe-Brown), among others. We can understand all these dualities (or variations on one duality) as an attempt to replace a static jural structure by processes of integration and exclusion, of solidarity and its suspension – or by a consciously irreconcilable balance between a world of (dynamical) jural social norms and a world of situational (dis)placements – a *Lebenswelt*, so to speak.

A further – and last – radical attempt to establish the priority of procedures of transformation and identification is undoubtedly represented by Steiner's reflection on an alternative theory of economics. Here too a certain duality is recognizable, which corresponds to what he characterized as the duality of each social structure. Steiner himself defined economics as 'a system of production and distribution of units of value' (SWII: 161). His article on the 'Classification of Labour' (SWII: 174–180) can therefore be seen as a contribution to the question of production; and a cursory look reveals that his contribution is limited to a careful classification of work forms, a classification, however, that focusses on the 'principles of linking and layering situations'. What in most theories before Steiner appeared as a norm of typical social relations – the so-called 'division of labour' – is re-interpreted here as a principle of 'linking and layering situations'.

The 'Notes on Comparative Economics' (SWII: 160–173), on the other hand, are devoted to the distribution of 'units of value', but here predominant focus is on what Steiner called a 'translation' of units of value, one might also say – in accord with the ending of the taboo lectures – on a 'classification and identification of transgressions'. It would be presumptuous to want to summarize Steiner's portrayal of economic 'translations' which is already an extreme condensation of a general theory and hardly less ambitious than Mauss's 'Essai sur le don' (if for no other reason than because Steiner's draft replies to that of 'the gift' with almost underhand precision and subtlety). In studying the influence of Steiner's economic theory, we find striking proof of a relation between the economic 'translation' of units of value and the chief principle of transformation and identification. Adler and Fardon have characterized this relationship as follows:

Steiner's notion of 'translation' perhaps needs to be located somewhere between a strictly scientific concept on the one hand and Cannetti's affective concept of 'transformation' or 'metamorphosis' on the other, namely his key idea of *Verwandlung* – a German word Steiner also uses in similar contexts. (SWII: 51)

Paul Bohannan, the editor of the 'Notes on Comparative Economics', touched on this potential retranslation, for in his own article on the economics of the Tiv he writes, in reference to Steiner, 'I shall call those exchanges of items within a single category "conveyances" and those exchanges of items from one category to another "conversion".[12]

Steiner conferred questions of 'transformation' onto his concepts of economic transactions and called them 'translation'; Paul Bohannan rendered Steiner's 'translation' as 'conversion' so as to distinguish it from 'transactions' – his 'conveyances'. A close reading of the 'Notes on Comparative Economics' shows how far the 'translations' or 'conversions' of Steiner's units of value are especially about one transformation that gives rise to a world-wide series of identifications, namely sacrifice.

VI.

In the same year as his thoughts on economics, 1950, Steiner composed a longer notation, less a statement than an essay that he found important enough to re-write on the typewriter:

The curiosity of a child is expressed in two ways: it wants to know what is 'in' or 'under' and 'how something happens'. Even when the child is thoroughly familiar with how something functions and runs, driven by curiosity it still wants to take the thing apart. Even when it knows exactly the main circumstances of a process, exactly because it knows its sharply defined difference so well, it wants to observe the short connecting phases, wants to see how a new kind of coal turns to ashes, how a liquid turns to ice, how the dead bird lying on an anthill is reduced to a skeleton. Curiosity still consists of the two desires, to take apart and to be present, and these desires correspond to the still magically separated two categories of mystery: kernel and transformation.
The separation of these two kinds of mystery is demonstrated by one fact. The child does not expose something only to observe it: that would be ra-

---

[12] Paul Bohannan, 'Some principles of Exchange and Investment among the Tiv,' *American Anthropologist*, 57 (1955), 60–70 (p. 65).

tional research. The child can neither interrupt the process of disclosure and dissection as long as it is interested, nor does it want to intervene in a transformation that it observes. If this does happen, then it is not as part of the action, but in full awareness that a rule of the game has been badly overturned.

In this regard one regulation is noteworthy that results from the logic of magic: at the site of an initiation (*Einweihung*) – which is after all a ritually shaped transformation – a picture is not supposed to be revealed. An associated idea is that in times of transition, of transformation – such as a new moon or New Year's Eve – we can get a glimpse of the future. During such critical transformation points, nothing must be disclosed or interfered with. In this way it is already postulated psychologically that, during a transformation crisis, every disclosure, every look, concerns transformation itself. Thus, by a weakening of the basic experience, the time of peril can become directly suitable for a glimpse into the future. The farm maid, who hacks a hole in the ice on New Year's Eve and looks into the pond, sees the new year. Certainly the type of mystery that can be listened in on and the type that has to be disclosed cannot get any closer without coinciding and thus making room for the object of rational research.

Yet the development does not lead from a magical bipartite mystery to a unified object of rational research in order to stop there. The mature adult finds a new magic. He learns that intense, observant participation discloses and dissects him too. In observing a transformation he can be the one to break into pieces (*zu zerbröckeln*). Once again there is kernel and transformation, but the transformation takes place in the outside world and the kernel is within him. To know that these transformations and this kernel are the same, the last grand mystery – this is the new magic [...] And it is so exciting that any nostalgia for the infantile precursor quickly disappears [...] (50 III 37)

This 'essay on kernel and transformation' can be glossed in different ways. I will concentrate on those aspects in which this outline contains a kind of parable of (Steiner's) anthropology. There is an axiomatic-hermeneutic scheme that is also noticeable in Steiner's outline of economic translations. A dichotomy is set down, its application carried out, the dichotomy – according to its own game rules – deposed to another place or rather punctured, and then amazingly reversed or rather turned inside-out (here: from observed kernel to the kernel of the observer) so that it may end with a new identification – and at this point something like a promise appears (as in the economics draft). It seems to promise something practical, 'the new magic' – but this time too it seems to be, above all, about the good fortune of theory (Greek *theoria*), the promise of 'observing participation'.

The method of 'participant observation', of ethnographical field-work, from which Steiner felt himself painfully excluded during his years at Oxford, has undergone transcription here into an 'observing participation'. The 'last grand mystery' of this observing participation is – one could say – the *tat tvam asi* of anthropology itself: that subject and object are not separable in its research, and that they may therefore coincide in a 'kernel of transformations' and a 'transformation of the kernel' during the process of observation.[13]

The 'transformations' of this notation are quite explicitly what van Gennep encompassed in his *rites de passage*: initiation is the 'ritually shaped transformation', and 'transformations' or 'passages' are also all 'periods of transition', for example, the New Year. At the same time, the issue is the transition within a life cycle, the passage from child to mature adult, the passage from a childish to a mature 'magic'. The starting-point of this notation and its dissection of 'kernel and transformation' lies, however, not only in van Gennep's book but in a whole school of central European ethnology, and if you will, in the 'nostalgia for an infantile precursor'. Steiner was able to take over the dichotomy of kernel and transformation, as well as the whole question of a 'magic' empowered by 'transformation', in exactly this form from Leo Frobenius's *Kulturgeschichte Afrikas* (there is even a certain tone of imitation and mockery).[14]

However, one often finds repeated 'puncturing' of his own (always polemical) dichotomies in Frobenius, but never an 'inversion' such as Steiner performs here. Frobenius aligned himself throughout on the side of those cultures that he – whether rightly or not – identified with a preference for kernel and disclosure (for secret societies, masked terror, sacred royalty, hieratic emotions), and he painted the cultures of 'transformation' – at least in his *Kulturgeschichte Afrikas* – as the suspect carriers of an anti-hierarchical 'magic'.

---

[13] 'Now what we call Social Anthropology is empirical sociology par excellence: and the conundrum – what objectivity can there be in an enquiry where subject and object are identical: socially conditioned man and the social conditions of man? – that conundrum is solved by us as far as it can be solved at all: we are investigating kinds of social life quite different from the one which conditioned us.' (SWII: 216)

[14] See Leo Frobenius: *Kulturgeschichte Afrikas* (1933), here following the reprint of the 1954 edition (Wuppertal, 1993). See esp. pages 184–185, 286, 282, 302, and: 'it doesn't especially concern us where poetry takes its themes, its building material. What is crucial is which outlook is given expression, which outlook and which "principle". The principle is in both cases the forebear, the forefathers, and for these the resolute Ethiopianism never recognizes the transformation themes of magic – never! It recognizes only the simple appearance in nature, say, of the fruit, in which the kernel lies within a peel. For transformation – where magic speaks of a change in form – the poetry of mysticism cites "shedding skin". From primitive Ethiopia to the German fairytale.' (pp. 255–256)

Thus, we can speak of this 'essay on kernel and transformation' as a multiple and playful homage, and of a multiple 'invocation and exorcism' of Steiner's ethnologies, disguised as an essay on magic. And I believe that the question here is also one of a homage to Steiner's new way of thinking, that is, a certain self-homage – not for nothing is the name 'Steiner' invoked in the 'break-up' (*zerbröckeln*) of the observing 'kernel' and in the affirmation of this break-up as a sign of maturity. For, in fact, the fission of social structures through their transformations, their dualities and pluralisms and forms of 'status change' had become the actual field of work of Steiner's social anthropology. And Steiner had quite rightly been able to sense a clear affinity between his method of an analytical dissection of social structures and his preferred research object of 'fission through transformation', which he set apart from the reduction to a (scientific or jural) anthropological 'kernel'.

Steiner's affirmation of 'fission' – of terms, of society – was for him presumably also the affirmation of a principle that makes social life worth living. In another notation dated November 1948 Steiner presses on towards such a principle of living together by an interpretation of his name. Or, one might say, that it is an issue of living together that allows an interpretation of his name.

If you wanted to compare society with stone, then it would be possible to say of sociability: it only exists on the surface, on the plane of splits or fissures. The more fissures, or, as one says: the more easily split-able, the more sociability. (48 XI 144)

VII.

How do Steiner's efforts to understand transformation and identification compare to those of his friend Elias Canetti as expressed in the latter's theory, or series of stories, 'Die Verwandlung' (Transformation) in *Masse und Macht* (Crowds and Power, 1960)?[15] I shall mention Canetti's own homage to Steiner only briefly; it is a homage that has remained largely unnoticed. Although both the 'Notes on Comparative Economics' (which presented a theory about German inflation to compete with Canetti's) and *Taboo* had already been published, there is no mention of Steiner in the bibliography of *Masse und Macht*. Moreover, the word 'taboo' is never mentioned in *Masse und Macht*. Where similar phenomena are dealt with (for instance the word 'totem' is prominent),

---

[15] Elias Canetti: *Masse und Macht* (Munich: Carl Hanser, 1993 [1960]), pp. 395–455. Translations by the author and Jeanne Haunschild. Page references appear in the text.

taboo's place is taken by words like 'sparing' (Schonung, p. 423) and 'prohibition' or 'avoidance'. (One could almost say: the word taboo is avoided.)

And yet – at least so it seems to me – Steiner's name does appear in *Masse und Macht*, and just where it is required to appear: in the context of 'transformation' and between 'taboo' and 'slavery'. Here, Steiner's name intersects with Canetti's own name (in a double transcription that runs through both of their works). The literary memorial to a friendship, Steiner's and Canetti's, is in the transcription of the two names: stone and dog.

The last two headings in the chapter 'Die Verwandlung' are called 'Verwandlungsverbote' (transformation prohibitions) and 'Sklaverei' (slavery). The chapter 'Verwandlungsverbote' is framed by the Australian unity of mythical transformation (already called the 'transformations' of Dreamtime by Spencer and Gillen) and the ritual 'prohibition of their appropriation' (p. 449). What mediates between the mythical transformations and the prohibition of their appropriation are rites of passage, especially the transition from one age group to the next: 'It is possible only by way of special initiations, and these, however, are felt to be transformations in the actual sense of the word' (pp. 450–451). Canetti sketches a short comparative theory of the institutional link between transformation and transformation prohibitions. We could even translate this Canetti term into Steiner's: 'the classification and identification of transgressions' (SWI: 214).

For Canetti, the institutional apex of this type of prohibition is the Indian caste system:

Here membership in one caste absolutely excludes any social transformation. [...] The consequence of this system is astonishing; its exact study would make it possible to recognize all moments of social transformation. Since they must all be avoided, they are carefully registered, described and researched. The positive side-effect of such a system of complete prohibition is the fact that one could precisely deduce what makes up a transformation from one class into a higher one. 'A Study on Castes' from the standpoint of transformation is indispensable; it is overdue. (p. 451)

This project not only comes very close thematically to Steiner's own analysis of 'caste systems' in his thesis (which I cannot elaborate here), Canetti also adopts Steiner's method of studying institutional differences *ex negativo* (discussed above). That means exactly using 'the positive side-effect' of such 'institutionalized negations' to 'precisely deduce' what a specific system of prohibitions negates and how it can be overturned.

One can hardly call this a coincidence, so it is no surprise to learn that this chapter ends with a conceptual formula that brings together 'identification' with 'transformation prohibition' and with transformation itself. The story and the comparison take us back to Australia, to Canetti's 'totem', but via a South African book that played an important role in the friendship between Canetti and Steiner:

> It seems that exactly man's talent for transformation, the increasing fluidity of his nature,[16] was what disturbed him and made him reach out for firm and unchangeable restrictions. The fact that he felt on his own person so many strange signs – recall the knocking sounds of the Bushmen[17] – that he feared surrender to the alien and had to turn into it [...] had to awaken in him an urge for permanence and strictness, which could not be stilled without transformation prohibitions.
>
> In this context one tends to think of the stone economy[18] of the Australian aborigines. All the deeds and experiences, the fate and the wanderings of their ancestors have been absorbed by them into the land and become firm, unchangeable memorials. [...] In the external and monumental features of the country that remain immobile, many smaller stones participate, which are kept and saved for sacred places. Each of these stones is passed on from one generation to the next. It means something quite special: its meaning or its saga is bound to it; it is the visible expression of this saga. As long as the stone preserves its sameness, the saga does not change. In this concentration on the permanence of the stone, something here – and this is in no way alien to us – seems to me to express the same profound wish, to comprise the same necessity, which has led to all kinds of transformation prohibitions. (p. 453)

If this is a homage to Steiner, then – one might object – it is a very ambivalent and also defensive one. The theory of transformation prohibitions (or the classification and identification of transgressions) is here, as it were, invoked and exorcized. The very alienation experiences of hunters and gatherers (Bushmen and Australian aborigines) made them feel how important was the counterbalance of something that 'preserves its sameness', is identifiable and permanent. And these are the transformations: at once fluidity and stone. This em-

---

[16] The 'fluidity' of transformation and 'primitive mentality' in general is an essential – quasi-terminological – keyword of Lévy-Bruhl's; the association of metamorphoses and water is, however, obviously found in other interpretations of metamorphosis, e. g., in Jacob Burckhardt's *Griechische Kulturgeschichte* (2nd edn., 1898).

[17] This reference is based on Canetti's interpretation of 'Bushman Presentiments' from Bleek and Lloyd, *Specimens of Bushman Folklore* (1911).

[18] Shortly after this 'stone economy' – in a discussion of the connection between 'the division of labour' and slavery – Canetti mentions 'man's transformation household' (Verwandlungshaushalt, p. 441); and, herewith, almost all of Steiner's main topics are mentioned in one transcription: economics, prohibition, the division of labour, slavery, and transformation.

phasis on the durability of stone lacks the counterweight of a possible fission. But here Canetti does indeed approach, in his own way, Steiner's paradoxical way of thinking: only here – and this may be the one place that Canetti can be said to impute *sociological* realism to 'transformation' – only here in Australia (but by implication universally) are transformation and transformation prohibition one and the same, and thus coincide analytically. Invocations of 'transformation' are at the same time exorcisms; localizing and isolating transformation in stone, at the same time a protection against its dangers and a rendering of it conjurable from the stones. 'As long as the stone preserves its sameness', identification and dis-identification, group membership and localization, are so to speak two 'functions' of the unity between transformation and transformation prohibition, 'but as no society can afford to keep them separate, we find them expressed in the same terms' (SWI: 188).

Perhaps it is here – in Canetti's invocation of this 'stone age' of transformation – that we find not only a homage and memorial, but also a quotation from his discussions with Steiner:

The reflection on language is not complete if we don't seriously consider how people want to protect themselves by their words and surround themselves with the husks of communication, or, better, of ostensible communication. The French and Spanish cavemen probably protected themselves by painting, by objectification of, the animals they hunted, against an unavoidable identification with their prey, among which they constantly roamed, creeping up on them dressed in their pelts. Each of the paintings on the cave wall says: 'I *can* you, but *am* not you [Ich *kann* Dich, aber ich *bin* Dich nicht]. You are in me. But also outside of me. But you are not me. I push you to my periphery. You are that which I observe out of my mercy.' If we accept this occurrence, we cannot relate it only to painting. Are there not verbal configurations set up in speech that have just as little to do with communication as these paintings? Do such as these not have to exist? (48 XII 74)

(Translated by Jeanne Haunschild; revised by Richard Fardon)

THE DIALECTICS OF NAMING

Franz Baermann Steiner's Critical Engagement with Myth, Value, and Redemption

Michael Mack

I. VALUE

This essay discusses Steiner's critical stance toward themes and concepts which permeate his anthropological and literary work. My emphasis is on poems written by Steiner between 1940 and 1952. In his lyrical cycle *Eroberungen* (Conquests), in particular, Steiner seems to question the ethical and intellectual foundations of his anthropological and literary projects. This multi-faceted as well as fragmentary aspect of Steiner's oeuvre also unveils a refusal to fall prey to the temptation of a reductionist explanation of human existence. This is not to say that Steiner refrained from theorizing. On the contrary, he developed a complex sociology of danger. Steiner's sociology of danger presupposes the acknowledgement of an all-encompassing fact, namely, that value in a postlapsarian world cannot be conceived without its relation to danger. Value thus describes actions that help to alleviate suffering. In a letter to Georg Rapp, Steiner makes clear that 'suffering as such is not a value'. He defines value, however, as 'everything that contributes to the alleviation of suffering, everything which gives us strength to overcome suffering, everything which can make suffering cease' (SWII: 116). As anthropologist as well as poet Steiner attempts to come to terms with the dangerous that causes death and suffering. Apollo, the god of poetry, also practices medicine.

Anthropology, on the other hand, seems to be a value-free science. How can an anthropologist then presume to help alleviate suffering? Like his friends Elias Canetti and H. G. Adler, Steiner too rejects an understanding of science as being 'value-free'.[1] With Steiner, however, the term value has rather ironic

---

[1] For a discussion of Canett's and Steiner's critique of positivism see Michael Mack, *Anthropology as Memory. Elias Canetti's and Franz Baermann Steiner's Responses to the Shoah*, Conditio Judaica 34 (Tübingen: Niemeyer, 2001), pp. 149–157.

connotations. Does value not depend on suffering? Only a world in which suffering did not exist would therefore be truly value-free. Such a world, however, has not yet come into being. As a result, the human quest for knowledge cannot do without addressing issues related to 'value'. By analysing how value depends on suffering Steiner casts moral philosophy into a rather sober mode of thought. He in fact demolishes a German idealist divide between nature and freedom. Rather than conceptualizing 'value' as the overcoming of natural conditions, Steiner argues for protecting humanity's place in nature. This rather humble undertaking is more complex and difficult than it would seem to transcendental philosophers like Kant and Hegel.

Steiner was indeed cognizant of its complexity. Faced with the untold destruction of human life during the Second World War in general and the Nazi genocide in particular, he formulated a critique of civilization. In his aphoristic essay 'On the Process of Civilisation' (1944; SWII: 123–128), Steiner focuses on humanity's domination of nature. According to Steiner, by attempting to control natural dangers one actually extends them to the human sphere where their destructive potential intensifies within the course of 'history's progress'.

The term 'civilisation' thus describes 'the march of danger into the heart of creation' (SWII: 128). By rendering human society increasingly dangerous until it reaches the point where a single individual is able to exert the destructive power which it required societies to unleash in the past, the progress of civilization propels an increase in suffering. Humanity loses its place in nature. Steiner thus articulates his sense of despair vis-à-vis such blindness to humanity's self-destructive potential:

> Whoever recognises this [i. e. that 'the process of civilisation' is 'the march of danger into the heart of creation'] lives in the black night of despair, illuminated only by the star of a dual discipline:
> regarding man, who was created in His image;
> regarding society, whose boundaries are immutably set forth in the covenant. (SWII: 128)

The reference to a star, which illuminates Steiner's night of despair, might well include an allusion to Franz Rosenzweig's dazzling book *Der Stern der Erlösung* (The Star of Redemption, 1921). This study responds to the carnage perpetrated on the battlefields of the First World War. Against the background of the war, Rosenzweig affirms both a theology of creation and a Jewish philosophy of law. The teaching of the being created in 'His image' in Steiner's text seems to refer to a theology of creation, the concomitant plea for 'boundaries' that 'are immutably set forth in the covenant' seems to allude to the covenantal law revealed at Sinai. Significantly, Rosenzweig's book closes with the call 'Ins Leben' (Into life). Life is exactly what Steiner sees threatened by civilization's 'march into the heart of creation'. Whether Steiner actually had *Der Stern der Erlösung* in mind when he wrote about his 'Stern einer Doppellehre,' (Star of a dual discipline) cannot be explored fully here. It should, however, be noted that, in Steiner's late poetry, socio-religious concepts like a covenantal community seem to be conspicuous by their absence.

How can we account for this apparent tension between Steiner's anthropological project and his late poetry? This tension seems particularly odd if one takes into account that Steiner worked on his 'taboo' lectures between 1950 and 1952. In these lectures he formulates his sociology of danger. There is no such thing as taboo as such but only ways of avoiding danger:

> Danger is narrowed down by taboo. A situation is regarded as dangerous: very well, but the danger may be a socially unformulated threat. Taboo gives notice that danger lies not in the whole situation, but only in certain specified actions concerning it. These actions, these danger spots, are more challenging and deadly than the danger of the situations as a whole, for the whole situation can be rendered free from danger by dealing with or, rather, avoiding the specified danger spots completely. (SWI: 213)

Here Steiner warns against any attempt to control danger in a totalitarian manner. Steiner cautions against attempts to master danger as such. This kind of undertaking all too easily gives rise to a perception of one's innocence, which one then contrasts with the threat posed by the other. Rather than arguing for the mastering of danger in the outside world, Steiner advocates a certain type of action, in which the self and not the outside world assumes responsibility for the avoidance of encounters with danger. As Steiner makes clear in 'On the Process of Civilisation', he sees tendencies to such control in modern Western societies. According to Steiner, though, in the modern Western world, danger is to be eliminated by attacking anything that might be conceived of as dangerous. Attempts to control a dangerous situation lack any form of 'value'. The very act of domination in fact extends the sphere of suffering and death deeper into a societal sphere, rather than helping to alleviate it.

Danger as 'a socially unformulated threat' increases the risk that a specific society may turn totalitarian. It does so when a community sets out to attack all possible 'sources' from which the unknown danger seems to originate. Countering such totalitarian behaviour, Steiner advocates specific actions by which one avoids rather than attacks manifestations of the dangerous. In so doing, he contrasts the empirical with the conceptual, and the context-specific with the categorical. While this seems sound, it begs the question whether his sociology of danger is not itself based on concepts and categories. Does it not also incorporate a theory of law?

As we have seen, Steiner advocates 'boundaries' that 'are immutably set forth in the covenant'. Immutable boundaries, however, seem to depend on firmly established categories and concepts. What Steiner describes here appears to be far removed from context-specific actions. On the contrary, he affirms an intransigent and fixed way of ordering the external world. How can we understand this apparent contradiction in Steiner's formulation of the sociology of danger?

II. Myth and Danger

In order to fully understand the sociology of danger we have in fact to examine Steiner's poetry. In his poetry the theme of danger unfolds within stories about specific communities, as can be seen in poems like 'Die Warner' (The Warners), 'Kenez im Nebel' (Kenez in the Mist), 'Nach der Wüstenschlacht' (After the Desert Battle), 'Elefantenfang' (Elephant Round-up), and 'Der Aufseher' (The Overseer). These stories are therefore myths: they describe the specific ways in which a society deals with danger in the external world. The centrality of the theme of danger in his lyrical work is not only exemplified by the fact that Steiner dedicated a whole section of his poetry to this theme; danger also features in other poems and most conspicuously in 'Leda' (AsP: 257). In contrast to his predecessors (Spencer, Yeats, and Rilke), Steiner embeds the Leda myth into the social setting of a village environment.[2] Having been raped by Zeus, Leda returns to her village, where her parents ask her whether she has seen the glory of the gods. With Leda the whiteness that her parents attribute to the divine transforms itself into darkness:

Da rief sie aus: 'ich war im dunkel, ja!
Ich wund vor dunkel! nehmt den schleim von mir,
Was ich nicht sah, soll nimmer mehr geschehn,
Ihr einzigen, o wascht mich wieder rein!'

(Then she cried out: 'I was indeed in darkness! / Darkness had made me sore! Take the slime from me, / What I did not see, must never happen again. / You, the only ones, oh wash me clean again!')

Instead of purifying her, Leda's contact with the god has defiled her (schleim / slime). The powerful touch of the god is dark (dunkel / darkness). As in the above quotation from *Taboo*, danger is characterized as being indefinable, imperceptible: Leda says that she could not see what was done to her ('Was ich

---

[2] See Jeremy Adler, '"The step swings away" and other poems by Franz Baermann Steiner', *Comparative Criticism*, 16 (1994), 139–168 (pp. 144–145).

nicht sah' / What I did not see). The divine has the attributes of power – 'Mit wilden flügeln,' (With wild wings) 'Peitschte den schaum hoch, riesensäulen stäubend' (Whipped up the foam, spraying the giant pillars) – and the neologism 'riesensäulen' (giant pillars) that Steiner created to describe the effect of Zeus's forceful movements underlines the ineffable, indescribable nature of danger.

These conceptualizations of the 'dangerous', however, may themselves produce the forces they were meant to help to control. In the process of naming danger one may actually 'create' danger. Steiner is indeed aware of the difficulties involved in subdividing the world into the dangerous and the harmless. As we will see, in 'Begegnen' (Encounter), in 'Im Anfang' (In the Beginning), and in his lyrical cycle *Eroberungen*, Steiner bemoans the various divisions into which the created world has been compartmentalized by means of differences between linguistic sign systems. Societal subdivisions may produce divisions between particular communities. These political separations may, in turn, help to promote warfare and therefore danger and suffering.

Steiner addresses this potentially dark aspect of the discourse concerning boundaries to the dangerous in his powerful poem 'Elefantenfang' (AsP: 249). This poem is itself the result of detailed sociological studies of elephants. Steiner took notes from Alice Hart's *Picturesque Burma* (1897) and from Otto Stein's *Elefantenjagd im alten Indien* (Elephant Hunting in Ancient India, 1921). These notes report how human captors manage first to lure male elephants through the enticement of females, how the wild elephants are in this way led to a place from which escape is impossible. In both Hart and Stein, Steiner found descriptions of how finally the captors crawl beneath the elephant cows and entice them to attack their wild male companions. In this way the malicious enticement by the human hunters turns the female elephants into murderers of their own species whereas their usual behaviour is characterized as benign and supportive.[3]

In Steiner's poem the elephants wound their companions with enjoyment ('Strafte mit lust' / Punished with relish). Following Hart and Stein, Steiner divides elephants into two categories. However, whereas Hart and Stein contrast 'females' with 'males', Steiner establishes a binary opposition between the tame ones ('zahme tiere'), and the wild ('wildlinge'). Ironically, the wild fall victim to the violence of the tame. The expression 'wildlinge' is closely associated with the term 'die Wilden,' the German equivalent for 'the sav-

---

[3] Alverdes refers to these characterizations in *Social Life in the Animal World* – a book that was in Steiner's library – when he writes: 'According to Burger (p. 225), the instinct to help a sick companion is stronger in elephants than in any other species of animal [...]'. Alverdes, *Social Life in the Animal World* (London: Paul Trench and Trubner, 1927), p. 134.

ages'. Grimm's *Deutsches Wörterbuch* defines 'Wildling' as a 'savage' in the true sense – 'Ein wilder Mensch […] ein "Wilder" im eigentlichen Sinn' (A wild man […] a 'savage' in the true sense of the word) – giving as an example North American savages – 'Indianische Wildlinge' (Indian savages). If 'wildlinge', as Grimm confirms, refers to the 'Wilden,', to the 'savages', then 'the tamed animals' resemble the 'civilized', that is to say, people living in the modern 'civilized' world who have supposedly 'tamed' their sexual and aggressive drives. But in Steiner's poem, the 'civilized' irrationally wound the 'savages', who are hungry. The opening of the poem dramatizes categories that are used to subdivide the world into the dangerous and the harmless. These names are employed as concealment beneath which hides the reality of violence and injury. The accusation that the 'other' is dangerous serves to justify endangering the life of those who are classified as strangers. Actions do not cohere with the names given to those who perform them. The 'tame' elephants threaten to wreak destruction on the wild ones:

> Die zahmen tiere drohten schweigend,
> Köpfe gesenkt vor schwarzem meer,
> Das rastlos mahlte in der friedung,
> Gellte, schnob.

> (A silent threat came from the tame ones, / Heads lowered against the grey-black sea / That milled and milled within the palisade, / Trumpeted, snorted.)

The threat posed by the tame ones makes nonsense of the word 'zahm' (tame). The root 'Friede' in the term 'friedung' (palisade) ironically evokes 'peace', whereas the word in fact denotes an enclosure or prison. The 'Doch' (But) with which the second stanza begins marks, in an ironic manner, a turning away from 'peace':

> Doch als die wildlinge, bemeistert
> Von hungertagen und verschnürter welt,
> Nicht kraft mehr fanden, alte angst verstanden,
> Ließ man die zahmen zu.

> (But when the wild ones, wholly overcome / By days of hunger and a world strung tight, / Found no more strength, convinced by an ancient terror, / The tame were let in.)

The fear of the wild elephants, whose health has been damaged by starvation and anxiety, caused by their imprisonment, paradoxically justifies the letting loose of the tame elephants. The latter are well-fed with both food and hatred. The socially constructed scenario in which the 'zahmen' are made to attack 'wildlinge' reflects constructions that establish binary oppositions, of which the one between the dangerous and harmless is a key example. This construction of a divide between the dangerous and harmless – between the savage and the civilized – in itself constitutes danger, since it incites to hatred and violence. The tame and well-fed elephants are incensed to fury by the otherness of the wild ones. They are thus wild, raging with fury:

Erbarmungslos der wohlgenährten haß
Dem waldgeruch galt, dem fernherkommen:
Strafte mit lust.

(And pitiless the hatred of those well-fed / Turned on the forest smell, provenance from afar, / Punished with relish.)

Strikingly, Steiner leaves out the captors who entice the female elephants to attack their male companions as narrated in the anthropological sources. The absence of a third party focuses the attention on the binary opposition between 'tame' and 'wild'. One might note that Steiner is here anticipating a deconstructive method; he illustrates the way in which language perpetrates violence. Derrida has drawn attention to how, in the hands of the Nazis, language itself turns into a murderous instrument.[4] In Steiner's poem, the 'wild' animals are killed exclusively on account of the signification of which they are the carriers. However, Steiner does not only question the complicity of linguistic denotation in the perpetration of violence. He also undermines ways of perception in which those who are different are associated with repellent physical characteristics (like smell). 'Otherness" ('fernherkommen' / provenance from afar) provokes violence: the 'wildlinge' are seen as coming from afar, they smell of the forest ('Waldgeruch'), of the uncivilized and it is exactly this air of strangeness that causes the hatred of the 'zahmen tiere'. In calling the 'zahmen' 'wohlgenährt' (well-fed) Steiner emphasizes the irrationality of such aggression, which recalls the fate of the Jewish people in their own imprisonment in the Second World War.

As I have mentioned, this deconstructive move by which Steiner analyses how the imposition of categories on living beings that are perceived to be dangerous results in the infliction of death and suffering on those who are named thus, seems to conflict with his advocacy of localizing the dangerous. However, one needs to distinguish between prejudicial categories, and those which avert danger. As we have seen in the previous section, Steiner affirms the necessity of the latter kind of limits.

---

[4] For Derrida's discussion of the Nazi attempt to erase the name of otherness, see, 'The Force of Law: "The Mystical Foundation of Authority"', in *Deconstruction and the Possibility of Justice*, ed. by Drucilla Cornell et al (London: Routledge, 1992), pp. 3–67 (pp. 59–60).

This affirmation and a belief in the differences between premodern and modern forms of life offer a sharp contrast to some postmodernist assumptions concerning non-difference and indifference. Here, however, I will focus on Steiner's deconstructive methodology in his poetry, most of all in his *Eroberungen*. Steiner's critique of binary oppositions dramatizes his concern not to confuse limits to the self-empowering or self-aggrandizement of man with the establishment of geographical and other boundaries that contain and avert danger.

Steiner's critique of national boundaries unfolds within an examination of language. He questions the process of 'naming' as well as the construction of nationhood in *Eroberungen*. As an autobiographical poem,[5] *Eroberungen* refers back to Wordsworth's *Prelude*[6] and shares with the latter a deep interest in an investigation of the nature and the workings of memory. The poet transfers his memory to the reader, so that the experience saved in the act of memorizing can be repeated in a non-identical manner. The title of the poem is therefore ironic: the whole poem undermines the concept of 'conquests', arguing for an enactment of the idea of gift and of sacrifice instead. The very narrative of the poetic cycle illustrates the practice of giving and sacrificing. The poet's sacrifice consists in the destruction of his memories. At the same time, memory, though lost to the poet, survives in the life of all those readers to whom it has been given. In their lives, some of the poet's experiences may live on.

By handing his private memories to the public, the poet sets out to establish a bridge between selfhood and community, between what Buber calls *Ich und Du* (I and Thou). The allusion to Buber's famous philosophical essay of 1923 is indeed a point of reference here. Buber's 'Thou' is both human and divine. By establishing a dialogue with one's neighbour one does not lose the eternal 'Thou'. On the contrary a meaningful relationship to the 'mundane' opens a glimpse of the divine. Pertinently, Buber defines 'myth' as the correlation between the everyday and the eternal.[7] In a sense, the mythical constitutes the dialogical. In handing down his personal memories to the public, Steiner engages in a dialogue. *Eroberungen* performs the very act of myth-making, as understood by Buber, by bridging the gap between personal and communal memory.

Here the tasks of the anthropologist and the poet meet. The poetic 'I' of *Eroberungen* also establishes relationships between different kinds of commu-

---

[5] In an unpublished letter of 5 April 1948 to the critic Rudolf Hartung, Steiner characterizes *Eroberungen* as a metaphysical, autobiographical poem.
[6] As discussed in Jeremy Adler, '"The steps swings away" and other poems', and Katrin Kohl in the current volume.
[7] See Martin Buber *On Judaism*, ed. by Nahum N. Glatzer, with a new Foreword by Rodger Kamenetz (New York: Schocken, 1995), p. 106.

nities. He thus leaves the realm of his own upbringing, the Western world, and becomes one with the other of the 'primitive'. Significantly, Steiner links this closeness between self and other to his childhood reading. As an anthropologist, Steiner works for the recognition of the inseparability of different ways of life and the need not to discriminate against people whom language denotes as separated or 'other'. Indeed, Steiner inserts into *Eroberungen* a variation on the Robinson Crusoe myth in which he dramatizes his own experience as an anthropologist. The episode describes the encounter between a captain who has been bound to the mast of his ship and a foundling from an island. The foundling narrates from his experiences of this 'alien' place:

> Wie er vor langen jahren von schwarzen stürmen
> Geschleudert worden auf ein gefürchtetes land
> Das dann sein eigen wurde.
> Wie er verwuchs mit der wildnis!
> 'jener gefiederte baum zum beispiel
> Ist ein bewährter freund.
> Die tosenden affen im astwerk lieben wir beide.' (AsP: 346)

> (How, many long years ago, he had been hurled / By black storms onto a land he feared / That then became his own. / How he grew together with the wilderness! / 'that feathered tree, for example, / is a proven friend, / We both love the raging monkey in the branches.')

Strikingly, Steiner undermines the projection of danger onto a foreign country, refusing to accept the geographically constructed boundaries of nationhood, or the biologically erected boundaries of 'race'. These boundaries create danger in that they erect further oppositions between man and man. Steiner has only contempt for philosophies such as Social Darwinism (subscribed to by the Nazis) which made use of biological or geographical 'facts' for the shaping of a value system. In a short aphorism, Steiner marks off 'truth' ('Wahrheit') from the biological.[8] In Steiner's anthropological encounter with the 'other', all false separations dissolve: the foundling grows at one with the wilderness. This account of an identification with what seemed to be split apart and unbridgeable, has a religious impact on the captain, who sighs the words:

> 'ich fuhr nicht vergebens.
> Du also machst mich fromm'. (AsP: 346)

> (I did not sail in vain. / You make me pious.)

---

[8] Steiner expresses this in aphoristic form: 'More human effort lies behind the invention of the concept of "truth" than behind any other abstraction. It is the first entirely un-biological concept, and the premise for many others.' (SWII: 239)

An anthropological encounter in which two separated ways of life unite is driven by a theological concern: the attempt to find a way back to a prelapsarian, creaturely existence, in which man is created according to His image. Every war, every act of violence removes us further from a creaturely existence. The endeavour to bridge rifts between different people (so as to prevent the perpetration of violence) cannot be dissociated from the biblical account of man's creation in His image. Human life is meaningful since it is related to a spiritual point of reference. As such it must not be violated. Myth establishes this correlation between the mundane and the eternal. Steiner's revision of Robinson Crusoe establishes a myth, precisely because it describes how the mundane experience of a shipwreck offers glimpses of the eternal.

The episode in the *Eroberungen* closes with the word 'fromm' (pious), and thus underlines the religious dimension of the experiences narrated. Hearing how the foundling grew at one with what had been perceived as dangerous and wild, the captain realizes a correlation between the empirical and the spiritual and thus becomes pious. In this way Steiner's Robinson myth recalls what Buber understands by religious experience. The captain finds traces of the divine in this world. Buber describes humanity's relation to God as follows:

> One does not find God if one remains in the world; one does not find God if one leaves the world. Whoever goes forth to his You with his whole being and carries to it all the being of the world, finds him whom one cannot speak.
>
> Of course, God is 'wholly other'; but he is also the wholly same: the whole present.[9]

God seems to reside in the in-between. He cannot be found in any kind of totality. Buber thus locates religious experience in the relational, that is to say, in the correlation between opposites. The construction of either a dualism or a monism empties life of a spiritual point of reference. The 'I' of the *doppelgänger*, however, allows for the coexistence of two entities in peaceful unity. Steiner's 'Der Einsame' (The Lonely Man) inhabits a borderland and is double-faced:

> O anfang der heimat:
> Wie innig sind die keime der schuld
> Und jene ersten und breiten unsichern grenzen der fremde,
> Wohnliche grenzen, in welche der frühe einsame
> Doppelgesichtig sich einbaut.
> Er duldet nicht trennung,
> Hält hüben und drüben im liebenden aug, solang ers vermag. (AsP: 355)

---

[9] Martin Buber, *I and Thou*, a new translation with a prologue 'I and You' by Walter Kaufmann (Edinburgh: Clark, 1970), p. 127. Further references appear in the text.

(O beginnings of home: / How intimate are the seeds of guilt / And those first, expansively uncertain boundaries of alterity, / Homely borders, into which the lonely man / Soon installs himself with his double-face. / He does not tolerate division. / He maintains both here and there in his loving eye, as long as he can.)

Steiner's early 'lonely man' (who moves into adulthood) does not accept the separation which the symbolic system imposes on the created world and, though he cannot remove the borders which a postlapsarian humanity has established, he succeeds in dwelling amongst them rather than conniving at geographical separations. Here, Steiner sees in the process of naming the causes for separations that promote violence, and undermine value. By contrast, the poet seeks to restore unity, meaning, and value.

III. LANGUAGE

Names establish national boundaries, concepts of friend and enemy, and as such they contribute to the violence exerted in wars and genocides. By contrast, children are free from guilt on account of their ignorance of 'names':

Heimat, heimat des herzens …
Die verwobene schuld
Ist im leben die heimat auf der wir wachsen.
Die kinder sind heimatlos.
[…]
Sie, die sich noch nicht gehören, die staunenden:
[…]
In ihrer welt ist nicht fremde von heimat geschieden, (AsP: 354)

(Home, home of the heart … / The entangled web of guilt / Is the home of life in which we grow. / Children are homeless / […] / They who do not yet possess themselves, / Are filled with wonder: / […] / In their world, alterity is undivided from home.)

Steiner traces certain actions that cause suffering to national separations between peoples. In a paradoxical manner guilt unites humanity by causing divisions amongst various communities. Guilt is thus the homeland in which we grow up. For the concept of the 'home' can be used to demonize those who live outside of it. In this way, the 'homely' contrasts with the 'uncanny'. Any attempt to erase that which is perceived to be uncanny, however, results in violence. However, since communal identities are grounded in the concept of a homeland, they can easily give way to friend-enemy oppositions, which can then degenerate into violence. The home as birthplace of potential guilt thus constitutes the opposite of the values that Steiner seeks.

Steiner's poem contrasts the home of the 'heart' with the notion of 'home' as a geographical and national place of birth. In Steiner, 'heart' symbolizes all that man experiences, be it bodily or spiritually. The individual in a pre-modern community collects in his or her heart taboos and other rituals which delineate the avoidance of specific dangers and powers. 'The home of the heart' therefore denotes the way of life that the child acquires in following the directions concerning limits to certain forms of action performed in community rituals.

In his poetry, Steiner thus critically reflects on the concern with social cohesion and community. An examination of *Eroberungen* thus demonstrates that, although addressing political concerns, Steiner argues against a certain type of politics. If, in *The Concept of the Political* (1932), Carl Schmitt defines the political as the struggle between two camps, or the confrontation between friend and enemy, then Steiner's thought opposes politics – the Schmittian and sometimes Nietzschean glorification of power as such – with a theology that tries to limit the range of danger which man unleashes in his bid for omnipotence.[10] Whereas Schmitt theologizes politics, Steiner politicizes theology. In the former, theology provides the struggles of political life with a metaphysical justification: after the Fall, man must of necessity perpetrate violence, otherwise peace would create a paradisal condition, which would be blasphemous.[11]

Both the *Eroberungen* and Steiner's sociology of danger constitute a strong affirmation of the rituals laid down in the Hebrew Bible. He shows how non-Jewish pre-modern societies enacted rituals which helped to save life precisely through the avoidance of danger and unrestricted power. From a theological perspective Steiner's conflation of the Jewish with the 'primitive' – in the sense of premodern – and the 'Oriental' is justified. Indeed, the Biblical scholar Jacob Milgrom has shown that the P strand in *Genesis* obliges the whole of humanity – not only the Jews – to the strict keeping of taboos (i. e. blood prohibition)

---

[10] See Julien Freund, 'Schmitt's Political Thought', *Telos*, 102 (1995), 11–42, (p. 14).

[11] For Jacob Taubes' discussion of Schmitt's critique of secularization see, *Die politische Theologie des Paulus* (Munich: Fink, 1993), pp. 86–97; see also Heinrich Meier, who has described the relation of theology to politics in Schmitt's thought as follows: 'In the end, politics needs theology not to realize a goal but to provide a foundation for its own necessity.' In *Carl Schmitt & Leo Strauss. The Hidden Dialogue*, trans. by J. Harvey Lomax, ed. by Heinrich Meier (Chicago: University of Chicago Press, 1995), p. 55; for a discussion of Schmitt's failure to link his theology to Biblical writings, see Wolfgang Palaver, 'Schmitt's Critique of Liberalism', *Telos*, 102 (1995), 43–71, (pp. 66–67).

against endangering life on earth.[12] Both Steiner's critique of language and his sociology of danger need to be seen against the background of a Jewish prohibition against murder. As we have seen, in *Eroberungen*, Steiner contrasts the holistic and 'nameless' perception of the child with an adult world in which binary opposition emerges as a result of a split between signifier and signified:

> Damals durchpulste das herz die einheit der bilder,
> Leben vom leben waren hände wie tor,
> Gesichter der menschen wie züge der berge,
> [...]
> Hatten alle das einzige schicksal der welt,
> Einmal geschaut, waren alle bilder
> Schon verbunden und vom selben herzen gespeist.
> Dann doch aus bildern entschälte sich jäh das sondergeschick,
> Bilder von dingen fielen,
> Dinge beharrlich wurden,
> Meßbar und fremd, auf vergleiche und ablauf bezogen.
> Mit geduldigen blicken rührte das kind an die heile welt,
> Aber sie warfen ihm einen namen zu
> Und ein kleineres deckt er von jahr zu jahr. (AsP: 355)

(In those days, a unity of images pounded through the heart, / The hands were the life of life, a gate; / The faces of man were the procession of hills, / [...] / As they all shared the common fate of the world, / Once observed, the images / United, nourished by a single heart. / Yet then an individual fate emerged abruptly from the images, / Images fell from things, / Things grew persistent, / Measurable and strange, related to comparison and change. / The child breached the untouched world with patient gaze, / But it gave him names / And now from year to year the world he covers diminishes.)

This critique of procedures that render the created world measurable, comparable, and static recalls Buber's notion of the 'Es' (It). If the truly mythical consists in establishing a bridge between that which seemed to be separated, then the principle of the 'Es' affirms a quantifiable compartmentalization of life. The relation of the 'Ich' (I) to the 'ewiges Du' does not proceed in a measurable mode, since the eternal Thou does not know 'Maß und Grenze' (measure and limit, p. 160). The encounter between 'Ich' and 'Es' by contrast unfolds accord-

---

[12] See Jacob Milgrom, *Studies in Cultic Theology and Terminology* (Leiden: E. J. Brill, 1983), pp. 47–48, (p. 48): 'The P strand in Genesis also indicts the human race for its *hamas* (Gen. 6: 11). Because the Noachide law of Gen. 9 is the legal remedy for *hamas*, it probably denotes murder (as in Ezek. 7: 23), though in subsequent usage, especially under prophetic influence, it takes on a wider range of ethical violations. Thus, the blood prohibition proves that P is of the opinion that a universal God imposed a basic ritual code upon humanity in general.'

ing to the principle of 'Trennung' (discreteness, p. 74). It is this kind of principle which Steiner sets out to question in his critique of naming.

The process of signification divests the image of a thing from the thing itself, and shows thing and image to be arbitrary. Thus 'naming' alienates the subject from the surrounding world. Things have become dead, measurable objects without any personal connection to the subject. The splitting between the 'I' and the world goes hand in hand with the gap between signified and signifier. Through this rupture between image and thing, language can be used for violent, dangerous ends.

IV. REDEMPTION

From Steiner's perspective poetry attempts to do justice to suffering, that is, to all inhumane social practices on this earth and at this time. There is, as we have seen, an apparent tension in Steiner's intellectual project between anthropology and poetry. If the anthropologist is mainly concerned with families, that is, with tribal communities, then his poems attempt to counteract the violence that might issue from possible clashes between different social units in which myths are instrumentalized. Here we find a messianic strain in his poetry that implicitly questions his anthropological approach, thus highlighting the multi-dimensionality of his intellectual project.

In the poem 'Begegnen' (Encounter) we find another kind of mythical element, one that could be called messianic, even though it seems to be rather removed from the messianic vistas of a redeemed social world. Unlike 'Elefantenfang' and other poems, 'Begegnen' appears to have a radically subjective focus. The poem opens with a description of a landscape that makes room for the psychic scenery of the poetic voice:

Langsamer zauber des frühlings löst die wurzeln,
In wehenden lichtern rötet sich das land,
Schatten werden freundlich:
Welch fremdling ist das leben in der welt. (AsP: 304)

(Slow enchantment of spring loosens the roots, / Under fluttering lights the land turns red, / Shadows become friendly: / What a stranger life is in the world.)

What kind of landscape is this? The beginning of the poem prepares for the messianic hopes at its end. The slow moving pace of the first line describes a letting go, a letting loose, a gradual separation of roots from their surrounding, the presently existing world ('Langsamer zauber des frühlings löst die wurzeln'

/ Slow enchantment of spring loosens the roots). In this light the world appears friendly to the poet. However, life, as it is lived now remains a stranger in the world: the statement 'Welch fremdling ist das leben in der welt' (What a stranger life is in the world) sums up a major theme in Steiner's poetry that we have also encountered in 'Elephantenfang' and *Eroberungen*. These poems describe the process by which members of a minority are turned into strangers. In 'Begegnen' Steiner broadens out the notion of strangeness in a radical manner in calling life on earth a 'Fremdling' (stranger). Thus the impression of an outspoken subjective point of view does not bear out critical investigation. On the contrary, Steiner juxtaposes a descriptive tone with a critical mode.

As in the childhood myth of *Eroberungen*, in Steiner's 'Begegnen' language causes a violent rift between life and world. The charge against naming affects the self-depiction of the poet:

> Ich habs gewußt: mich hat das schweigen übervorteilt.
> Zu keiner verbesserung kann ich mich entschließen.
> Habs gewußt: mich haben die worte betrogen,
> Wenige waren es, doch hohles leid folgt. (AsP: 304)

> (I knew it: silence has cheated me. / I cannot decide in favour of any improvement. / I knew it: the words have betrayed me / They were few, yet hollow pain will follow.)

If the writer distrusts language and depicts himself as knowledgeable on account of his silence, why does he then try to communicate with the reader? In these lines, the poet associates language with suffering. Words thus seem to lack the capacity to alleviate pain.

Words betray life by causing suffering ('hohles leid folgt' / hollow pain will follow). The poet qualifies this stark view, when he calls 'distress' the nourishment of names: 'Not, namens nahrung' (AsP: 304). Thus language seems to fail in its attempt to do justice to what is done to life in an unredeemed world. The distress caused by suffering nevertheless feeds the usage of names. In absorbing the stress of distress, in not turning away from the sight of suffering, but by giving it a voice, a voice that enables empathy, poetry might very well be the silence of which the poet speaks. Its voice might then be voiceless and hesitant.

Steiner's poetry does not say anything insofar as it remains silent. Rather than speak, it absorbs life-pressure and delineates life's precarious position in an unredeemed world. Steiner's notion of silence also implies a silencing in that it, as it were, lays names to rest. The poetic voice of 'Begegnen' radicalizes Steiner's critical procedure insofar as it takes leave from a world in which human agency is supposedly free, but cannot escape the nets of a brutalizing system that turns life into a stranger:

Kennst du des stimmlosen zögern, das zögern aus gewißheit?
Kennst du ein schließen der augen, den urlaub aus der freiheit
In andre freiheit?
Leid ohn verengung hat mich dies gelehrt.
Ich sah die netze des jägers überm erdreich des verfolgten,
Unter erden sah ich des verfolgten gänge als netze;
Und ich bins, den kein netz hält, was oben ist, ist unten,
Ein urlaub aus freiheit in freiheit. (AsP: 304–5)

(Do you know the voiceless hesitation, the hesitation born of certainty? /
Do you know the closing of eyes, the holiday from freedom / In another
freedom? / Pain without constriction taught me this. / I saw the hunter's
nets above the soil of the persecuted, / Below the earth I saw the paths of
the persecuted like nets: / And it is I, who holds no net, what is above, is
below, / A holiday from freedom in freedom.)

By tearing himself free of all nets, the poet frees himself from a structure that
does violence to life. It is this kind of structure that figures in his critique of
naming. Poetry enables the mode of freedom that consists in closing one's eyes
so that the contours of a future messianic world can be perceived, in which life
is no longer a stranger. Silence describes this act of suspending the nets that
bind the violent and suffering elements of a dangerous and therefore compartmentalized, unredeemed world into a seemingly coherent whole. If the myths
in Steiner's poetry unfold such nets in a critical manner, 'Begegnen' points to
a future redemption. In 'Begegnen' Steiner rejects comfort. He depicts himself
as a man who suffers but who rejects 'Verbesserung' (improvement):

Zu keiner verbesserung kann ich mich entschließen,
Bin ohne bedeutung, da eine welt annoch unsichtbar
Auf stirnen zu rasten kam meiner gelübde.
Ich habs gewußt, daß es sich also verhält:
O engel, engel, es ist nicht dieser lenz, nicht dieser ... (AsP: 305)

(I cannot decide in favour of any improvement, / Am without meaning, for
a world still invisible / My oath came to rest upon brows. / I knew it, that
it would behave thus: / O angel, angel, it is not this spring, not this ...)

The angel is a messenger of a new messianic world that speaks in silence,
namely, as absence. The poem, which communicates in a mode that silences
messages, does so by thematizing its refusal to participate in the process of
naming. Silence thus empties the world of naming, making room for another
world in which life and sense are not violently divided as they are in the
present.

II. Cultural Context

Franz Baermann Steiner's First Work, *Die Planeten*, in Its Czech Literary Context

Robert B. Pynsent

At first sight it appears strange that a young student of Oriental languages at the German university of Prague should choose to translate and publish what a prolific, but minor Czech writer, Josef Maria Emanuel Lešetický z Lešehradu (1877–1955), initially intended to be his last work in verse.[1] I wish here to say something about the literary background against which Lešehrad matured as a poet, and in so doing demonstrate how Steiner was, perhaps unconsciously, contributing to a tradition of Prague writing that began during the *fin de siècle*. I shall also suggest reasons Steiner may have been attracted to this really rather dull verse drama, which Lešehrad conceived of as a self-mythicizing spiritual autobiography.

The mostly indirect associations of Franz Steiner with the Prague literary scene of the 1890s are manifold and, given political developments in Prague after the Munich Agreement, imbued with tragic irony. Two writers prepared the way for the Czech Decadents and Symbolists among whom Lešehrad initially tried to belong. The first was Jaroslav Vrchlický (1853–1912), whom the Nineties *avant-garde*, whether Decadent or Naturalist, rejected. Vrchlický was a *nom de plume*; his real name was Emil Frída, which sounded Jewish, and so during the Second World War, the Royal Bohemian Society of Sciences published a genealogical study of the poet in order to 'dispel the rumour' (klep o židovském původu) that he had been a Jew.[2] The second of the writers who prepared the way was Julius Zeyer (1841–1901), a prosperous German Jew, brought up as a Roman Catholic, who learnt Czech from his nanny. The Nine-

---

[1] At the end of the seventh and last volume of his collected verse works, which includes 'Planety', Lešehrad declares that he had spent his whole life working on his 'simple, lucid' poetry and that he had written poems for the 'innumerable brethren' and for 'future generations' so that it can be elaborated and refined by their 'dreams and deeds'. Emanuel z Lešehradu, *Most nad světem* (Prague: Srdce, 1932), p. 107. All translations are the author's.

[2] Karel Doskočil, *Původ Jaroslava Vrchlického* (Prague: Královská česká společnost nauk, 1944).

ties Decadent *avant-garde* more or less adopted Zeyer as its patron. The centenary of his birth in 1941 became an occasion for Czech anti-Nazi celebration.[3] Vrchlický, while predominantly concerned with introducing the forms and concerns of Romance literature into Czech, was also a translator of Persian verse, exploited Indian themes and wrote a major epos on Bar Kokhba and the destruction of Jerusalem. In connection with Lešehrad's preoccupation with esoteric thinking, one might mention that Vrchlický was something of an admirer of Joachim of Fiore[4] and also wrote a verse drama on the Polish Faustus, Twardowski. He was, however, not particularly interested in occultism – though he did have a nasty occult experience with a ring mounted with a scarab.[5] Lešehrad was an acquaintance of Vrchlický's and they corresponded between 1899 and 1907. Both Vrchlický and Zeyer were fascinated by mythology, though Vrchlický never had the money to do much travelling to visit the locations where this mythology had been born. Zeyer spent much of his life outside Bohemia, mainly in Paris, but also elsewhere in western Europe, in Russia, Asia Minor, Central Asia, and North Africa. He also studied Oriental languages, particularly Sanskrit – after having failed his matriculation. Later on, he became a serious student of Japanese culture. Much of Zeyer's writing consisted in the reworking of Czech, Celtic, French, Arabian, Egyptian, Japanese, and Jewish legends. Though Zeyer very rarely published anything in German, he did have close links with German literary circles in Prague. He was godfather to Rainer Maria Rilke whose first sweetheart, Valerie von Rhonfeld, was his favourite niece. Towards the end of his life, Zeyer also became a close friend of the writer, Růžena Jesenská, aunt of Kafka's beloved, Milena Jesenská. Julius Zeyer was, together with another baptized Jewish writer, Jakub Arbes, primarily responsible for the introduction of the late nineteenth-century Western 'occult revival' into Czech literature. He first came into contact with French 'spiritism' in Paris in the early 1870s and esoteric thought is evident, predominantly in his fiction, from 1874 till his death. As far as this, my little aetiology of Franz Steiner's adoption of the occultist Lešehrad, is concerned, the most important of Zeyer's flights into the esoteric was his frequent attendance at the meetings of the Blue Star Lodge (Blauer Stern / Modrá hvězda). This Lodge held its meetings in the flat of Gustav Meyrink on Ferdinandova (now Národní) Avenue in the block on the plot which now houses

---

[3] Among the publications that appeared were: [Anon.], *Český bibliofil Juliu Zeyerovi* (Prague: Spolek českých bibliofilů, 1941); Eva Jurčinová, *Julius Zeyer. Život českého básníka* (Prague: Topič, 1941); and J. Š. Kvapil, *Gotický Zeyer* (Prague: Petr, 1942).

[4] See Marjorie Reeves and Warwick Gould, *Joachim of Fiore and the Myth of the Eternal Evangel in the Nineteenth Century* (Oxford: Clarendon Press, 1987), particularly p. 298 and pp. 323–325.

[5] Karel Weinfurter, *Paměti okultisty* [1933] (Brno: Pohlodek, 1999), pp. 146–148.

the British Council.[6] The most prolific Czech exponent of occultism in the Blue Star Lodge, Karel Weinfurter (1867–1942), became the self-proclaimed and commercially the most successful leader of Czech occult circles between the wars, when his chief works were translated into English and German. One of Zeyer's best loved books, the *Bhagavad Gita*, was translated into Czech by Weinfurter. Adler and Fardon inform us of Steiner's love for the work, which he read in German (SWI: 34). At the end of 1941, the Gestapo arrested Weinfurter and held him for three months; he died three weeks after his release.[7] The Blue Star Lodge was founded in 1890 by Weinfurter on the inspiration of Meyrink, the German banker author of occultist novels in which Steiner also had an interest (Adler and Fardon, SWI: 27).[8] In 1891, the Lodge became the home of the Prague Theosophical Circle; the Pragers were introduced to the teachings of Mme Blavatsky by the Viennese Theosophist, Baron Adolf Leonhardi and initiated into Theosophical rites by the ascetic Viennese industrialist, Dr Friedrich Eckstein, and the Styrian morphine-addict Count Leiningen-Billigheim, but they abandoned Theosophy when Annie Besant became the movement's leader and Rudolf Steiner split off into his Anthroposophy. In the mid-1890s Meyrink introduced Weinfurter and his fellows to some of the ideas of the imaginary Anglo-Indian Brotherhood of the Sad Bay. Weinfurter and his followers became enthusiasts of the Sad Bay, since in pre-history this Brotherhood had allegedly founded Prague. Czech mediaeval chroniclers (for example Dalimil, in 1314) had derived the name Prague (Praha) from *práh* (threshold). This indicated, writes Weinfurter, more or less following Bulwer Lytton's Rosicrucian novel *Zanoni* (1841), that Prague contained the entrance to the underworld. Allegedly the name of the Indian city Allahabad (*recte* city of God) had the same meaning.[9] Perhaps the best known Czech occultist novel based on this was Josef Šimánek's (1883–1959) *Bratrstvo Smutného Zálivu* (Brotherhood of Sad Bay, 1918).[10] Here we learn that Prague, naturally enough at one point labelled 'the heart of Europe', is soon to become the centre of the occult-

---

[6] The gossipy occultist professor (since 1989) of psychology at Prague Universitiy, Milan Nakonečný, claims that the first Blue Star Lodge was founded as a Martinist Lodge, in Budějovice (Budweis) in 1895. See his *Novodobý český hermetismus* (Prague: Vodnář, 1995), p. 12.

[7] Jiří Scheufler, *Mystický učitel Karel Weinfurter a jeho doba* (Olomouc: Přátelé duchovních nauk, 1991), p. 33.

[8] On the establishment of the Lodge, Weinfurter writes something that smacks strongly of the *kaisertreu* behaviour of ordinary 'patriots': 'it was a secret lodge, but we announced its founding to the directorate of police.' *Paměti okultisty*, p. 62.

[9] Karel Weinfurter, *Tajné společnosti okultní, mystické a náboženské* (Prague: Naňka, [1933?]), p. 231.

[10] Weinfurter informs us that Šimánek and the prolific writer of sugary romances, sometimes with minor occult motifs, Quido Maria Vyskočil, were his only close literary friends, *Paměti okultisty*, p. 151.

ist movement for the whole civilized world.[11] Such notions are by no means dead: the Slovak writer, Peter Pišťanek, has recently made fun of them in his effervescent satirical novel, *Rivers of Babylon 3* (original title in English, 1999). For Weinfurter, one of the most important strands of esoteric thinking for the Czechs is embodied in Rosicrucianism and Freemasonry. Weinfurter's acquaintance, Lešehrad, was making Freemasonry a major theme of his writing from the beginning of the 1920s onwards; he introduced the theme with his novel-cum-occultist handbook *Mučedník touhy* (A Martyr of Desire, 1920) and his *Pokus o historii Bratrstva Růže a Kříže* (Attempt at a history of the Brotherhood of the Rose and the Cross, 1921).[12] Weinfurter maintains that Freemasonry had been 'simply tolerated' in the Monarchy, had not been allowed to flourish until after the establishment of Czechoslovakia,[13] just as Lešehrad maintains that the Czech Rosicrucians had gone into exile after the Battle of the White Mountain (1620). In fact, just as it was a patriotic fashion to leave the Catholic Church in the new republic, so becoming a Freemason was a patriotic act. The first foreign minister and second president of Czechoslovakia, Edvard Beneš, was a conscientious Mason. The fact that in Bohemia, Enlightenment Freemasonry was associated with the National Revival and particularly with the compiler of the first modern Czech grammar, the former Jesuit novice Josef Dobrovský (1753–1829), no doubt helped lend Czech Freemasonry its patriotic hue. Indeed, a collection of Masonic verse published not long after Hitler's assumption of power as a New Year's greeting for 1934 begins with a poem on Dobrovský.[14]

---

[11] Josef Šimánek, *Bratrstvo Smutného Zálivu a jiná próza* (Prague: Topič, 1918), pp. 16 and 51.

[12] This marginally scholarly compilation with a nationalist message has as its full title *Pokus o historii Bratrstva Růže a Kříže v Čechách ve styku s Jednotou Českých Bratří* ([Prague] Král. Vinohrady, Sfinx, 1921). Though treating the Rosicrucians in Bohemia, the Freemasons are, naturally, frequently mentioned. He makes nothing of the fact that Jan Amos Comenius introduced the Rosicrucian element into English and then, indirectly, Scottish Freemasonry. That surprises one given the book's message – the Rosicrucians are joint bearers with the Unitas Fratrum of Czech national 'progressive' spirituality and pedagogical excellence. Lešehrad wrote this book under the auspices of another esoteric group, the Silver Circle, who claimed to represent the revival of the Czech spirituality which was naturally coming about amongst the sensitive with liberation, the establishment of the new Czechoslovak republic. The circle or ring represents the horizon the mythological pseudo-Moses Forefather Čech saw from Říp hill, the bronze ring St Wenceslas clung onto on the Stará Boleslav (Bunzlau) church-door when being assassinated, the ring of fire surrounding John Huss's death, and so forth. Throughout the work Lešehrad blends occultism with more or less Masarykian nationalism. The Czech Fascist Jan Rys (Josef Rozsévač, 1901–46, executed) condemns Lešehrad as one of the 'white Jews' propagating Masonic ideology in his fiction. Jan Rys, *Židozednářství – metla světa* (Prague: Zednářská korespondence, 1938), for example, pp. 17 and 44.

[13] Weinfurter, *Tajné společnosti okultní*, p. 181.

[14] Josef Vrba, *Modrý chrám. Cyclus zednářských veršů* (Prague: Ervín Glaser, 1933), unpaginated. The Masonic lodge in Pilsen bore the name Dobrovský.

In both his verse and his esoteric pantheist thinking, his would-be Leib-
nizian spiritual materialism, Lešehrad came under the influence of two poets, one Czech and one German. Both had close links with the Decadent
journal *Moderní revue* (founded 1894), where Rilke had also published. The
central inspiration of both these poets, Otokar Březina and the Karlsruhe-
born Alfred Mombert, was the late nineteenth-century perception of the failure of religion. Reactions to this failure informed much of the work of the
two leading Czech Decadents, Karel Hlaváček and Jiří Karásek, the latter of
whom also acquired a serious interest in Jewish mysticism, and wrote occultist novels. Lešehrad did not begin contributing to *Moderní revue* until
1899, a year after the publication of his first volume of verse, and a visible
sense of the failure of religion develops in him only towards the end of the
first decade of the twentieth century. Březina, whose earliest verse shows
clear signs of Decadent pessimism, soon develops, on the basis of his reading of European and Indian philosophical mystics, a form of religious
thought which combines monotheism with a belief in the brotherhood of all
creatures, organic and inorganic, past and present. His conception of inherited memory, often close to Freud's conception of the *Es*/id, and to today's
notion of genetic memory, involves all human beings becoming aware of
their past experiences, shared for example, with flowers or stones, and having at least an inkling of their future experiences. He tries to demonstrate in
his verse and, especially, his lyrical essays that all art aspires to the manifestation of divine knowledge. Březina inspired Lešehrad with this thought;
Lešehrad, however, certainly never attempts Březina's majestic, often well-
nigh impenetrable alexandrines, with an imagery based on oxymoron and
dissociation. So heroized was Březina by the Czech critics that the sardonic
Viktor Dyk wrote in an epigram that 'everyone praised him, but no one read
him' (Každý ho chválil, nikdo nečetl).[15] Březina was extensively translated
into German, first his last completed collection, *Ruce* (Hands, 1905) by Otto
Pick in 1908; Pick translated another collection in 1920, *Stavitelé chrámu*
(Builders of the Temple, 1899). In the same year Franz Werfel and Emil Saudek translated *Větry od pólů* (Winds from [both] Poles, 1897); the same two
published a translation of his essays, *Hudba pramenů* (The Music of Springs,
1903) in 1923.[16] The Austrian writer and literary commentator Franz Blei reacted to Březina's verse thus:

---

[15] Viktor Dyk, *Satiry a sarkasmy* (Prague: Samostatnost, 1905), p. 50.
[16] For details of the publication of Březina in German, see Josef Vojvodík, *Symbolismus im
Spannungsfeld zwischen ästhetischer und eschatologischer Existenz. Motivische Semantik im ly-
rischen Werk von Otokar Březina* (Munich: Sagner, 1998), p. 345.

$$\text{BŘEZINA} = 2 \times 2 = \tau \left[\frac{d\sigma}{d\tau}\right] + \frac{\tau^2}{2} \left[\frac{d^2\sigma}{d\tau^2}\right] + \ldots (d\sigma_1 + d\sigma_2) = 4$$

Blei means that Březina expresses simple things in a complicated manner, not that he is stating the obvious.[17] Březina's conception of inherited memory finds an original elaboration in Rudolf Richard Hofmeister's occultist novel depicting the evolution of humankind from aquatic creatures to marsupials to *homo sapiens, Eopsyché* (1927). Hofmeister's 'Eopsyché' bears a resemblance to the combination of astral self and soul that makes up the Spirit of an Erstwhile Man in Lešehrad's 'Planety'.

Alfred Mombert knew Saudek's translation of Březina's *Ruce*, and particularly admired the poem 'Kolozpěv srdcí' (Round-song of hearts) which Richard Dehmel had declaimed to him, 'with enormous pathos' (s ohromným pathosem).[18] Mombert was hardly a Prague poet; he spent only three days in the city as Lešehrad's guest in November 1906. On the other hand, he was so to speak, discovered by *Moderní revue*. In its first years the Decadent journal really did represent Prague, not just Czech, literature, since it published German as well as Czech poets in the original language, amongst them Mombert. More important than that, it published the first critical appreciation of Mombert's verse in its January 1896 number. The author was the predominantly German-writing Pole, Stanisław Przybyszewski, allegedly the founder of Expressionism, but best known for his Satanism. Przybyszewski later published translations of Mombert's verse in his Cracow periodical *Życie* in 1899, nearly a year before Lešehrad published his first versions in the Prague *Studentské směry*. Lešehrad was to visit Mombert in Heidelberg in 1907, 1912, and 1931; he maintained a correspondence with him from 1899 until 1940 when Mombert, as a Jew, was arrested by the Gestapo and deported with his sister to the internment camp in Gurs in south-western France. Thanks to the efforts of friends, in particular Hans Carossa and Hans Reinharts, Mombert and his sister were moved to an internment sanatorium in April 1941 and eventually in October, were permitted to go to Switzerland. By now Mombert was a sick man and he died in April 1942.[19]

Lešehrad appears to have imitated Mombert in his desire to write his collections as if they had been planned as a cycle. Indeed, Lešehrad pursued his

---

[17] Franz Blei, *Das große Bestiarium der Literatur* [text based on 5th -8th impression, 1924], ed. Rolf-Peter Baacke (Hamburg: Europäische Verlagsanstalt, 1995), p. 27.

[18] Emanuel z Lešehradu, *Hovory s Nebeským hodovníkem* (Vršovice: Živný, 1939), pp. 28–29.

[19] Ulrich Weber, 'Bio-bibliographische Zeittafel', in Alfred Mombert, *Hundert Gedichte vom himmlischen Zecher*, ed. by Elisabeth Höpker-Herberg (Karlsruhe: Ebeling and Schirnding, Badische Bibliotheksgesellschaft, 1992), pp. 117 and 123.

project with great vigour from the 1910s onwards. Not only did he transfer poems from collection to collection, often in more or less radically altered form, but when he decided in 1931 that all his work hitherto had been a cycle (one cannot but think of Milan Kundera half a century later), he pared down his early collections (particularly those up to 1909) until they constituted a fraction of their earlier length.[20] Otherwise, Mombert's influence lay mainly in concepts and images; this was also the case with Březina's influence. Lešehrad has nothing of the irony evident in Mombert, particularly in the latter's early verse, and unlike Mombert with his often eccentric deviations from syntactic and morphological norms, Lešehrad, particularly in his verse from *c.* 1910 onwards, writes such simple, unlively Czech that it verges on the prosaic. Franz Steiner's German lyricizes Lešehrad's Czech lexically (for example, the use of the poetic words 'harren' and 'Fittich', where Lešehrad has the everyday Czech words for 'wait' and 'wing'), and by clipping sentences frequently, removing German definite and indefinite articles, Steiner makes stylistically more complex verse than Lešehrad, something far closer to Mombert than the original. Lešehrad, at least in 1912, considered *Die Schöpfung* (Creation, 1897, revd edn, 1902), Mombert's greatest work,[21] but once he moved into his esoteric mode around 1910, he appears to be striving for a perception of self already expressed in 'Das reine Sein' (Pure Being) from Mombert's first collection *Tag und Nacht* (Day and Night, 1894), that is 'ein von der Schlack gereintes Ich' (a self cleansed of dross).[22] It is probable that Lešehrad takes up the myth of eternal return from Mombert rather than Nietzsche, for I have noticed no Nietzsche echo in Lešehrad's prose or verse, which is of itself fairly uncommon among writers linked with *Moderní revue.* Lešehrad also has an unusually large proportion of images based on the sea for a Czech poet, and I imagine that Mombert has something to do with that, especially since Lešehrad also sometimes associates the sea with Creation, and primal chaos, like Mombert. The role that the sun and the moon play symbolically in Mombert's verse is similar to their role in Lešehrad's later verse, but here the moon is nothing like as ubiquitous as in early Lešehrad prose and verse, where it forms a well-nigh obligatory backdrop to any thought, deed or emotion. (It was not for nothing that Jiří Karásek called Lešehrad's pre-1910 verse 'lunatic poetry' [Lunatická poesie].)[23] In particular, some lines from Mombert's 'Der Denker' (The Thinker, 1901) look forward to 'Planety':

[20] See Emanuel z Lešehradu, *Kosmická pout' I* (Prague: Srdce, 1931).
[21] Lešehrad, *Hovory s Nebeským hodovníkem,* p. 21.
[22] Alfred Mombert, *Fremder, der du dies liest bei der Nachtlampe. Ausgewählte Dichtungen* (Saarbrücken and Treves: Edition Thaleia, 1989), p. 22.
[23] In his preface to Lešehrad, *Kosmická pout' I,* p. 2.

Hierum wogt ewiger Triumphgesang.
Hier ruht der Schlafend-Träumende
Auf der Spitze einer goldenen Pyramide
Um die tiefen Flanken kreisen strahlend die Planeten.[24]

(Eternal songs of triumph surge. The sleeping-dreaming one rests here / on the tip of a golden pyramid. / Gleaming, the planets circle round the deep flanks.)

Indeed, these lines may have constituted the ultimate inspiration for the 'mystical' pyramid in 'Planety', however frequently Lešehrad had encountered the mysteries of pyramids and triangles in his occult studies.

Lešehrad published two books of translations from Mombert. And today, if Lešehrad is alive in Czech culture for something it is for his translations. In a tribute to Lešehrad on his sixtieth birthday (15 November 1937), the major representative of the inter-war *avant-garde*, František Halas, remembers his translations of Mombert, Mallarmé, Whitman, but especially his *Moderní lyrika francouzská* (Modern French lyric verse, 1922).[25] The still standard history of Czech literature by the Nováks recognizes Lešehrad's importance as a 'paraphrasing' (parafráze) translator, otherwise condemning him as an 'enthusiastic translator, superficial interpreter and tireless imitator of modern west European verse' (horlivý tlumočník, povrchní vykladač a neúnavný napodobitel moderní lyriky západoevropské).[26] Another standard work refers to the 'excessive aestheticism' (předmírou artismu) of his early verse, and claims that none of his 'original verse was ever attractive for readers, since it suffered from a lack of any individual, characteristic liveliness of ideas' (Jeho původní poesie nebyla nikdy pro čtenáře přitažlivá, trpěla totiž nedostatkem osobitějšího myšlenkového života.).[27] In the Academy history of Czech literature (finished at the end of the 1960s, but the fourth volume banned and thus not published until after the Changes), he is mentioned very briefly four times, but only once with some indication of who he was, that is as 'an epigone of the Symbolist and Decadent movements' (epigon symbolistického a dekadentního hnutí).[28] In the most recent more or less standard history of Czech literature, Lešehrad is not men-

---

[24] Mombert, *Hundert Gedichte*, p. 108.
[25] 'Poděkování E. Lešehradovi', in *Imagena*, ed. by František Halas and Ludvík Kundera (Prague: Československý spisovatel, 1971), p. 289.
[26] Jan V. Novák and Arne Novák, *Přehledné dějiny literatury české*, 4th rev. edn. (Olomouc: Promberger, 1936–39), pp. 928–929.
[27] Jaroslav Kunc, *Slovník soudobých českých spisovatelů. Krásné písemnictví 1918–45*, 2 vols (Prague: Orbis, 1945), I, 468.
[28] Jan Mukařovský, ed., *Dějiny české literatury IV. Literatura od konce 19. století do roku 1945* (Prague: Victoria Publishing, 1995), p. 637.

tioned at all.[29] In a review of an early collection, Karásek characterizes all his early verse as abounding with images and stylistic frills, 'the invention of which gave him little effort'; 'in Mr Lešehrad a mood gives birth to a poem and nothing is as alien to him as the effort to want a poem to evoke a mood' (U p. Z Lešehradu nálada rodí báseň, a nic ho není tak vzdáleno, jako úsilí, aby básní teprve chtěl vzbuzovat náladu.); Karásek does see him, however, as beginning to express some energy in contrast to the pallid tones of his earlier verse.[30] In 1900, S. K. Neumann writes of his having 'set up a factory for the mass production of verse' (Zařídil si velkovýrobu veršů). 'He does not merit our serious attention' (Nezasluhuje vážné pozornosti), Neumann continues, 'he did not have the slightest idea about the significance or task of writers; he was just a sportsman. Resquiescat in pace' (neměl ponětí o významu a úkolu spisovatelově, byl pouhým sportsmanem; resquiescat in pace).[31]

The frequency of such judgements would appear to make it all the more remarkable that Franz Steiner should choose to translate Lešehrad. In fact, however, poems by Lešehrad were learned by rote in Czechoslovak schools well into the 1940s, and a particularly popular collection was *Písně na pobřeží* (Songs on a Shore, 1900). Recently an academic critic, while dismissive of Lešehrad's optimistic verse of the period following the Great War, has written of the remarkable records of dreams in *Písně na pobřeží.*[32] While *Písně na pobřeží* still contains Decadent imagery, and Decadent ideas like the eternal nature of frustration, a poem like 'Vise' (Vision) introduces Mombertesque images of spiritual liberation within the framework of a Decadent autostylization (the *persona* is the lord of a manor). Furthermore, the image of the dead poet whose soul lives on a star in eternity where he gives birth to a new humanity of beautiful, muscular titans ('Metamorfosa') looks forward to the imagery of four later poems, including 'Planety'. The image marks the beginning of the semi-religious myth which appears to have appealed to Steiner. In an untitled poem from *Orfeovy proměny* (The Metamorphoses of Orpheus, 1931), which comprises poems from the period 1909–18, Lešehrad expands the image: 'In the spaces of the universe I wander / from ages to ages' (V prostoru vesmíru těkám / od věků do věků).[33] In the poem 'Jaro' (Spring) from 1911, he first produces at least the early stage of the poetic autobiography that will blend

---

[29] Jan Lehár, Alexandr Stich, Jaroslava Janáčková and Jiří Holý, *Česká literatura od počátků k dnešku* (Prague: Lidové noviny, 1998).

[30] Jiří Karásek, 'Z nové produkce poetické', *Rozhledy*, XI (1901), 251–252.

[31] Unsigned review in *Nový kult*, 3, 1900, reprinted in Stanislav K. Neumann, *Stati a projevy, I, 1893–1903* (Prague: SNKLU, 1964), pp. 261–262.

[32] Luboš Merhaut, *Cesty stylizace. (Stylizace, 'okraj' a mystifikace v české literatuře přelomu devatenáctého a dvacátého století)* (Prague: Ústav pro českou literaturu Akademie věd České Republiky, 1994), p. 36.

[33] Emanuel z Lešehradu, *Orfeovy proměny* (Prague: Srdce, 1939), p. 36.

with the astral wandering of 'Planety'. He had searched for 'truth' (pravdu), 'for knowledge of the meaning of existence' (poznání žití), in books, but all he had found was 'empty, dead words' (slova [...] prázdná a mrtvá). Then he turned to the universe itself, casting out 'lyrical bric-à-brac, dreamt words, and poses' (básnické cetky, vysněná slova a pósy) and discovered his 'pure essence' (podstatě ryzí). In the universe, he had found 'eternal return, / the laws of terrestrial matter, the all-governing greatness of the spirit' (odvěký návrat, / zákonnost pozemské hmoty, vševládnou velikost ducha), and he glows with 'universe-bred love' (vesmírnou láskou).[34] In *Píseň modrého paprsku* (The Blue Ray's Song, 1910) he describes his period of 'lunatic poetry' thus:

Noc, v níž jsem se narodil,
měsíc postříbřil,
[...]
Od té chvíle neuhas'
v mých očích jeho jas.[35]

(The moon silvered / the night on which I was born / [...] / From that moment its bright light / was not extinguished in my eyes.)

This is taken up in the key autobiographical passage in 'Planety', in the words of the Moon:

Já střežila jej něžně při zrození
a rozesmála jej v trudném mládí
[...]
V mém třpytu bloudil v chvílích zanícení
a učil znát se oblast neskutečna,
jež však mu byla pouze šerou branou,
jíž vešel v jiný svět [...]
a stal se pěvcem slunné skutečnosti
(*Bolestni*)
Pak, nevěrný, již na mne zapomenul.
Jsem pro něj snem. Ted' podléhá jen Slunci.[36]

---

[34] From 'Z "Ód"' first published in a selection of his verse: Emanuel šl. z Lešehradu, *Hudba srdce. Vybraná lyrika z let 1897–1911* (Prague: Hynek, 1912), pp. 73–76.

[35] Lešehrad, *Orfeovy proměny*, p. 15.

[36] Lešehrad, *Most nad světem*, p. 97; Emanuel Lešehrad, *Die Planeten*, translated from the Czech by Franz B. Steiner (Prague: Orbis, 1935), p. 30. Lešehrad also includes a factual autobiographical element in the verse drama when he writes of 'adventures of the heart', *Most nad svetem*, p. 74 ('Herzensabenteuer' in Steiner, p. 10). This refers to his collection of rather trivial short stories from 1900–14, *Dobrodružství srdce* (Prague: Mazáč, 1927). The 'Epilog' to *V dnech šerých* (In Grey Days, 1901), where a Pilgrim tells a young soul it must suffer more before it will be strong enough to follow him to the Sun might be considered the germ of 'Planety'.

(I guarded him tenderly at his birth / and gave dreams to his sad youth / […] / In my light he wandered in times of rapture / and learnt how to know the sphere of the unreal, / which was, however, only a twilight gateway for him / through which he entered another world […] / and became the singer of the sun's reality. / (*Painfully*) / After that he forgot me, unfaithful man. / I have become a dream for him. Now he is subject only to the Sun.)

The Sun means for Lešehrad not simply his post-war optimism, his vision of the First World War as a version of the primal chaos that will give birth to a new age with a New Man, but also abandonment of the old moon-god(dess) for a sun-god, a god that embodies the First Creator, the bright spirit of the Prime Mover, and the force of spiritual and material maturation.

This maturation depends on metempsychosis, an essential element of virtually all contemporaneous Czech occultist teaching, as far as I am aware. Metempsychosis constitutes a frequent theme in Lešehrad's verse before 'Planety' as well. The following words addressed to a disillusioned woman in the pre-Great War poem, 'Kolo osudu' (Wheel of Fate) express this notion as well as that of *karma*:

vše cos na zemi žila,
trpěla, myslila, snila,
přivezeš v příští své žití,
kterým ti souzeno jíti […][37]

(everything that you have lived / suffered, thought, dreamt on Earth / you will bring back in to the next life / that you are destined to lead […])

Unlike most Czech occultists, however, Lešehrad appears to have believed like a Jainist that a human being's soul may transmigrate into another form of matter. In the lengthy didactic poem, 'Hvězdný hudebník' (Stellar musician), he declares:

Kdo jednou zde na zemi byl,
v nějaké podobě žil,
stýská se věčně mu po ní,
stále se navrací zpět
v hostinný svět,
přeměněn v nerost neb v květ,
ve tvora vzhled: září neb zpívá neb voní.[38]

[37] Lešehrad, *Kosmická pout' I*, p. 44–42.
[38] Lešehrad, *Orfeovy proměny*, p. 45.

(Anyone who has lived in some form / here on Earth / eternally pines for the Earth, / and constantly returns / to the hospitable world / changed into mineral or flower, / or other creature: he glows or sings or wafts scent.)

By the time he writes 'Planety', which contains no evidence of this migration between forms of matter, Lešehrad suggests that one's soul or astral self moves from one world (star) to another: the trajectory of the soul is no longer that of a boomerang, but of a sky-rocket. Beside the motif of metempsychosis, Lešehrad frequently refers to another standard occultist notion, that the human being is a microcosm, that everything contained in the universe is present in him or her. This notion enters 'Planety' only once.

However one might judge the aesthetic qualities of 'Planety', it does represent a consistent, non-rational response to the failure of organized religion. That no doubt attracted Steiner. While comparing Steiner with Evans-Pritchard, Mary Douglas states: 'They were both interested in religious belief, both against idealism, both against materialism and rationalism.' (SWI: 6–7) Hence, also he abhorred nationalism, 'since nationhood had taken the place of religion', as he wrote to Gandhi (SWI: 131). In the Prague of the 1920s and 1930s, one could be Marxist, (as Steiner had been in his teens), and simultaneously be at least to some degree an occultist like Lešehrad. The Marxist dramatist, Jan Bartoš, was also an occultist, and indeed regularly told the fortune of the greatest twentieth-century Czech poet, Vítězslav Nezval, one of the few Communist Czech writers not to be expelled from the Party when it took the Stalin line in 1929. Nezval himself in his key work on the birth of the poet and poetry, *Podivuhodný kouzelník* (The Remarkable Magician, 1922), uses the number seven in an esoteric manner, the number of the days or ages of the creation of the world, as well as the number of colours conventionally in the rainbow; in the poem, which has seven *canti*, these colours more or less correspond to the seven 'higher' and 'lower' planets used in astrology. Furthermore, Nezval alludes to various literary figures beloved of occultists like the Lady of the Lake and Merlin, including the latter's birth in a crystal cave. In any case, Franz Steiner's apparent interest in occultism at this time in his life may represent an early sign of his interest in religion.

One of the first books Lešehrad was involved in editing while working for the publishing house Sfinx immediately after the First World War, when it produced only occultist books, was a study in Jewish mysticism.[39] Steiner, however, manifested an interest in occultism at around the same time as he began translating Lešehrad. Adler and Fardon inform us that 'he began a play with

---

[39] S. Arje, *Pojednání o židovské mystice*, followed by Heinrich Cornelius Agrippa von Nettesheim's *Kabala*, an extract from *De Occulta Philosophia*, trans. into Czech by Viktor Seifert ([Prague] Vinohrady: Sfinx, 1922).

Ramon Lull as the somewhat unlikely hero, the first act of which was presented at a public reading' (SWII: 88). The Catalan mystic Lull was the subject
of literary works by two earlier Czech students of the esoteric arts. Julius
Zeyer published his verse 'Ramondo Lullo' in his *Poesie* (1884) and Jiří Karásek
his prose *Obrácení Raymunda Lulla* (The Conversion of Ramon Lull) in 1919.
Ramon Lull was, then, a figure of mainstream Czech literature.

Whatever his publishing activities, it is not at all clear that Lešehrad, unlike
Zeyer and Karásek, was particularly interested in the Jews. 'Vzpomínky
starého zrcadla' (Memories of an Old Looking Glass) in the short-story collection, *Démon a jiné povídky* (The Demon and other Stories, 1911) manifests something like that typical element of Czech anti-Semitic stereotyping, the portrayal of the Jew as the destructive modernizer. Here an impoverished noble-
man marries a fat, but rich, Jewish woman who throws out all the antique
family furniture and replaces it with hideously modern pieces. On the other
hand, in a volume comprising his 1920s collections of verse, he has a poem
entitled 'Dceři ghetta' (For a Daughter of the Ghetto). One could show ill-will
and maintain that, at least at first sight, what we have here is the stereotyping
of the beautiful young Jewish woman in the manner of the clearly antisemitic
Walter Scott in *Ivanhoe*. Lešehrad's depiction of the girl's dark eyes manifest-
ing a longing for Jerusalem is certainly a convention of Czech literature. Nevertheless, Lešehrad's unusually majestic verse here serves to render even her
conventional luxuriance serene. Furthermore, he introduces Steiner's perception of Jewish servitude. A 'prisoner of northern climes' (zajatče severních
krajů), she longs for her 'distant, sunny fatherland' (slunné otčině dálné), and
in her veins runs the blood of her 'wandering, crushed forbears' (bludných a
zkrušených předků). The narrator of the poem stylizes himself as a lovelorn
musician who wishes to sing to her, accompanying himself with 'the sighs of
his ivory harp' (vzdechů sloňové harfy).[40] Especially given the fact that
Lešehrad very rarely writes such straightforward erotic verse, I would maintain that 'Dceři ghetta' constitutes a eulogy to an ancient religion that has survived, unlike European Christianity.[41] One might find another tenuous link
between Lešehrad and Steiner in another group of 'wanderers', the Gypsies.
By the time Steiner went to Subcarpathian Ruthenia to study the Gypsies, it

---

[40] Emanuel z Lešehradu, *Slunovrat. Zpěvy* (Prague: Srdce, 1931), pp. 14–16.
[41] Jan Zábrana went with his fellow-writer Viola Fischerová and the future president Václav
Havel to visit Lešehrad a few weeks before he died. In Zábrana's account, Lešehrad's attitude to Jewishness in his old age was, perhaps, ambivalent. He was by then hard of hearing and used a silver ear-trumpet. When he cannot understand something Fischerová is
saying, he asks Havel and Zábrana, 'What is that Jewess nattering about?' (Co tam ta
židovka kecá?); Jan Zábrana, *Celý život (I). Výbor z deníků 29. dubna 1948–5. listopadu 1976*
(Prague: Torst, 1992), p. 320. Still, Nakonečný claims Lešehrad joined the Communist
Party in 1948, *Novodobý český hermetismus*, p. 225.

had become fashionable for Czech intellectuals, Jewish and Gentile, to travel there to observe the Hasidim. Lešehrad also manifests a minor interest in Gypsies, though it amounts to little more than a watered-down Romantic attraction. In the poem, 'Cikáni' (Gypsies), he portrays them desiring ever to roam into distant parts, their 'lungs, full of song' (zpěvnou hrud'), their hearts of 'distress' (tísní).[42] Steiner expresses similar sympathy – but without the sentimentalization: 'travelling, travelling, travelling … no home anywhere. […] Insight, but no happiness' (Adler and Fardon, SWII: 14). It is important to Steiner that Gypsies originally came from India (Adler and Fardon, SWI: 56); Lešehrad manifests no interest in that fact. Perhaps particularly significant in Steiner's notes on the Carpathian Gypsies is the fact that he evinces Czech nationalism, for he refers to the Hungarians as the 'Magyar hordes' (Adler and Fardon, SWII: 14). Quite coincidentally, that was the sort of language Zeyer used of the Hungarians;[43] in Steiner's days, Edvard Beneš was the chief Czech propagator of magyarophobia. Lešehrad also had his moments of mythopoeic nationalism, and not only in the nationalist occultism of *Pokus o historii*. Immediately after the First World War, for example, Franz Ferdinand's assassin had borne the banner of humanity, and prepared the way for freedom and a Joachite 'new gospel' (nové evangelium).[44] Much more significant for understanding Lešehrad's spiritual proximity to Steiner is the Czech poet's reaction to German occupation. His collection, *Jen víra* (Only Faith, 1940), which appeared exactly a year after the German troops marched in, constitutes probably the strongest published expression of hatred for the occupiers and encouragement for the Czechs that I have ever read.[45] It is an irony all too typical of the times that the publishers with whom Lešehrad brought it out, EMNA, were charged with collaboration immediately after the war.[46]

---

[42] Lešehrad, *Kosmická pout' I*, p. 338.

[43] In the 'mystical' short story 'Samko pták' from *Tři legendy o krucifixu* (1892), Zeyer writes of the Hungarians as 'a Mongol horde that still today suffocates these tormented people [the Slovaks]'; Julius Zeyer, *Tři legendy o krucifixu* (Prague: Unie, 1906), p. 77. This attitude to the Hungarians constituted something of a nationalist cliché; thus, for example, in his 1894 vademecum for 'patriots', Štech writes of the Hungarians as a 'savage nation'; Václav Štech, *Národní katechismus aneb Co má věděti každý Čech*, 6th edn (Prague: Otto, *sine anno*), p. 11.

[44] 'Nápoj volnosti', in Lešehrad, *Orfeovy proměny*, p. 88. But we remember that the Rosicrucians also thought of a coming 'golden age' similar to the Age of the Spirit Joachim was expecting.

[45] The politician prelate Bohumil Stašek did publish a sermon that was just as strong in August 1939, *Kázání na pouti u svatého Vavřinečka* (Prague: Vyšehrad, 1939). Immediately after preaching this sermon, Stašek was arrested; he spent the war in Dachau.

[46] Michal Bauer, 'Soudní řízení s V. E. Coufalem a skupinou EMNA', *Tvar*, X, 20 (2.12.1999), 14–15.

That Steiner did feel close to Lešehrad is evident from his two letters concerning the translation of 'Planety' that are held by the Museum of Czech Literature in Prague.[47] In the first letter, from 27 September 1933, he is offering Lešehrad some translations in response to a conversation they had in the spring of the same year. In the second letter, from 5 May 1934, he apologizes to Lešehrad for not having kept his word; in March he had promised the translation in three weeks. He had completed the first two sections of 'Planety' and the three poems from the later collection, *Škeble oceánu* (Shells from an Ocean, 1934), which Lešehrad had selected to be appended to the verse drama. Steiner's dissertation had been accepted, but he had to do 'einige Kleinigkeiten' (a few minor changes) by the end of May. The translation was 'viel zu ernst' (far too serious) a matter for him to be able to work at it off and on between making corrections to his dissertation. He promises Lešehrad that he is thinking of him. The second letter is somewhat less formal than the first, which suggests that their friendship has become closer.

Steiner's German is more elevated than the Czech original. Indeed, in the very first speech, the Czech word for 'singer' (*pěvec*) is translated into the positively Wagnerian 'Sängerheld' (hero-singer). That is, however, counterbalanced when Lešehrad's somewhat archaic expression for 'fecund matter' (*žírná hmota*) becomes 'Dingwelt' (living world). Since Steiner appears to have an excellent command of Czech, one assumes that what could be errors are actually intended as improvements. So, 'where the light of the heights dazzled him' (kde oslňovalo jej světlo výšin) (which is opposed to 'in the depths in which darkness wanted to consume him' [v hloubkách, v kterých tma ho pozřít chtěla]) becomes 'wo Kraft ihm wurde von der Licht der Höhen' (where he gained strength from the light of the heights). Steiner appears to intend to contrast the heights with the depths, perhaps thus showing himself less occult-minded than Lešehrad. Only at one point does Steiner seem to have changed too much:

Já přísnou krásou Věčnosti byl dojat,
v ní objímá se všechno při zrození,
v ní shledává se všechno při svém skonu,
a v ní se věky věkův odehrává
i neustálá svatba hmoty s duchem.

---

[47] I am grateful to the director of the Literature Archive at the Museum, Dr Naděžda Macurová, for supplying me with photocopies of these letters. They constitute deposit no. 4485 in Lešehrad's own collection of letters and literary documents mainly from the nineteenth and twentieth centuries. See Jarmila Mourková (ed.), *Lešehradeum. Sbírka literárních a historických dokumentů* (Prague: Literární archív Národního muzea, 1963), p. 182.

(I was moved by the serene beauty of Eternity: / in it everything embraces at birth: / in it everything meets in its death, / and in it forever and ever there takes place / also the unceasing marriage of matter and spirit.)

Steiner interprets the 'it' as beauty instead of Eternity. His first line runs 'I became aware of the eternal, severe beauty' (Die ewige strenge Schönheit ward mir kund); the fourth and fifth lines run: 'therein at all times is celebrated / the marriage too of matter and spirit' (darin in allen Zeiten wird gefeiert / die Hochzeit auch des Stoffes mit dem Geist).[48]

Steiner's translation of Lešehrad's unrhymed dramatic poem seems to me to have been a young man's experiment with poetic language. Given Lešehrad's wide contacts in the world of publishing and his own reputation as a translator, Steiner's translation was bound to appear in print. Furthermore, it was published by Orbis, where Paul/Pavel Eisner worked. Eisner was a great propagator of Czech literature among the German-speaking peoples. *Die Planeten* had no impact on the imagery and vision of Steiner's later verse. Nevertheless, Lešehrad's theme, his mythic exposition on the physical meaning of death for the soul, would always be close to Steiner's anthropological interest in religion. Furthermore, given that occultists, albeit normally in an amateur fashion, were great students of non-Christian religions, and sought insight into the nature of humankind's relationship to the world of spirits and the godhead among these religions, it would not be outrageous to suggest that Steiner may have been interested in translating such verse for that very reason. Occultism may have joined with his study of Oriental languages in inspiring a passion for anthropology. That may, however, not be as significant for Steiner as the fact that he used this translation also as an apprenticeship for his own *Eroberungen* (Conquests).

---

[48] Lešehrad, *Most nad světem*, pp. 74 and 96; Lešehrad, *Die Planeten*, p. 29.

PAINTING AUTHORS

The Portraits of Elias Canetti, Iris Murdoch, and Franz Baermann Steiner by Marie-Louise von Motesiczky

Ines Schlenker

It might be quite appropriate to call Marie-Louise von Motesiczky a 'well-kept secret'. Only a relatively small circle of people know her paintings and a smaller circle still are aware of her connection with figures like Elias Canetti, Franz Baermann Steiner, and Iris Murdoch. The substantial body of work Motesiczky left at her death in 1996 includes striking portraits of all three. In particular Elias Canetti, who entertained a friendship with Motesiczky that lasted for more than fifty years, was a favourite if not an easy and often evasive subject-matter for the artist.

Marie-Louise von Motesiczky was not a prominent figure in the British art scene. Although the few solo exhibitions in England, for example at the Goethe Institute in London in 1985, were extremely well-received by the press and substantially enlarged the number of admirers of her work in this country, it is fair to say that Motesiczky achieved the status of a widely accepted artist only in her native Austria. After several solo exhibitions, a major retrospective at the Österreichische Galerie im Belvedere in Vienna in 1994 celebrated nearly seventy years of the artist's work. Her undisputed place in the canon of Austrian art was once again proved by her prominent inclusion in the exhibition *Jahrhundert der Frauen* at the Kunstforum in Vienna in 1999. Numerous paintings are in private collections all over the world and in several public collections, such as the Tate Gallery in London, the Fitzwilliam Museum in Cambridge, the Stedelijk Museum of Modern Art in Amsterdam, and the Österreichische Galerie im Belvedere.

Motesiczky's relative obscurity in this country can be attributed to several factors: her emigré status left her without the established network of professional support and her style of painting, a kind of Expressionism that was founded on her training with Max Beckmann, met with lack of interest. Furthermore, Motesiczky did not actively push her work into the public sphere and was, rather, content with focusing on creating new art works. Her awareness and ambivalent evaluation of this fundamentally lonely situation which, however, also contained unique artistic possibilities is expressed in the following autobiographical observation:

In der Malerei fehlte jede Konfrontation. Isolierung ist ein Wort. Es klingt traurig, kann aber auch etwas sehr Schönes sein. Ob die Isolierung gut oder schlecht war, weiß man erst viel später.[1]

(In painting there was no confrontation. Isolation is a word. It sounds sad, but can also be something very beautiful. Whether isolation was good or bad, one can only tell much later.)

This paper intends very briefly to introduce Marie-Louise von Motesiczky as an artist, before considering the relationship between Motesiczky, Canetti, Steiner, and Murdoch and discussing some of the artworks that these sitters inspired.

I.

Marie-Louise von Motesiczky was born in Vienna in 1906.[2] Her father, Edmund von Motesiczky, a gifted amateur cellist, died when she was only three. Her mother came from an extremely wealthy Jewish family of bankers, industrialists, and scholars who played a vital role in the intellectual and artistic circles of Vienna; they included the philosopher Franz Brentano and Robert von Lieben, the inventor of the amplifying valve. Motesiczky's grandmother Anna von Lieben was one of the earliest patients of Sigmund Freud and thus a crucial inspiration for the creation of psychoanalysis.

Having left school at the age of thirteen, Motesiczky continued her education privately, visiting art schools in Vienna, The Hague, Frankfurt, and Paris before being accepted in Max Beckmann's master class at the Städelschule in Frankfurt in 1926/27. Beckmann, whom she had already met in her teens, was to have a shaping influence on her art and also became a lifelong friend. During the following decade Motesiczky quietly practised her

---

[1] Marie-Louise von Motesiczky, 'Etwas über mich', in *Marie-Louise von Motesiczky*, exh. cat. (Vienna: Österreichische Galerie im Belvedere, 1994), pp. 13–16, (p. 15). Unless otherwise stated, all translations are the author's own.
[2] The biography is based on documents from the archive of the Marie-Louise von Motesiczky Charitable Trust and on Richard Calvocoressi, 'Introduction', in *Marie-Louise von Motesiczky: Paintings Vienna 1925 – London 1985*, exh. cat. (London: Goethe-Institut, 1985), pp. 59–63.

art in Vienna. When, in 1938, Hitler marched into Austria, Motesiczky immediately left for Holland, together with her mother. Their flight would eventually take them to England the following year, where they settled in Amersham during the war years. Her brother Karl, who remained in Austria, managed to send on her paintings – as a result some of the early works have survived. Karl subsequently became active in the resistance. During an attempt to smuggle refugees into Switzerland he was denounced and sent to Auschwitz where he perished soon afterwards.[3] After the war Motesiczky moved to London and eventually purchased a house in Hampstead where she settled for the last thirty-six years of her life and continued to work steadily on her paintings.

Besides Max Beckmann, Oskar Kokoschka, whom the Motesiczkys knew in Vienna and later frequently met in England, came to be a decisive influence on Motesiczky's work. Although she never studied with him, his constant encouragement and comments on her works gave her guidance and support. Yet, despite the impact of two such masters of modern German art, Motesiczky very soon developed her own distinctive style. The strongest works can be found among her portraits and self-portraits. The group of works depicting her mother Henriette, spanning some fifty years and comprising about twenty paintings and numerous drawings and sketches, is outstanding in its honesty and directness. Motesiczky faithfully chronicles her mother's changing face and ultimate descent into extreme old age – she lived to be 96 – with an empathy and boldness that sometimes seems almost brutal. The 1936 drawing *Hunting* shows a strong, matronly figure in a boat, engaged in one of her favourite pastimes. Two decades later, the mother still presents an impressive, almost manly, pipe-smoking figure in *Henriette von Motesiczky* (1959). Here, the onset of old age can faintly be detected in the wearing of a wig, from which a few strands of hair have managed to escape. The painting *From Night into Day* of 1975 (Tate Gallery, London) shows the mother, now in her mid-nineties, retiring in bed. Together with her hair she has lost all former energy. Only the whippet, a constant companion, provides a reminder of her hunting days. Finally, extreme helplessness can be seen in the shrivelled body and almost childlike features of *Mother with Baton* of 1977 (Arts Council of Great Britain). Abstaining from beautification and idealization and with a passion for truth, Motesiczky succeeds at boldly depicting her sitter 'objectively' with all the unsightly consequences of old age.

---

[3] Christiane Rothländer, University of Vienna, is currently preparing a Ph. D. on Karl von Motesiczky.

II.

Like Motesiczky and her mother, another pair of refugees from Nazi-occupied
Europe sought shelter in Amersham in the early 1940s: Elias Canetti and his
wife Veza. Soon a remarkable friendship developed between the painter and
the couple. Veza Canetti expressed her admiration for Motesiczky in the dedication of an as yet unpublished novel:

> Mein Roman 'The Response' ist der Malerin Marie-Luise Motesiczky ge-
> widmet. Denn der leise Zauber, der von ihr ausgeht, hat mich zu einer Fi-
> gur angeregt und ihre Feinheit hat meine Wildheit gebändigt und die Figu-
> ren und die Musik meines Buches bestimmt.[4]

> (My novel 'The Response' is dedicated to the painter Marie-Luise Mote-
> siczky. The soft magic that emanates from her has given me an idea for a
> figure and her refinement has tamed my wildness and determined the fig-
> ures and the music of my book.)

Yet it was Elias Canetti who was to become a crucial influence on Motesiczky's
life. Their long-lasting and intellectually stimulating friendship survived the
death of Veza, and Canetti's subsequent founding of a family with his second
wife, Hera, although it was extremely painful for Motesiczky to come to terms
with the fact that her own hope of marrying Canetti would remain forever
unfulfilled.

Motesiczky met Canetti as a relatively young and unknown writer – his
first novel *Die Blendung* (The Deception) had been published in German a
few years before – and was to support him throughout his career emotionally and practically as well as financially. Canetti frequently worked in Motesiczky's house and in this way became intimately familiar with her oeuvre. Each was very appreciative of the other's work. Canetti often lavished
effusive praise on Motesiczky's latest paintings as several of her diary en-
tries and his hand-written book dedications to her show. Over the years,
Canetti's different ways of addressing Motesiczky indicate a growing distance in their personal relationship yet also his continued dedicated support
for her artistic output. In the 1950s and 60s he addresses her as 'Muli', a pet
name for Motesiczky, his friend and lover, and comments on and praises individual works. Later on, when he did not see her so regularly, he would
write to her as 'Maler Mulo', refering to Motesiczky, the painter, and encour-
age her to carry on working. Motesiczky showed her appreciation of, and

---

[4] Undated note by Veza Canetti: archive of the Marie-Louise von Motesiczky Charitable
Trust.

108

Plate 1. Marie-Louise von Motesiczky, *Self-portrait with Canetti* (mid-1960s), Marie-Louise von Motesiczky Charitable Trust, London.

easy familiarity with, Canetti and his writings by including a copy of one of his books in the still-life *Orchid* of 1958. The spine of the book is labelled 'Pio', Motesiczky's nickname for Canetti. Ten years earlier, in *In the Garden* (1948), Canetti had been included in a domestic scene showing Motesiczky and her aunt Ilse, engaged in rather imaginary gardening. As the German title *Familienbild* (family portrait) implies, Canetti was by then seen as part of the Motesiczky family. Yet, his frowning looks, detached stance, and slightly disapproving attitude suggest that he did not feel comfortable at being thus appropriated. The painting *Self-portrait with Canetti* (Plate 1) of the mid 1960s further comments on the strained relationship between the poet and the painter. Having completed her work, her brushes washed and neatly arranged like arrows for use in the anticipated struggle, Motesiczky depicts herself patiently waiting for Canetti to finish his newspaper. He, however, is thoroughly engrossed in his reading and does not notice his expectant companion. The rift between the two characters and the palpably awkward atmosphere is exemplified by their representation in two almost separate parts of the canvas.

Iris Murdoch could have been introduced to Motesiczky by Canetti, an intimate friend for a number of years, or by Franz Baermann Steiner, to whom she was linked by a close friendship towards the end of his life, and who knew Motesiczky as a friend of Canetti's.[5] Murdoch's appreciation of, and interest in, Motesiczky's paintings spans several decades and reached an early climax in 1963 when Murdoch commissioned Motesiczky to paint her portrait. A postcard from 1986 still expresses Murdoch's curiosity about new paintings with the concise wish: 'Wd like to see you and pictures!' While certain characteristics of Steiner and Canetti (their Central European origin and charismatic Jewish personality as well as more specific individual traits) appear in several characters of Murdoch's novels, a painting by Motesiczky, together with a de Kooning and a Kokoschka, captures the essence of the remodelled interior of a formerly musty and old-fashioned house in the novel *The Book and the Brotherhood* from 1987:

> The drawing room [...] was now painted a glowing aquamarine adorned with a huge scarlet abstract by de Kooning over the fireplace and two colourful conversation pieces by Kokoschka and Motesiczky.[6]

---

5 On the relationship of Murdoch with Steiner and Canetti see Peter Conradi, *Iris Murdoch. A Life* (London: Harper Collins, 2001), pp. 317–375.

6 Iris Murdoch, *The Book and the Brotherhood* (London: Chatto and Windus, 1987), pp. 536–537. For more detailed information on the relationship of Murdoch and Motesiczky and the creation of the portrait see Ines Schlenker, 'Painting the Author: The Portrait of Iris Murdoch by Marie-Louise von Motesiczky', *Iris Murdoch Newsletter*, 15 (2001), 1–4.

The *Portrait of Iris Murdoch* (Plate 2), that belongs to St. Anne's College, Oxford, was completed in 1964. On the occasion of leaving St. Anne's in order to devote her time fully to her novels and becoming an honorary fellow of philosophy in 1963, Iris Murdoch commissioned Marie-Louise von Motesiczky to paint her portrait. As a parting gift to the college, Murdoch was willing to pay the difference between the college's contribution and Motesiczky's normal fee. By that time, having just published her sixth novel, Murdoch had become a well-known and established figure on the English literary scene. She chose Motesiczky as an artist she personally admired and thought undervalued in this country. With this commission she hoped to help increase Motesiczky's reputation and make her more familiar to a wider audience: 'I admire her work very much & I think she is not well enough known in England. (She has a big reputation in Austria where she originally comes from.)'[7] Motesiczky portrayed Murdoch facing the viewer, the head turned to the right with an absent, dreamlike expression on her face and a slightly windblown air about her whole presence. Fittingly, she is seated before a background of an animated dark sea on which the prow of a ship can be made out, cutting diagonally across the picture plane. With the ship, the emblem of St. Anne's College, Motesiczky chose an accessory for the background that clearly defines its context and also marks the occasion the portrait was to commemorate. The painting's reception was nevertheless ambivalent. One viewer, for example, allegedly mistook the ship for an aeroplane crashing into the sea. The historian Marjorie Reeves, who frequently passed the portrait hanging outside the Senior Common Room at St. Anne's, found it a 'powerful portrait' but felt that the overall 'ship-wrecked' appearance of the sitter did not adequately capture the various aspects of Murdoch's personality.[8] Murdoch, however, who did not see the portrait until it was nearly completed, found it uncannily prescient. She noted in her diary: 'I think it is wonderful, terrible, so sad and frightening, me with the demons. How did she know?'[9]

It was through Canetti that Motesiczky met Franz Baermann Steiner during the war years in Amersham.[10] The painter and the anthropologist and poet possess several similarities: both came from fully assimilated Jewish families, both had suffered great personal tragedies (the early loss of father or sister and

[7] Iris Murdoch to the Principal of St. Anne's College, Oxford, 25 June [1963]: personal file, St. Anne's College, Oxford.
[8] Marjorie Reeves to Ines Schlenker, 18 June 2000: archive of the Marie-Louise von Motesiczky Charitable Trust.
[9] Iris Murdoch: unpublished diary entry 16 February [1964], kindly made available by Peter Conradi; partially quoted in Peter Conradi, *Iris Murdoch. A Life*, p. 374.
[10] Alfons Fleischli: 'Franz Baermann Steiner. Leben und Werk' (dissertation, University of Freiburg, Switzerland, 1970), p. 30.

Plate 2: Marie-Louise von Motesiczky, *Portrait of Iris Murdoch* (1964),
St Anne's College, University of Oxford.

subsequently of brother or parents to the Nazis), both were greatly attached to their native homelands and now forced to live in exile. Neither received the recognition they deserved during their lifetime. Their friendship led to infrequent visits and seems to have created enough trust for Steiner to send Motesiczky samples of his work.[11] Several poems by Steiner survive in the Motesiczky estate; the earliest date from 1942 or before, while the last selection was written in the early 1950s. Motesiczky is full of praise for the painterly technique applied in the poems. In 1942, for example, she writes:

[D]anke ich ihnen für ihren lieben Brief und für die Gedichte. Sie sind sehr, sehr schön. Man kann sie nicht beantworten, denn sie sind vollendet, man kann auch nicht für sie danken, es sei denn man könnte selber dichten. Das kann ich nicht, doch würde ich mich in der Sprache der Malerei ausdrük-ken, so würde ich sagen, dass sie zum Leben erwachten Bildern gleichen, die man mit geschlossenen Augen ansieht. Man atmet sie ein, Geräusche dringen bis in's Ohr wärend aus dem Dunkel, leise sich bewegend das Bild aufsteigt. Die Augen wandern im Garten vom Himmel hinab zum rasen u. wieder empor zu den Bäumen – u. wenn man sie wieder öffnet, meint man, man sei selber in dem Bild gewesen.[12]

(I thank you for your kind letter and for the poems. They are very, very beautiful. One cannot reply to them because they are perfect, one also cannot express one's thanks for them unless one can write poetry oneself. I can't do that but if I were to express myself in the language of painting I would say that they resemble paintings that have come alive and that one sees with closed eyes. One breathes them in, noises reach the ear while the painting arises from the dark, moving slightly. The eyes wander in the garden from the sky to the grass and back again up to the trees – and when one opens them again one seems to have been in the painting oneself.)

In the face of this comment it is not surprising that Steiner practically gave up poetry and took up drawing as a pastime himself in 1950 when he became increasingly disillusioned with his situation as a poet. In a letter to Canetti he remarks on his new interest: 'Drawing gives me a lot of pleasure. [...] Human groups interest me most of all' (Adler and Fardon, SWI: 96). To H. G. Adler,

---

[11] On the occasion of a visit by Steiner and the singer Engel Lund to Amersham in August 1945, Motesiczky noted in her diary on 4 August 1945: 'Engel Lund u. Steiner angekommen. Spatz.[iergang] mit Steiner [...] Steiner isst heimlich Pfeffermünz Zuckerln. Lund schläft bei St. [einers] Geschichten.' (Engel Lund and Steiner arrived. Walk with Steiner [...] Steiner secretly eats peppermint drops. Lund goes to sleep during Steiner's stories): archive of the Marie-Louise von Motesiczky Charitable Trust.
[12] Marie-Louise von Motesiczky to Franz Baermann Steiner, 5 February 1942: private collection, London (partially published in Dokumente, AsP: 428).

Steiner confesses that painting and drawing indeed took precedence over writing for a while – as well as opening up new ways of seeing and perceiving the world around him: 'Zeichnen und Malen ist mir jetzt das Wichtigste geworden. [...] jeder Spaziergang zeigt mir neue Dinge in der gewohnten Umgebung. Ich hatte früher nur Flächen gesehen und keine Linien; und das ergibt ganz andere Rhythmen.' (Drawing and painting has now become most important for me. [...] each walk shows me new things in the familiar surroundings. I formerly only saw planes and no lines; and this results in completely different rhythms.)[13]

While one portrait exists of Murdoch and several of Canetti – both on his own and with others (Motesiczky's *Elias Canetti* of 1960 is in the collection of the Historisches Museum der Stadt Wien and her 1992 *Portrait of Elias Canetti* belongs to the National Portrait Gallery in London) – Franz Baermann Steiner is only depicted in a painting alongside Canetti, *Conversation in the Library* (Plate 3). This, however, is one of the most characteristic works in Motesiczky's oeuvre. Just as the *Portrait of Iris Murdoch* chronicles the end of Murdoch's career at St. Anne's, on a much larger scale the painting *Conversation in the Library* (1950) is testimony to a lost world. The two writers are involved in a heated discussion. It takes place in a room full of books, presumably the artist's studio in the Motesiczky house in Amersham where a sizeable portion of Canetti's vast library was kept. Jeremy Adler poignantly describes the painting:

> Canetti, mighty and straddle-legged, with his left hand in the pocket and the right behind the bowed head, hair tousled, looks at the floor in front of him; Steiner, slight, stands to his right like a fencer taking his guard, the oversized, almost bald head in profile, the right eye sharply looking into the distance, the red mouth like an arrow pointing inwards, the right arm bent, the hand stretched out, open, demonstrating. Thus, entangled in a battle of words, the two appear like mutually intertwined opposites, and follow, each for himself, a common goal.[14]

When Canetti and Steiner met again in England, their friendship soon became close. Apart from an intensive and regular exchange not only on questions of

---

[13] Franz Baermann Steiner to H. G. Adler, 23 May 1950; quoted in Fleischli, p. 33.

[14] 'Canetti, mächtig und breitbeinig, mit der linken Hand in der Tasche und der rechten hinter dem gesenkten Kopf, blickt mit zerrauftem Haar vor sich auf den Boden; Steiner, schmächtig, steht rechts vor ihm wie ein Fechter in Positur, der übergroße, fast kahle Kopf in Profil, das rechte Auge scharf in die Ferne blickend, der rote Mund wie ein nach innen gerichteter Pfeil, der rechte Arm gebogen, die Hand ausgestreckt, offen, zeigend. So wirken die zwei, verstrickt im Wortgefecht, wie ineinander verschränkte Gegensätze, und verfolgen jeder für sich ein gemeinsames Ziel.'; Jeremy Adler, 'Die Freundschaft zwischen Elias Canetti und Franz Baermann Steiner', *Akzente*, 42/3 (1995), 228–231, (p. 228).

poetry and scholarship, but also on the problems of everyday life in exile, their many shared and varied interests, especially in myths, their similarities in the method of working and – most importantly – their 'massive and extraordinarily wide-ranging scholarship' (Adler and Fardon, SWI: 17) as well as a pronounced passion for books and book-hunting must have provided endless food for discussion. The intellectual exchange certainly benefited both: while, for example, Steiner started to write numerous little essays and aphorisms at Canetti's suggestion,[15] he, as a professional anthropologist, would have been an invaluable help to Canetti who was conducting his extensive research for *Masse und Macht* (Crowds and Power, 1960) at the time. In a letter to Motesiczky of the late 1940s, Canetti praises Steiner as the only scholar able to grasp the consequences of his own thoughts.[16]

It would have been appropriate for Motesiczky to situate Canetti and Steiner, as she knew them, in a room full of books. She associated Canetti's learnedness with books and the intensive study of them. She might even have seen the books as a kind of rival for Canetti's attention – a battle she had resigned herself to losing since reading and especially writing always took precedence over Motesiczky. Books also provided a recurring theme in the poems Steiner gave to Motesiczky. They can characterize a room or a mood, as for example in *Herbstmorgen im Zimmer* (Autumn Morning in the Room) of 1943:

Bücherrücken stehn im morgengold,
Bilder wachen auf aus gelben wänden.[17]

(Book spines stand in the morning gold, / Pictures awaken on the yellow walls.)

Books can also become a consolation in solitude as in the 1934 poem *Die Neige* (The Closing):

Der abend geht zur neige.
Wer kühlt die müde stirne?
Ins dunkel schneidet bang der lampe lichtkreis.
Nur alte bücher warten auf die hand. (AsP: 25)

(The evening draws to a close. / Who will cool the tired brow? / The lamp's circle of light cuts fearfully into the darkness. / Only old books wait at hand.)

---

[15] Fleischli, p. 28.
[16] Elias Canetti to Marie-Louise von Motesiczky, n. d. [May 1948]: archive of the Marie-Louise von Motesiczky Charitable Trust.
[17] The poems refered to here are held in the archive of the Marie-Louise von Motesiczky Charitable Trust.

Another example is *Ohne Staunen* (Without Surprise) of 1945:

In der abendsonne zittert die bunte reihe der bücher:
Bin von euch müd worden.
Jetzt neig ich mich über des gartens durstigen rand. (AsP: 171)

(The bright row of books trembles in the evening sun: / I have become tired of you. / Now I lean over the thirsty edge of the garden.)

Ernst Gombrich, a Motesiczky family friend, always imagined Steiner as a veritable 'bookworm', eating his way through the stock at the British Museum (Adler and Fardon, SWI: 18). Equally, Motesiczky was aware of the common passion for book-hunting that kept Canetti and Steiner in constant competition. Most importantly, the books stand for the immense knowledge amassed by Canetti and Steiner over the years.

This allusion to their intellectual force stands in striking contrast to the physical characterization of the two figures. While an anonymous critic once thought of Canetti and Steiner as a 'gnomic couple'[18] and Canetti referred to this depiction of himself as a caricature,[19] it would be wrong to treat them as cartoons. They could instead be seen as psychological studies conducted in a simplified, slightly naïve style. Like the series of paintings Motesiczky made of her ageing mother, *Conversation in the Library* is a prime example of the artist's method of poignant characterization, and of her bitter truthfulness. Canetti, himself no giant, was, nonetheless, an impressive figure. John Bayley described him as follows: 'Squat, almost dwarfish, with a massive head and thick black hair, he looked like a giant cut short at the waist, what the Germans call a *Sitzriese*.'[20] Canetti, himself, was chiefly fascinated by Steiner's qualities as an interlocutor and not by his physical appearance. In his usual biting style, Canetti reminisces:

Sein Leben war von seiner Figur bestimmt, er hatte keine. Er war klein und so schmächtig, daß man ihn beinahe übersah. Besonders häßlich war sein Gesicht: niedere, fliehende Stirn, ohnmächtige Augen immer in unwillkürlicher Bewegung. Die Sprache weinerlich, selbst wenn nichts zu beklagen war. Weniger einnehmend als er konnte kein Mensch in Erscheinung treten. Aber dann sprach man mit ihm, und er hatte, auf seine langsame und scheinbar leidenschaftslose Art, immer etwas zu sagen. Es war immer klar und konkret und jeder Rhetorik bar. Es bestand aus seinem Gehalt, nie irgendwelchen Mitteln der Wiedergabe.[21]

---

[18] 'Enchantment drawn from Life', *Ham & High*, 29 November 1985.
[19] Elias Canetti to Marie-Louise von Motesiczky, 17 September 1954: archive of the Marie-Louise von Motesiczky Charitable Trust.
[20] John Bayley, *Iris. A Memoir of Iris Murdoch* (London: Duckworth, 1998), p. 118.
[21] See p. 253 in the current volume.

Plate 3: Marie-Louise von Motesiczky, *Conversation in the Library* (1950), Marie-Louise von Motesiczky Charitable Trust, London.

(His life was determined by his figure, he had none. He was small and so slight, that one almost overlooked him. His face was particularly ugly: low, sloping forehead, powerless eyes in constant involuntary motion. His voice was tearful, even when there was nothing to complain about. There cannot have been a less winning human being.
But then you talked to him, and, in his slow and apparently passionless manner, he always had something to say. It was always clear and concrete and free of any rhetoric. It was always original, never reliant on any means of expression.)

Steiner himself was well aware of his physique. He explained his plans to do fieldwork among the pygmies as follows: 'All my life I have been a little man, I want to know what it feels like, just for once, to be a big man' (Adler and Fardon, SWI: 88).[22] It is exactly this discrepancy between corporeal appearance and intellectual greatness that Motesiczky is able to capture.[23]

But there is a further dimension to the painting. Although not physically included in the painting, Motesiczky is nevertheless obscurely present as the invisible third party. Indeed, in a preliminary sketch for the painting, she reveals her partially hidden figure behind the more prominent Canetti. Modestly keeping in the background, she is but an observer of the scene, which in this version does not yet figure Steiner. By later omitting herself entirely, she manages to distance herself from the sitters and to gain a more objective perspective.

In her portraits of Canetti, Steiner, and Murdoch, just as in so many of her other works, Motesiczky succeeds in standing back and dissociating herself from her subject-matter – her friends or her mother – while at the same time, with integrity and courage, managing to relate to them sympathetically. As an intensive observer of her surroundings, Motesiczky creates portraits that are extremely honest – and sometimes seemingly crude. They nevertheless seem to capture the sitter's true identity and the situation they find themselves in.

---

[22] The comment was presumably made around 1950.
[23] An observation by Motesiczky on a trip to Portugal is telling in this context: 'Es giebt tatsächlich Leute die wie die Gespenster vom Steiner aussehen u. kleinwinzige Pärchen – eine sehr schöne Rasse ist das gerade nicht – aber vielleicht sind alle Rassen zunächst mal recht hässlich u. die schönen Exemplare muss man sich dann erst suchen gehen. Ein reitzendes kleines Kindermädchen sah ich mit einem weissen Häubchen in einem Park – u. sehr spanisch – aber gleich kam so ein schielender Steiner u. setzte sich zu ihr.' (There are really people who look like ghosts of Steiner, and tiny little pairs – it is not a particularly beautiful race – but perhaps all races are basically really ugly and one must seek out the more attractive examples. I saw a charming little children's nurse with a white cap in the park – and very Spanish – but immediately there appeared a squinting Steiner who sat down next to her.): Marie-Louise von Motesiczky to Elias Canetti, [?] September 1954: archive of the Marie-Louise von Motesiczky Charitable Trust.

FRANZ BAERMANN STEINER'S INFLUENCE ON IRIS MURDOCH

Peter J. Conradi

On 16 December 1952 Iris Murdoch wrote to a friend that she was not in good shape at present, having

> lately lost, by death, the person who was closest to me, whom I loved very dearly, whom I would very probably have married, if things had gone on as they were going. I can't at the moment see how one recovers from such a loss.[1]

She referred, of course, to Franz Baermann Steiner, and, around the same time tried to console herself in her journal by evoking his voice and intonation. One phrase among many hit her. His way of asking *What ees it*? Two months later on 27 January 1953, Murdoch made the following journal entry: 'Am I excessively "open to influence"? Franz influenced me very much.' This essay attempts to open the question of what that influence was, a question vexed by the inconvenient fact that there were so many Jewish refugees who were important to her.

She made many friends among expatriates. An Anglo-Irishwoman whose father never acquired English friends, she identified with the condition of exile. At Badminton school from 1932 to 1938, she and her peers had understood earlier than most, she later claimed, what was happening under Hitler. Her high-minded head-mistress had invited to Badminton after *c.* 1936, as well as Indians such as the young Indira Ghandi, *Mischlinge* like Chitra Rudingerova. Then at Oxford from 1938 to 1942, Czechs, Austrians, and elderly German Jews – 'scholars' she called them, 'with long hair and even longer sentences'[2] – flooded the streets and buses. 'East London and East Europe,' she noted,

---

[1] Iris Murdoch to David Hicks, 16 December 1952. All references to letters and to journals cited in this essay are from unpublished sources, and, apart from the Murdoch-Hicks run – which is in the Modern Mss Department of the Bodleian Library – in private hands. Journal references in this article are for this reason identified solely by date throughout.

[2] Iris Murdoch to David Hicks, 21 March 1941.

'jostle for Lebensraum on the pavements of the High & Corn.' It used to be said that on the buses of North Oxford one needed to speak German.[3] Murdoch wrote around 1940 that the internment of refugees who had been fighting fascism, some suicidal, drove her 'frantic', and in March 1945 'I find my pro-Semitism becoming more & more fanatical with the years.'[4]

If the Serb and Slovene refugees who became her friends (some life-long) in front-line UNRRA camps in Austria between December 1945 and June 1946 are excluded, together with the Palestinian Wasfi Hijab and the Indian Kanti Shah, both students of Wittgenstein at Trinity College, Cambridge and friends from her year there in 1947 to 1948, eight major expatriates remain, all of them Jewish, many of them major scholars in their fields. The most important was arguably Elias Canetti, known since 1952, to whom she dedicated *The Flight from the Enchanter* in 1956. He is a shadowy presence behind many of her best books. She had joined the Classicist Eduard Fraenkel's famous, long-running seminar on Aeschylus's *Agamemnon* in October 1938, and was to dedicate her novel *The Time of the Angels* to Fraenkel in 1966. The Hungarian economists Thomas Balogh and Nickie Kaldor were both friends from 1943 onwards. To Georg Kreisel, the eminent Austrian mathematician and friend of Wittgenstein whom she met in 1947, she dedicated *An Accidental Man* in 1971. She probably met the ancient historian Arnaldo Momigliano during the war. His parents were killed by the Nazis after 1943. In 1987 she dedicated the *Message to the Planet* to him. Their friendship was important to Momigliano over many years: Murdoch and Momigliano were holidaying in Italy in August 1952, their third such trip, at the time that Franz Steiner was making his second – and last – trip to Spain. Canetti and Franz are the remaining two expatriates.

Franz Steiner's diary-entry 'Enter Iris Murdoch' suggests that he and Murdoch met on Friday, 11 May1951, a year during which they appear to have met six times, mostly for a drink in the Lamb and Flag pub. For her part, she first mentions this new acquaintance in her journal ten months later in February 1952. On 22 January1965 she wrote of her colleague the German-Jewish teacher of philosophy at the RCA, Frederic Samson, that he 'is the latest of my Jewish teachers, of whom the first was Fraenkel and the most beloved Franz'.[5]

It is no accident that she wrote of her Jewish *teachers*. Reverencing her father, Murdoch thirsted for fatherly guidance for the intellectual she was becoming. Hence her need for gurus, for the same qualities on a yet more august

---

[3] Mark Amory, *Lord Berners: The Last Eccentric* (London: Chatto and Windus, 1998), p. 179.
[4] Iris Murdoch to David Hicks, 8 March 1945.
[5] This list leaves out of account Wittgenstein's ex-pupil and antagonist Friedrich Waissmann, whose wife and son both committed suicide, Oxford's first professor of engineering Hans Motz, and the Marxologist Georg Lichtheim who also killed himself. She was close to both Motz and Lichtheim.

and majestic scale. Fraenkel and Momigliano were pre-eminent in their field; Murdoch believed Canetti to be a genius. As for Franz, Adler and Fardon's *Selected Writings* make clear how much his early death deprived us of. These Central European refugees that Murdoch admired, pitied, and collected, had lost their culture, their language, their homes, sometimes their families when these had been gassed, their money, their professions, their papers, their way of life. They were wounded patriarchs, deprived even, in many cases, of the ability to fight. The British attitude towards them was by no means uniformly generous. 'What are they doing taking jobs away from our boys who are away at the front?' was a common reaction. Small surprise if some of them could be difficult.

Uniquely among her expatriate friends, Franz Steiner shared Iris Murdoch's interest in religion. It was a topic much in his mind at the end of his life. Franz noted (14 November 1952): 'A highly interesting conversation about Jewish mysticism and Chassiduth [& the] absolute necessity of bringing together non-gnostic elements of Jewish mysticism [...]'. Iris Murdoch asked him on Saturday, 15 November whether he believed in God. He could not use the word 'believe' because, among other things, it misinterpreted his relationship with God: he could only say that he loved Him. Very lamely he skirted around the most important thing for him, wondering how he could talk about such heart-felt matters, 'least of all to this seriously questioning angel'. So he spoke about his understanding of Judaism, in painfully brittle words; the dual relationship of God – to the individual as creator, and to the people as spouse (Gefreier).[6] Then she spoke: about her ignorant 'groping'; her feelings of guilt because of her past life; her ties to the Anglican Church. Only within the framework of *that* church could she imagine a realization of the religious life. He listened, half turning away, silently praying that all might not be lost. His heart was thumping a grand march of breathlessness. 'Thank God she didn't see how things were with me.' His journal suggests that they read Kafka's story 'Josephine, the Singer' together.

Murdoch wrote to the poet Michael Hamburger that neither Franz nor Canetti were to be found in her work, and often stoutly maintained that she did not draw her characters from life, a practice she held to be morally abhorrent; when friends saw themselves in her books, 'this was generally vanity on their part'.[7] In 1982 she echoed Canetti in maintaining that 'true writers encounter their characters *after* they've created them',[8] something which appears to have

---

[6] Steiner's handwriting is very difficult to decode: 'Befreier' would be deliverer.

[7] 1982 radio interview with Susan Hill

[8] Elias Canetti, *Aufzeichnungen 1942–1985* (Munich: Hanser, 1993), 'Die Provinz des Menschen', p. 103: 'Die wirklichen Dichter begegnen ihren Figuren erst, nachdem sie sie geschaffen haben' (1946).

happened after she had created Anne Cavidge in *Nuns and Soldiers* (1980) and then met an ex-nun Sister Ann Teresa whose career had unknowingly prefigured Cavidge's. Among those offended by the ageing eponymous Bruno of *Bruno's Dream* (1969), had been the critic Lord David Cecil, her Badminton headmistress BMB, the writers J. B. Priestley and Elisabeth Bowen – the differences between these four suggesting that she had 'universalized' the condition of old age successfully: BMB was the most sporting. Her already fragile friendship with the philosopher Donald MacKinnon, her Greats tutor and most important mentor, was dealt a death blow when he believed he had been treated satirically in another novel. Since at least two others close to MacKinnon were offended by this characterization, the uncomfortable possibility that she had drawn an unconscious portrait suggests itself.

Moreover she more than once consciously broke her own rule. Her journals openly acknowledge that Hugo Belfounder in *Under the Net* (1954) is a portrait of Wittgenstein's premier pupil, Yorick Smythies. Yet there can be no absolute congruence between fiction and real life, and the ways the former feeds the latter are – of course – much more various that through the writing of *romans-à-clef*. Even where a character or situation can indeed be traced back to one in 'real-life', this does not always necessarily deepen our understanding of the book. She certainly borrowed a certain 'situational logic' from her friends' lives.

There are five places where the inspiration of Franz, or of something about his ideas, seems visible. The most direct portrait, it may be, is in *The Nice and the Good* (1968), the first of her novels to recall Shakespearian comedy and romance, in its lyrical meditation on the themes of love, forgiveness, and reconciliation. The action is divided between a wicked court at Whitehall and its pastoral cousin, Trescombe, a Dorset Arden in a green world, its characters each wrestling with some unhappy past *karma*. Paula has suffered the disfigurement of her husband by her lover, Mary Clothier the inadvertent death of her husband in a street accident after a furious row. Mary is given Murdoch's figure: 'Though not formally beautiful, Mary had as a physical endowment a strong confidence in her power to attract'.[9] She loves and tries to console the Central European Willy Kost. Opinion is divided as to whether Willy comes from Vienna or from Prague. Willy is given Franz's slight build, his accent, and throughout the book the precise question Murdoch commemorated him with shortly after his death, *'What ees eet?'* He is short in stature, his face small and brown, his nose thin, his hands dainty and bony.

For the anthropologist Mary Douglas, Franz single-handedly invented the 'sociology of danger' (SWI: 3–15) and that reading of 'taboo' that relates it, not

---

[9] Iris Murdoch, *The Nice and the Good* (London: Chatto and Windus, 1968), p. 95.

to aberration, but to the sacred. He became because of what he had endured, both sacred and taboo, coming from the place where Nazism undid all taboos, so questioning the idea of the sacred itself. The camp-survivor Willy Kost in *The Nice and the Good*, inspired by Franz, is both sacred and taboo. His Trescombe neighbours leave anxious gifts outside his cottage door, unconsciously appeasing a source of danger, propitiating one whose ill luck makes him an object of holy dread.

Much about their friendship recalls Steiner and Murdoch. When Mary brings Willy a posy of sweet nettles and arranges them in a wine-glass, he comments that, if only he were a poet, he would write a poem about that – a direct reference to the gentians Iris brought and arranged in a wine-glass for Franz on his return from Spain in 1952, and the poem 'Enzian brachte sie mir' (She brought me gentians) with which he commemorated this. Like Franz, Willy teaches Mary German, which they read together. Iris also gives Willy one habit of Frederic Samson, that of jigging around the room to Mozart. What seems none the less most like Franz, albeit dramatically transmuted, is the guilt Willy nurtures about betraying out of fear two people to their deaths in Dachau. This seems inspired by Franz Steiner's guilt about abandoning his parents in 1938. Murdoch awards him a poetically just ending when he is pursued at the end by the passionate and needy young Jessica Bird, into whose troubles he has earlier made a dramatic intervention.

This is not the first occasion, however, that Steiner haunts Murdoch's work and world. Rosa Keepe's sense of being split, in *Flight from the Enchanter* between Mischa Fox and Peter Saward, borrows, her journals suggest, from her own guilt, after Franz's death, at her association with Canetti. Saward, in the first draft called Kostalanetz, and writing a history of the Jews, is anglicized in the second and trying to decode an archaic script. I will return to one reading of this act of decrypting at the end of this short essay. Peter, like Franz, is a scholar-saint in his 40s, whose beloved sister had died in late childhood, and who, also like Franz after the loss of his thesis in 1942, at the end has to re-start his work. He is dying of TB as was Franz of heart failure, and Rosa's proposal of marriage to him on the last page, just after she has dreamt that he is dead, reflects Canetti's singular version of Franz's last days.[10]

The triangular opposition between Fox, Saward, and Rosa reappears, reworked, in *A Fairly Honourable Defeat* (1970), a brilliant rewriting of *Much Ado about Nothing* in late 1960s London. Here the trio are Julius King and Tallis Browne fighting for the soul of the latter's wife Morgan, partly based, in her naive belief in the power of love, on the Iris Murdoch of *c.* 1950. Tallis, like

[10] See p. 254 in the current volume, but see also Peter J. Conradi, *Iris Murdoch: A Life* (London: Harper Collins, 2001), Chapter 13, which throws doubt on Canetti's reliability.

Peter Saward and like Franz, grieves for a sister who died when she was 12, believes in the power of goodness, and is given a line of Franz's that long amused Iris and John Bayley. Franz, frequently interrupted when drafting a new lecture, would come to the podium to find only the words 'In my last lecture I ...' written there.[11] Tallis has the identical habit. Like Saward, Tallis is also inspired by John Bayley, and here given his snub-nose. The revelation, in chapter twenty-one, that Tallis's sister was raped and killed by a sex-maniac comes on the same page as the disclosure that Julius spent the war in Belsen, a symmetry, found sensational by some, which is meant to bear out Simone Weil's hard-nosed belief that affliction degrades all but the saintly.

One of Franz's themes, later picked up in Mary Douglas's *Purity and Danger* (1966), is the relation between what is forbidden and what is sacred. As Dan Jacobson understood, this too is the theme of *A Severed Head*. In an early draft of *A Severed Head*, started in 1959, the anthropologist Honor Klein is an expert on taboo. Murdoch possessed the 1956 book of Franz's lectures with this title, published with Evans-Pritchard's introduction. Honor has for years had incestuous relations with her half-brother Palmer Anderson, and is perceived herself both as taboo, and as sacred, by the hero with whom she at the end is enslaved. 'Everyone in the book is enslaved,' Murdoch commented. This emphasis on slavery in Murdoch's 'closed' novels owes something to Franz's English doctorate, entitled 'A Comparative Study of Forms of Slavery', something else to the Canetti of *Masse und Macht* (Crowds and Power, 1960), and much to Simone Weil's view of Plato, in which the force trapping mankind in the Cave is selfish love.[12]

Iris Murdoch could look steadily, as the novels show, at the terrible aspects of human existence. The relationship with Franz doubtless strengthened this. Steiner's greatest poem 'Gebet im Garten' (Prayer in the Garden) remains to Michael Hamburger 'one of the few valid and adequate responses in poetry to events literally unspeakable and beyond the range of good sense, decorum or realistic presentation', a long poem that 'exposed the raw nerve of his anguish and of his faith'.[13] Here Franz utters the unspeakable by negating the will and identity of the speaker; the dead can de 'uttered' only from a posture of complete self-abasement. The poet, 'wounded' into his own inwardness must bear witness to the transcending of all taboos, to the defilement of all that is held

---

[11] See John Bayley, *Iris: A Memoir of Iris Murdoch* (London: Duckworth, 1998), p. 54.
[12] For excerpts from Franz's doctorate, see SWII: 155–9. For an expansion of the general point about Murdoch's use of the motif of slavery, see both my *Iris Murdoch: A Life* and *The Saint and the Artist: A Study of the fiction of Iris Murdoch* (London: Harper Collins, 2001), *passim*.
[13] *Franz Baermann Steiner: Modern Poetry in Translation*, New Series, no. 2, with translations and an introduction by Michael Hamburger (London: King's College London, 1992), p. 19

sacred, accepting his own spiritual death as a condition of witness – a martyr taking on himself the world's pain.

Iris Murdoch recalls that Franz influenced her, especially her views on religion, but does not vouchsafe *how*. Jeremy Adler suggested in the 1989 *Bookmark* three aspects: religiosity itself, guilt, and an impassioned sense of good-and-evil. Bettina Adler agreed that, coming from a harmonious home, Iris felt the evil of the world more keenly than most; and that Iris saw in Franz both an absolutely truthful attempt to see the evil of the world, and how, though 'none of us could cope with it', an understanding of the powers of good, in the Bible, in poetry, and in good things in the world, perhaps good people, was the only means we have of opposing it.[14]

In his last month, as already noted, to Murdoch's question as to whether he believed in God, he replied that he could not use the word 'believe' because, among other things, it misinterpreted his relationship with God: he could only say that he loved Him. This bears comparison with the servant, described as a natural mystic, in the 1986 Socratic dialogue *Above the Gods* who, when asked if he believes in God replies that he loves him because he is God. 'Even if he kill me, I love him.'[15]

This may link Franz, the most beloved of Iris Murdoch's Jewish teachers, with Fraenkel, her first, whose greatest work was on Aeschylus's *Agamemnon*, from which Iris twice in her own work quotes the great Hymn to Zeus.[16] In Iris's translation, this runs:

> Zeus, who leads men into the ways of understanding, has established the rule that we must learn by suffering. As sad care, with memories of pain, comes dropping upon the heart in sleep, so even against our wills does wisdom come upon us.[17]

Fraenkel wrote that in this hymn to Zeus '[Aeschylus] endeavours in a sublime effort to unriddle the ultimate cause of the fate and suffering of man'.[18] This may be the hidden meaning of the 'archaic script' that Peter Saward, *alias* Franz, in *Flight from the Enchanter* is also trying to unriddle. If Iris Murdoch argued later for a recovery of our sense of the sacred, Franz Steiner fed this, and taught her to view the world in terms of the relations between what is taboo or forbidden and what is holy. They held in common an essentially reli-

---

[14] *Bookmark*, 'A Certain Lady', BBC Television, 29 December 1989.
[15] Iris Murdoch, *Acastos: Two Platonic Dialogues* (London: Chatto and Windus, 1986), p. 96.
[16] The first occasion is in her novel *The Unicorn* (London: Chatto and Windus, 1963), Chapter 9, and the second, *Acastos* (op. cit.).
[17] *The Unicorn*, p. 80.
[18] *Proceedings of the British Academy*, LVI (1970 [1972]), 415–442, Gordon Williams's tribute to Fraenkel.

gious vision that reverenced difference or otherness and privileged the sense of wonder, a mistrust of systems and of modernity, a fascination with home-lessness, a belief that the ancient gods or powers now reappear as impersonal forces (Adler and Fardon, SWII: 74). For both, the truth must be grounded in pain.

III. POETRY

FRANZ BAERMANN STEINER AND SPAIN

'The Prayer in the Garden' and Manrique's 'Coplas a la muerte de su padre'

Carol Tully

Towards the end of his life, when Franz Baermann Steiner was already a sick man with hardly more than a year to live, his first visit to Spain gave him a new lease of life. Consider, for example, the following extract from a letter dated 5 August 1951, written while Steiner was in the Galician village of Cangas de Morrazo:

> Nur wenige Tage sind vergangen, seit ich landete, aber es scheint eine lange Zeit, denn ich habe so viel gesehen u. bin in einem Taumel der Begeisterung [...] Die 14 Jahre in England sind von mir abgefallen, wie eine Krankheit oder eine alte Haut; die Leute sagen: Sie sind jung, Usted joven! Freuen Sie sich! Und tatsächlich, habe ich noch kein Wasser getrunken, u. ohne die geringsten Beschwerden eine Nacht bis 4h durchgetanzt.[1]

> (Only a few days have passed since I landed, but a long time seems to have passed, I've seen so much and am reeling with enthusiasm. [...] The fourteen years in England have just fallen away like a sickness or an old skin; and people say: you are young, Usted joven! Enjoy yourself! And to tell the truth I still haven't touched a drop of water, and have danced through the night until 4.00am without the slightest problem. [SWI: 96])

This from a man who had for years been suffering from chronic ill-health. So enamoured of the Spanish way of life was Steiner that he followed his ten week sojourn in Galicia and Andalucia in 1951 with another visit in 1952. Yet the time Steiner spent in Spain towards the end of his life and, indeed, the interest he displayed in the nation and its culture for many years are rooted in a set of cultural connections which signify far more than mere enjoyment.

---

[1] Steiner to Isabella von Müller-Aichholz, Cangas de Morrazo, 5 August 1951. All translations, unless indicated otherwise, are the author's own.

To draw together the threads of Steiner's relationship with Spain is a complex task and in endeavouring to complete it, one is inevitably drawn to the past. In many ways, Spain is the most oriental of all the Western European nations, its culture, at least in part, the product of eight hundred years of Moorish rule. It is also the homeland of the Sephardic Jews and for many centuries boasted a rich Jewish tradition centred around cities such as Toledo and Zaragoza. Given its cultural complexity, once so heavily influenced by Eastern ideologies, Spain can perhaps be said to offer the proudly oriental Steiner a multi-ethnic touchstone, a focus for his ideal of 'Oriental collectivism' which complements his own Sephardic roots and stands in stark contrast to the 'Western individualism' of post-Kantian idealism still prevalent in twentieth-century Europe (SWI: 82–83). This philosophical affinity is shadowed by a potential connection of a more personal nature. The near mythical image of early medieval Spain, with its many fragmented kingdoms and cultures, as an era when Jew, Moor, and Christian once lived in harmony is – given the benefit of historical hindsight – more the product of modern romantic idealism and contemporary pragmatic economics than a true example of *convivencia*, that multi-cultural ideal 'supposedly typical of medieval Iberia'.[2] Nevertheless, perception of the period suggests a parallel, albeit flawed, to the 'Golden Prague' of Steiner's childhood where Jew, German, and Czech coexisted in one diverse community.

However, such potential idealistic explanations for Steiner's appreciation of Spain must stop here. Subsequent events in Spanish history, even before the Catholic Reconquest in 1492, are far less open to positive interpretation, given a level of official and unofficial anti-Semitic activity reminiscent of that experienced on an even greater scale by Steiner's generation some five centuries later. From the mid-fourteenth century onwards, as the Moorish grip weakened and power began to fall back into Catholic hands, life for Jews on the Iberian peninsula became increasingly uncomfortable. Indeed, the tactics employed were uncannily similar to those employed by the Nazi regime. For example, both Castile and Aragon banned all Jews from positions of authority within the court, official propaganda depicted the Jew as a source of social and moral evil, segregation was widespread, and in some areas Jews were forced to wear a badge. Inter-marriage was taboo and *limpieza de sangre* (clean blood) of utmost social importance. Violent attacks became more prevalent as the century progressed, something which, as Bernard Reilly points out, had as much to do with blind popular prejudice as it did with political gain:

---

[2] Bernard F. Reilly, *The Medieval Spains* (Cambridge: Cambridge University Press, 1993), p. 191.

[W]hen the attack came it was a popular phenomenon which responded to no official program whether of church, crown, or *cortes*. A mob attacked and destroyed the *aljama* [Jewish Quarter] of Estella in Navarre in 1328. Another attacked that of Gerona in Catalonia with less success in 1331. Royal troops massacred some Jews in Toledo in 1355. But the final storm broke in Seville where the archdeacon of Ecija, a member of the cathedral chapter, had been rabid in his preaching against the Jews since 1378. There on June 4, 1391, a mob sacked and burned the *aljama* and its synagogues and such Jews as survived were forced to accept baptism. As the news spread 250 Jews were killed in Valencia, 300 in Majorca, 400 in Barcelona. Reliable numbers elsewhere are lacking but at Gerona, Huesca, and Lérida, at Burgos, Madrid, Segovia, and Cuenca the pattern was the same. (p. 200)

Such sporadic violence continued but enforced conversion soon became the key means of controlling the Jewish population. Non-compliance would result in execution. This became law after the accession of Ferdinand and Isabel, the Catholic Kings, in 1492. Fearing Jewish unrest, they issued two edicts on 31 March 1492 which required all Jews who had not converted or were unwilling to do so to leave the country or face execution. The policy, which was masterminded by the Inquisition, was highly successful and by the summer of 1492, the Jewish population of Spain had effectively disappeared.[3]

Such extremes of intolerance seem to belong in the unenlightened age from which they came, yet modern Spain presented no more positive a picture. The Spain which Steiner came to know was already a fascist state under Franco, unsympathetic towards any minority, particularly the Gypsies, the subject of Steiner's own fieldwork. The notion of 'clean blood' still had a role to play in Phalangist rhetoric – a film scripted by Franco himself in 1941 bore the ominous title 'Raza' (Race). The fact that anti-Semitism continued to be rife is further underlined by the fact that right-wing groups in the early 1930s found themselves echoing fascist demands elsewhere in Europe for the closure of Jewish businesses – even though there were none in Spain.[4]

Despite the negative nature of Judeo-Hispanic relations over the centuries, the temperament and manners which Steiner found in modern Spain were nevertheless something with which he felt at ease and the positive impact of his experience there was clear for all to see, as Elias Canetti recorded as recently as 1992: 'Seine Briefe aus Spanien enthalten das Schönste, was er mir je schrieb' (His letters from Spain contain the most beautiful words he ever

---

[3] See John Edwards, *The Spain of the Catholic Monarchs 1474–1520* (Oxford: Blackwell, 2000), Chapter 6.

[4] See *Spanish Cultural Studies. An Introduction,* ed. by Helen Graham and Jo Labanyi (Oxford: Oxford University Press, 1995), p. 106.

wrote me).[5] Appreciation of modern Spanish manners notwithstanding, it was the hand of history which beckoned Steiner to Spain. His Sephardic roots meant this was in many ways a homecoming, a parallel to his visit to Jerusalem before the war. Close relations with Elias and Veza Canetti, both also Sephardic Jews, must have reinforced this side of his identity. The Canettis conversed together in 'Ladino' or 'Spaniol', the Spanish spoken by the Sephardic Jews, and were acutely aware of the significance of Spain to their heritage, both individual and collective. Canetti even claims that Steiner made the visit to Spain on his behalf: 'In Spanien wäre Steiner wirklich gern mit mir gewesen, und eigentlich war er dort für mich.' (Steiner would really have liked to be in Spain with me, and really, he was there for me). This is confirmed in Esther Frank's 'Erinnerungen an F. B. Steiner' (Memories of F. B. Steiner), where she reports the following: 'Wie F[ranz] in Spanien war, entschuldigte er sich wegen seines wenigen Schreibens, weil die Zeit hier für "Canetti gebührte"' (When Franz was in Spain, his excuse for not having written more, was that he was spending time there 'on behalf of Canetti').[6] Steiner, in this representative role, hoped to be able to visit the great Jewish pre-Reconquest cities and follow in the footsteps of the great medieval Jewish thinkers such as Maimonides (Adler and Fardon, SWI: 96–97). His impressions are recorded in his correspondence, in particular with his friend Isabella von Müller-Aichholz. There is no doubt that Steiner hoped for some kind of spiritual gain from his visit to Spain but he also experienced a refreshing release from the restraint of English academic life. So enamoured was he of life there that in a letter of 21 August 1951 Steiner even talks of a possible move to Spain, at least for part of the year. The ironic self-justification – 'Das sind keine Luftschlösser' – is poignant, for these plans would sadly remain 'castles in the air' and probably would have done so even without Steiner's untimely death.[7] Yet, his enthusiasm for the Spanish nation was boundless, not least because of the positive impact this multi-faceted culture had on his own creativity and aesthetic appreciation. It is almost as if Steiner is seeing things with new eyes:

> Die paar Tage haben wirklich meine Beziehung zum Barock geändert. Hier drängt sich fast alles zusammen, was es in Oxford, Salzburg, Prag Schönes

---

[5] See p. 255 in the current volume. Steiner's letters to Canetti are held in a private collection. There are four letters, one of which reaches ten pages, and three postcards from his first visit in 1951. These are dated: Cangas de Morrazo (Mid-August), León (31 August), An Bord der Rio Francoli, *en route* to Cádiz (12 September), Cádiz (22 September), and Gibraltar (24 September). There appears to be only one letter from his 1952 visit, dated 19 August and sent from Cangas de Morrazo.
[6] See p. 247 of the current volume.
[7] Steiner to Isabella von Müller-Aichholz, Cangas de Morrazo, 21–22 August 1951

gibt, u. manches Maurische dazu. Ich werde gewiss noch oft herkommen. Hier könnte ich Gedichte schreiben. [8]

(These few days have truly altered my relationship to the Baroque. Almost all the beautiful things in Oxford, Salzburg, Prague are crammed together with some Moorish influences added too. I will surely come here often. I could write poetry here.)

There was indeed a late flowering of poetry during Steiner's time in Spain which reflects the fusion of influences referred to here. This love of diversity and the discovery of cultural connections characterize his poetic oeuvre as well as informing his work as a scholar and anthropologist. This is encapsulated in his response to Spain, which evokes the joy and wonderment he experienced there. Whilst his affinity centres primarily on the historical legacy of his Sephardic roots and the accompanying sense of homecoming, there is also a clear fondness for the people, culture, climate, and traditions of the Spanish nation:

Ribadavia war eine Liebe auf den ersten Blick. Der Wein ist fast schwarz, sehr herb, mehr als ein Bordeaux, aber ohne dessen Blume; ein herrlicher Landwein. Im Mittelalter war er eine internationale Berühmtheit u. Ribadavia war das Zentrum des galizischen Weinhandels. Die Winzer u. Händler waren meist Juden, u. seit unserer Vertreibung ist es mit dem Städtchen bergab gegangen. Jetzt ist es ein fast unverändertes mittelalterliches Nest von 8,000 Einwohnern, sein Hauptteil ist das uralte jüdische Viertel mit seinen Laubengängen, Gewölben, palastartigen kleinen Häusern u. den Synagogen, die nun Kirchen sind. Ich kam gegen Abend an, fand ein Zimmer u. wusch mich, u. als ich die alten Strassen betrat, hatte die Dämmerung schon begonnen. Ich war wirklich wie verzaubert, der Sprung über 5 Jahrhunderte war ganz überraschend, ich ging durch die stillen Gassen, stand vor den Kirchen u. wusste vorerst nicht, warum sie mich so vertraut u. doch wieder unheimlich empfingen; dazu die jagenden Abendwolken – ein rechter El Greco-Himmel, u. hie u. da die schönen Frauenstimmen von den Balkonen, die herrlichen galizischen Volkslieder. Ich habe inzwischen viel schönes gesehen, aber der erste Abend in Ribadavia wird mir als das grösste Entzücken dieses ersten Teiles meiner Spanienreise erinnerlich bleiben.[9]

(Ribadavia was love at first sight. The wine is almost black, very bitter, more so than a Bordeaux, but without its fullness; a wonderful regional

[8] Steiner to Isabella von Müller-Aichholz, Santiago de Compostela, 8 September 1951.
[9] Steiner to Isabella von Müller-Aichholz, Oviedo, 2 September 1951.

wine. In the Middle Ages it was internationally famous and Ribadavia was the centre of the Galician wine trade. The vintners and merchants were mostly Jews and since our expulsion the little town has gone downhill. Now it is an almost unchanged medieval backwater with 8,000 inhabitants, the centre is the ancient Jewish quarter with its leafy walkways, arches, palace-like houses and the synagogues which are now churches. I arrived towards evening, found a room and had a wash, and as I walked out into the street, it was already nightfall. I was really quite enchanted, the leap over 5 centuries was most surprising, I went through the quiet alleys, stood before the churches and did not know at first why they were so familiar and yet drew me towards them in such an uncanny way; add to this the evening clouds chasing across the sky – a true El Greco sky, and here and there the beautiful voices of women from the balconies, the wonderful Galician folk songs. I have seen many beautiful things since then but the first evening in Ribadavia will remain in my memory as the most charming experience of the first part of my travels in Spain.)

Despite his enthusiasm for his new surroundings, Steiner is unsettled by the Reconquest practice of building churches on the foundations of mosques and synagogues. Victim of a subsequent persecution, Steiner is able to feel an affinity with his forebears which underlines the historical continuity which he is seeking by visiting Spain. There is a sense of discovery and belonging which is emphasized by the reference to 'unsere Vertreibung' (our expulsion). This is a search for the past in the present; a search for the history of the Jewish people in a modern fascist state. The irony cannot have been lost on Steiner himself.

It is just such a coming to terms with the past which, I feel, underlies the connection between Steiner and Jorge Manrique in the poems 'Gebet im Garten am Geburtstag meines Vaters' (Prayer in the Garden on my father's birthday, 1947) and 'Coplas a la muerte de su padre' (Verses on the Death of his Father, circa 1475);[10] the framing of a history both personal and collective which both writers link to the loss of a father. The titles alone suggest a connection and Canetti is quite convinced of Manrique's influence, writing again in 1992:

> Das 'Gebet im Garten am Geburtstage meines Vaters', das ich gestern – nach vierzig Jahren – wiederlas, hat mich sehr ergriffen. Es ist unter dem Eindruck von Jorge Manrique geschrieben, und nie war ein Einfluß legitimer.

---

[10] References to the poem will appear in the text and are taken from the following edition: Jorge Manrique, *Obras*, ed. by Antonio Serrano de Haro (Madrid: Alhambra, 1986), pp. 241–300.

(The 'Prayer in the Garden', which I read again yesterday after 40 years moved me greatly. It was written under the influence of Jorge Manrique and never was an influence more legitimate.) [11]

There are certainly philological grounds for Canetti's claim. Steiner's interest in Spanish culture extended to a good knowledge of both language and literature. His library suggests a predilection for the literature of the Medieval and Golden Age periods and he owned a copy of Gerald Brenan's *The Literature of the Spanish People* (1951). Steiner's Hispanist interests, including the link to Manrique, are recorded by Esther Frank in her 'Erinnerungen an F. B. Steiner'. She recalls fondly the hours spent with Steiner before the war learning Spanish and, in listing the many texts covered, makes clear reference to Manrique's work:

In einem Winter zu dritt ich, F[ranz] u Frl. Feit (Wiener Buchhändlertochter) gemeinsames Spanisch lernen. – Fernando war der Name einer Lektion. Eine andere Lektion über Herbst = Brumal. Das führte zum sonst sinnlosen Titel Fernando Brumal. Grammatik mit Riesenschritten. Lektüre zu Übersetzen Fabeln des 18. Jh. Dann die hl. Teresa, ihre Gedichte. Dann Luis de Leon 'La perfecta cassada' *[sic]* (Anweisung zum sel[igen] Leben einer Hausfrau), da ging es schon besser mit spanisch. Leon vertritt eine Soziologie der Stünde *[sic]*, beeinflußt von Aristotoles. F. interessierte sich dafür und wollte darüber schreiben. Er liebte Jorge Manrique regte mit seinem Gedicht an den Vater V's [d. h. F's] ent[sprechendes] Gedicht an. Er schätzte Lucanor, in engl[ischer]. Übersetzung die 'Celestina'. Es wurde gelesen der Literaturkritiker Menendez Pidal (verhältnismäßig leichtes Spanisch).

(One winter three of us, myself, F[ranz] and Miss Feit (daughter of a Viennese bookseller) learnt Spanish together. – Fernando was the name of one of the lessons. Another was called autumn = Brumal. That led to the otherwise meaningless title Fernando Brumal. Great strides with the grammar. Reading of 18th c[entury] fables for translation. Then the poetry of Saint Teresa. Then Luis de León 'The Perfect Wife' (Directions for the happy life of the housewife), by then it was already easier in the Spanish. León promoted a sociology of class, influenced by Aristotle. F[ranz] was interested in this and wanted to write about it. He loved Jorge Manrique inspired F[ranz]'s poem to the father with his own. He valued Lucanor, translation of the 'Celestina' in Engl[ish]. The literary critic Menéndez Pidal was read (relatively easy Spanish)).[12]

---

[11] See p. 255 of the current volume.

That Steiner had more than a passing interest in Manrique's work is further supported by the fact that Steiner owned a copy of Manrique's collected works, purchased in Oxford in 1945. Furthermore, a stanza from Manrique's 'Los fuegos qu'en mi encendieron' (The fires set alight within me) is used as a motto for Steiner's cycle 'Lieder aus dem Kreise Junia in der Art früherer Dichter' (Songs from the Circle of Junia in the style of earlier poets) which were written in Oxford in 1948 and then in various places in Spain in 1951.

However, to seek far-reaching biographical or even ideological parallels between Franz Steiner and Jorge Manrique is a largely fruitless exercise, excepting the fact that both lost their father at a relatively early age. Even this was under very different circumstances. Don Rodrigo Manrique died of natural, albeit rather unpleasant causes, from an ulcer which consumed a large part of his face. Steiner's parents were among the many to fall victim to the horrors of Treblinka.

Jorge Manrique lived from 1440 to 1479, at a time when Spain, or more accurately the Spains, were the scene of great turmoil. *Convivencia*, had it ever really existed, was by now a thing of the past. Internecine and inter-racial war raged throughout Manrique's lifetime and he was involved to the full. The year of his death saw the union of the crowns of Castile and Aragon which laid the foundations for the power base which would eventually overcome Moorish rule and signal the expulsion of the Jews from the Iberian peninsula. Relatively little is known of the life of the poet, except that he came from a wealthy Castilian noble family of the ancient Catholic Spanish tradition. He was a respected figure like his father before him and was awarded a number of positions of power during his short lifetime. Both poet and knight, he died a heroic death in battle at the age of thirty nine.

Such a life of swash-buckling action could not have been further from Steiner's experience and, indeed, the little we know of Manrique's activities as a Moor-slaying Catholic knight do not mark him out as a man whom Steiner would necessarily have admired, even if he was inspired by his poetry. The Catholic star was most definitely in the ascendant during Manrique's lifetime as the cycle of history saw the once unassailable Moorish grip on Spain loos-

---

[12] See p. 243 of the current volume. The imaginary figure mentioned by Frank was immortalized in the poem 'Fernando Brumal' (AsP: 159). Two of Steiner's poems make direct reference to Spain and Spanish culture: 'Porträt Quevedos' (Quevedo's Portrait, AsP: 231) and 'Zeilen in Cadix' (Lines in Cádiz, AsP: 327–328). 'Porträt Quevedos' was written in Oxford in 1948 with a second version being completed in 1952. The poem centres on the face of the poet Quevedo, drawing on the flawed ideals of the Spanish Golden Age with references to 'fromme ritter' (pious knights) and yet also to 'des gelehrten bitternis' (the bitterness of scholars), all of which Quevedo seems able to rise above. 'Zeilen in Cadix' was written in Cádiz and Sanlúcar de Barrameda in 1952 but betrays no clear Spanish influence.

ened in the face of a vigorous Christian revival. This change in the balance of power is something which would have given Manrique a very different approach to and experience of life from that of Steiner who was witness to the fate of his people in their darkest hour. This is highlighted by one further link between their respective fathers. Both were soldiers: Manrique's a valiant medieval knight, witness to the revival of Christianity; Steiner's an infantryman on the brutal Isonzo front during the First World War, witness to the defeat of the German-Austrian alliance. Here we are confronted with two lives and two generations experiencing life from opposite sides of a sadly timeless divide: the shared experience of history seen from the opposing perspectives of oppressor and oppressed.

I find myself concluding, then, that the connection between Steiner and Manrique is far more profound than that suggested by mere biographical coincidence. There exists instead a commonality at the core level of human experience – the loss of a parent, and all this implies. Loss is the central theme of both poems and is fore-grounded on two levels – personal and historical. By examining each of these levels in turn, it is possible to detect a number of connections as well as differences which inform the poems, both individually as deeply personal human responses, and collectively as examples of historical synchronicity, centring both on the loss of a parent and on the issue of cultural history.

The poets choose different narrative stances for their poems of remembrance. This variance in strategy reflects the differing experiences of the two men, and indeed, the differences in status and destiny of their respective fathers. Manrique provides an ostentatious portrait of his father, Don Rodrigo, proudly listing his many deeds and conquests in the glorious battle with the infidel:

Y sus villas y sus tierras
ocupados de tiranos
las halló;
mas por cercos y por guerras
y por fuerça de sus manos
las cobró. (pp. 289–290)

(And his towns and his lands / occupied by tyrants / he found them / yet through sieges and battles / and the strength of his hands / he reclaimed them.)

The right to possession is clearly justified in terms of good and evil as Don Rodrigo – single-handedly it would appear – defeats the tyrants who have dispossessed his forebears. This strength of will is further underlined as comparisons are made with the great men of days gone by, each of whom has at least one positive characteristic shared by Manrique's father:

En ventura, Octaviano;
Julio César, en vencer
y batallar;
en la virtud, Africano;
Anibal, en el saber
y trabajar; (p. 280)

(In courage, Octavianus / Julius Caesar in victory / and in battle / In virtue Africanus / Hanibal in knowledge / and endeavour)

In making such comparisons, Manrique locates his father firmly amongst the figures of legend and myth whose leadership has enriched humanity and provided inspiration for the development of civilization. Here is a man worthy of such company, recorded, like all those victorious in the course of history, in the most positive light. Yet, despite these lofty comparisons, Don Rodrigo is no man to shun the people. Manrique depicts his father as someone who recognizes the worth of his fellow man:

¡Qué amigo de sus amigos!
¡Qué señor para criados
y parientes!
¡Qué enemigo de enemigos!
¡Qué maestro de esforçados
y valientes!
¡Qué seso para discretos!
¡Qué gracia para donosos!
¡Qué razón!
¡Qué benigno a los sujetos
y a los bravos e dañosos,
un león! (pp. 278–279)

(Friend of his friends! / What a master to servants / and to family! / What an enemy of enemies! / What a master of brave / and the valiant! / What a mind to the wise! / What grace for the benevolent! / What wisdom! / What beneficence toward his subjects! / To the brave and destructive / what a lion!)

This stanza in particular establishes Manrique's father as a member of the ruling class in an age when the enemy was clearly defined, at least in the religious battle between Christian and Moor. This stands in stark contrast to the world of Steiner's father where the distinctions were less clear cut in a society in which friend or acquaintance might turn enemy to suit the changing political climate. However, the parallels surrounding the divisive potential of religious intolerance, especially when exploited for political gain, highlight another shared experience: that of a lifetime sullied by war, violence, and grief. Whilst the historical and ideological background to both poems cannot be ignored, it is this grief which is immediately clear to the reader.

Manrique's near apotheosis of his father, whilst owing much to the rhetorical requirements of his time, clearly conveys a deep love and respect. Steiner, whilst remaining markedly more circumspect in his depiction, communicates a similar depth of feeling. As with Manrique, Steiner's father is portrayed as a man to look up to, a man to be admired. Once more, a noble nature is described:

> Ich seh zu meiner linken hand
> Das vornehmste, das ich auf erden fand,
> Ich seh meines vaters schlichtes, genaues gesicht,
> Ich hör der worte leise klang,
> Die er zu der leiseren spricht; (AsP: 315)

> (At my left side I see / The noblest earthly presence ever shown to me / I see my father's strict and unassuming face / I hear the quiet cadence of those words / He speaks to her more quiet still;)

The reference here to Steiner's father's voice underlines the difference in perspective identified earlier. In recalling his father's voice, Steiner can only provide an imagined utterance with no recorded text. This evokes the situation of a man robbed of self-expression, unable to make his voice heard. Indeed, he is never named. Silence lies at the centre of Steiner's poem. References to sound and voice are either nostalgic – 'Einst hab ich gerufen' (Once I called out; AsP: 311) – or deny any authority – 'mit flüstern und verneigen' (amidst whispering and bowing; AsP: 311). Manrique's father, on the other hand, maintains a voice to the end and is even permitted the luxury of a comforting conversation with death before his eventual demise. In so doing, he concludes the following:

> Y consiento en mi morir
> con voluntad plazentera,
> clara y pura,
> que querer hombre vivir,
> cuando Dios quiere que muera,
> es locura. (p. 297)

> (And in consenting to die / with pleasing acquiescence / clear and pure / for a man to wish for life / when God's will is his death / is madness.)

Don Rodrigo's acceptance of death as the wiser will of God suggests a sense of grace, an acknowledgement of the inevitable. His death is seen as just, even by his grieving son. Where could Steiner find such grace when faced with the reality of Nazi Germany? The opposing experiences of oppressor and oppressed are again to the fore.

Beyond the direct reference in a single stanza, Steiner deals with the image of his father in a more subtle manner than Manrique, a tendency which is echoed in his refusal to make explicit reference to the Holocaust, preferring instead the distance of symbol and analogy. Whereas Don Rodrigo is depicted, and indeed eulogized as a man *of* the people, Steiner's father is very much seen as a man *among* the people, one of the many who suffered. His depiction in the narrative merges, therefore, with Steiner's evocation of the wider suffering of the Jewish community. This is clear in the invocation, which calls for those destroyed by the Holocaust to bear witness: here the noun 'herr' could refer to God, but equally to Steiner's father:

Zeugen, zeugen,
Schliesst euch in mein sagen ein, bleibt mir jetzt nah,
Lasst mich in wahrheit sprechen.
Ich will nicht sprechen um meines herzens willen
Oder für meinen herrn. (AsP: 315)

(Witnesses, witnesses / Join me in what I speak, be near me now / Let me speak truthfully / I would not speak now for my heart's own sake / nor for my master's sake.)

Steiner's call for truth relates the personal to the collective: he does not speak for himself or his father alone, but for the community as a whole. Manrique's depiction of his father as a leader of men, although clearly affectionate and awe-inspired, seems quite cold and aloof by comparison. As victor, he knows no collective misery and has no communal context within which to place his personal grief.

This difference in approach in terms of the personal is reflected in the way each poet places individual loss in its wider, historical context. Initially there seems to be commonality of purpose as both poets locate their experience of personal tragedy within the cycle of human existence. Indeed, both choose a cyclical form of poem, and they both begin their poem with a cyclical metaphor. Manrique focuses on the cycle of life itself, providing Spanish literature with one of its most famous opening lines:

Recuerde el alma dormida,
avive el seso y despierte,
contemplando

cómo se passa la vida,
cómo se viene la muerte
tan callando;
cuán presto se va el plazer,
cómo, después de acordado,
da dolor;
cómo, a nuestro parescer,
cualquiera tiempo passado
fue mejor. (pp. 241–243)

(Reawaken the sleeping soul / Revive the mind and awake / contemplating / how life has passed / how death approaches / so silently / how quickly the pleasure vanishes / how, once remembered, / it brings pain / how, it seems to us, / any time gone by / was better.)

Here Manrique chooses imagery which reflects the wider issue – that of life itself with all its trials and tribulations, pleasure and pain: the evaluation of human life in the general context of human experience. Steiner, seeking a narrower analogy, introduces the symbolic values associated with nature as he evokes the hues of Autumn bringing life to an end:

Durch goldfarbnen herbstrauch
Mildes licht strömt
In verklärter stille umwebt es die inseln der blumen
Sie haben noch die blauen, samtenen freuden, die letzten,
Können noch speisen die steifer gespreiteten falter
Mit nachhut der süße.
Das laub ist noch grün, doch die früchte sind eingebracht,
Apfel und birne gelöst aus den zweigen;
Leidlos und lautlos ist solche vollendung:
Es ist nach der reife. (AsP: 311)

(Through golden autumn haze / Gentle light flows down / In transmuted stillness it clings to the islands of flowers / They are left with the blue, the velvet joys, with their last, / Still can feed the butterflies more stiffly spreading their wings / With an aftermath of sweetness / Still the foliage is green, but the fruit have been picked and stored, / Apple and pear detached from the branches, / Painless and soundless each consummation: / The time after ripeness.)

This idyllic image is a cleverly understated introduction to a poem which goes on to reveal such misery and suffering. Would that life were always blessed with a such peaceful end – 'leidlos und lautlos' (painless and soundless), as

145

Steiner describes it. This is, however, not Steiner's experience and this first stanza stands in stark contrast to later descriptions of violence and misery:

Nun sind sie die schreie auf dem meer,
Wieder die not und das freiwild auf dem meer,
Geziefer gepresst zwischen faust und sturm,
Seelen halb aus den körpern gezogen,
Weib und kind zwischen fußtritt und wogen; (AsP: 313)

(And now there is this crying out at sea, / Once more distress and anyone's sport at sea, / Vermin squeezed between fist and storm, / Souls half pulled from the living flesh, / Woman and child between kicks and the wave's lash;)

Any notion that Steiner's poem might depend on nostalgia and valedictory rhetoric is shattered by the open violence of this passage.

Having begun, then, with the wider issue of the cycle of life, both poets then focus on more specific concerns. These once more highlight a difference in perspective. Manrique clearly frames the narrative of his father's life in its historical context and, whilst dealing at length with an individual, and for him highly significant loss, elaborates too on the trope common to the period: 'ubi sunt qui ante nos in hoc mundo fuere?' – where are those who lived on this earth before us?:

¿Qué se hizo el rey don Juan?
¿Los infantes de Aragón,
qué se hizieron?
¿Qué fue de tanto galán,
¿Qué fue de tanta invención
que truxeron?
Las justas y los torneos,
paramentos, bordaduras
y cimeras.
¿Qué fueron sino devaneos?
¿Qué fueron sino verduras
de las eras? (pp. 261–263)

(What became of King Juan? / Of the princes of Aragon / what of them? / What of all the gallantry / of the brilliance / they displayed? / The jousting, the tournaments / The adornments, decor / and chimeras? / Were they but distractions? / Were they but the finery / of the ages?)

The question 'ubi sunt?' is here directed at the passing of greatness and voices a sadness which is nevertheless accepting in tone. The focus is clearly on history and heritage. Manrique sees himself and his father very much in the context of this continuum. Death is part of the greater glory upon which this history must forcibly thrive. Steiner, on the other hand, makes few explicit references to his father or his people, but yet succeeds in bringing a deeply personal, raw edge to his evocation of the Holocaust which stands in stark contrast to Manrique's historical contextualizing. No evidence here of elaborate occasions or the names of lofty forebears, but instead the almost mythical evocation of a journey to the very limits of human suffering. In the following quotation, however, Steiner is not dealing with the horrors of the Nazi regime but instead, rather ironically given the poet's place of exile, refers to the attack by the British navy on shiploads of Jewish emigrés off the Palestinian coast in 1948:

> Siebenmal rammstoß in splittriges holz:
> Stählerne schnäbel, babels stolz.
> Zerbrochen planken und klammern,
> Zerborsten die wasserkammern.
> Stählerne schnäbel, babels stolz:
> Siebenmal rammstoß in splittriges holz.
> Kein tropfen, die augen zu netzen,
> Der säuglinge augen, die gase ätzen,
> Augen der mütter, hart im entsetzen.
> Kein wundes auge ungezählt,
> Der kleinsten wimmern ungeschmält.
> Denn alles leiden auf dem meer
> Ein schmerz ist um die herrlichkeit,
> In herrlichkeit sich wandelnd,
> Alles all verwandelnd. (AsP: 316)

(Seven thrusts of the ram into splintering wood / Beaks made of steel, the pride of Babel. / Broken the clasp and plank, the chair and the table, / Burst the reservoir, dried up the flood. / Beaks made of steel, the pride of Babel: / Seven thrusts of the ram into splintering wood. / Not a drop with which to cool the eyes, / The eyes of the children which gases cauterize, / Eyes of the mothers, hard in the midst of horror. / No wounded eye uncounted now, / No smallest infant's whisper left unheard. / For all the suffering out at sea / Is a pain for glory's sake, / Itself into glory turning, / Transforming everything.)

The glory described by Steiner is not that of one heroic man in the historical process, as is the case with Manrique's father, but instead that of martyrdom on an unprecedented scale. The suffering described is monumental in the true sense of the word and will stand as a testament to the suffering of the Jewish people. Steiner explains this section of the poem in a letter to Rudolf Hartung as an attempt to record 'das Zeitlose des Zusammenstosses zwischen dem Volk und einer Imperialmacht' (The timeless confrontation between the people and an imperial power). He chooses Babel as 'die erste Imperialmacht, die zur Feindin des jüdischen Staates wurde, und mit deren Name das Volk die Vorstellungen von Spachverwirrung, Sittenverfall, politischer Gewaltsamkeit und Exil verbinden' (The first imperial power to become an enemy of the Jewish state and with whose name the people associate linguistic confusion, loss of tradition, political violence and exile).[13] That this description is uncannily befitting of the later imperial powers of Reconquest Spain and Nazi Germany underlines the validity of Steiner's poetic trail of historical synchronicity. The depiction of death in Steiner's work reflects the difference in perspective emerging from this socio-political dialectic between oppressor and oppressed by denying the existence of the glorious, beneficent, and gentle death portrayed by Manrique:

> Rotborstige steinhand, stirn ohne leid,
> Augen aus totem stahl,
> Euch gibt es nicht zum ersten, nicht zum letzten mal,
> Wir sind mit euch in der welt. (AsP: 314)

> (Red-bristled hand of stone, smooth forehead without pain / Eyes with a dead steel leer / Not for the first time nor for the last time you appear / With you we live in the world.)

This encounter with inhumanity, the harbinger of death with its 'rotborstige steinhand' (red-bristled hand of stone), is presented as one of life's perpetual realities. Dispossession and destruction are nothing new. Those out at sea, whom Steiner chooses as the central focus of his meditation, the 'irrende geschöpfe auf dem meer' (straying creatures out at sea), are those who have been lost, who seek mercy and comfort and are in search of the promised land.

Yet this encounter with death is not the consequence, as is the case in Manrique's poem, of the rightful passage of life and time but instead a violent rupture in the history of a people and of humanity itself. There is an echo of the 'ubi sunt?' trope, which, I feel, provides the key to an understanding of Steiner's poem in the light of Manrique's work. What for Manrique remains a philosophical pondering when confronted with the death of his father from natural causes, becomes for Steiner a question upon which hinges the very essence of humanity in the twentieth century – ubi sunt? Where are they in-

---

[13] Steiner to Rudolf Hartung, Oxford, 14 March 1952.

deed, the millions who suffered, died, or simply disappeared? That the emphasis on truth found in Steiner's work is absent from Manrique's text helps to inform this difference in perspective. Whereas Steiner finds himself searching for answers and demanding explanations on behalf of the vanquished, Manrique is able to gloss over atrocity from the privileged position of victor. Steiner uses his text both to praise his father and to criticize the world in which he lives whereas Manrique's poem carries no critical emphasis at all, except perhaps to bemoan the fleeting nature of life.

Whatever Steiner's appreciation of Manrique might have been, it must surely be acknowledged that, in finding a model for his poem, 'Gebet im Garten', he also found a point of view which stands as the antithesis of his own experience. In so doing, he effectively establishes his text as a counter-type to Manrique's poem. It is significant that Steiner chooses this strategy to frame his only poetic response to the Holocaust – making use of a poem which sanitizes and glorifies oppression as a framework for one which seeks to record it in all its inhumanity.[14] In employing this ironic stance, Steiner throws light on the historical synchronicity of two great caesura in Jewish history, part of a chain of fissures, including the destruction of the Second Temple, stretching back into biblical times. The position of the Jewish people and, indeed, the Moorish population in fifteenth-century Spain has much in common with the experience of the Jews, Gypsies, and other non-Aryan minorities in Nazi Germany almost five hundred years later. Whilst these two poems function in parallel as examples of personal remembrance, commemorating the loss of a father, they function too as historical documents recording opposing perspectives in the creation of cultural history. Whereas Steiner seeks to salvage memory, Manrique seeks to sanitize it. He remains implicit in the historical amnesia which continues to plague Spain and indeed many other nations who have had the privilege of shaping the world's understanding of history from the vantage point of victory. Steiner was acutely aware of this imbalance and sums it up with characteristic clarity:

> Building up a culture also means, amongst other things: finding a standpoint from which to spread lies about death. (SWII: 231)

This aphorism in many ways underlines the complexity of Steiner's relationship with Spain and Spanish culture, one which, to some degree, also parallels his relationship to Germany and German culture. There is much to admire but also much to shy away from.

---

[14] For a discussion of Steiner's anthropological response to the Holocaust see: Michael Mack, *Anthropology as Memory. Elias Canetti's and Franz Baermann Steiner's Responses to the Shoah*, Conditio Judaica 34 (Tübingen: Niemeyer, 2001).

Steiner is not alone in seeking inspiration from Spain. He finds himself part of a tradition in German-speaking culture stretching back to Herder and Goethe. His search for the past echoes the Romantic search for identity in the early nineteenth century which saw medieval Spain as a lost Golden Age. Their apotheosis of Spanish culture was continued in the mid-nineteenth century by Eichendorff and Grillparzer but perhaps the most significant figure from Steiner's point of view was another Prague poet, Rilke. One of Steiner's most admired poets, Rilke was also greatly influenced by Spanish culture and found a sense of self during his time there in 1912–13, regarding Spanish influences as central to both his *Duineser Elegien* (Duino Elegies, 1912/1922) and the *Sonette an Orpheus* (Sonnets to Orpheus, 1922). The parallel between the two writers' experience of Spain is perhaps best underlined by their individual responses. Following his time there, Rilke expressed his sense of 'Heimweh nach Spanien' (homesickness for Spain).[15] In his letter to Canetti on his return to Spain in 1952, Steiner wrote that 'Ich bin zu Hause' (I am at home). Ironically, as with every other home he ever had, Steiner would never return there. Like Rilke before him, Steiner found only temporary happiness in Spain. Nevertheless, his experiences there and his understanding of the nation's culture undoubtedly helped him to begin to come to terms with some of the tragedy surrounding his own life and that of his people. Steiner's love of Spain and its culture is perhaps best understood in this light: as an attempt to uncover the past, perhaps seeking a cornerstone for his own identity as a Jew, a writer, and, in the case of his poem 'Gebet im Garten', as a son.

---

[15] J. Gebser, *Rilke und Spanien*, 2nd ed (Zürich: Oprecht, 1946), p. 22.

SHADOWS AND BORDERLANDS

A Motif in the Poetry of Franz Baermann Steiner

Rüdiger Görner

I.

Poets, it often seems, deal with shadows as one of their prime materials. Important features of their poetry resemble shadows re-shaped: shadows of suffering and memory; shadows of loved ones and images; shadows of experiences, knowledge, and imagination. A poem can, of course, never be identical with an underlying experience or emotion. But it prevents its shadows from fading by means of verbal crafting and engaging in a dialogue with its seemingly fleeting verbal intermediaries between light and darkness. Thus what the poet tries to establish between object and verse is but a shadowy correlative which can only pretend to be objective.

However, the poetic re-shaping of shadows is able, at times, to unleash an abundant effusion of the imagination:

Mein erker ankert in wolken der blütenwipfel;
[...]
Heftig vor ungefähr flimmert der rand des himmels.
Grenzen sind aufgebraucht: [...] (AsP: 183)

(My oriel is anchored in clouds of blossoming treetops; / [...] / Brightly the skyline flickers with almost and maybe. / Boundaries have been drawn: [...])

These lines from 'Zinnen' (Merlons) belong to Franz Baermann Steiner's second major cycle of poems, written between 1943–1946, *Mündung und Geleise* (Estuaries and Platforms). The oriel is a place in the house which provides the best outlook. It can therefore 'anchor' itself in the images which it enables its lonely inhabitant to see. When viewed from this lofty perspective traditional boundaries appear to lose their function. The speaker states that no such borders ever concerned him. What matters is the flickering of fictitious borders, the distant horizon, and the ultimate certainty: 'Dies nur ist fest: in deine hände ... in deine ...' (This only is certain: into thy hands ... into thy ...). These 'hands' could be those of the beloved, giving a sense of reassurance and trust that is associated with their gentle firmness. But the phrase also recalls the last words of Jesus according to Luke (23, 46): 'Father, into thy hands I commit my spirit.'

In Steiner's poem, though, the potentially religious connotations are given in an ellipsis. One could therefore argue with some justification that this poem, like many others by Steiner, operates in the sphere of the transient, presenting shades of the spiritual. The decidedly earth-bound delights of spring which condition the main parts of this poem are framed by imagery of the transient, such as the aforementioned view from the oriel into the distance, the flickering of the skyline, and the disappearing of boundaries.

Steiner's poems remind us of the close relationship between poetry and prayer. In fact, prayer is omnipresent as a motif in his lyrical work, albeit the human prayer may be 'confused' by the higher fact 'that there are truths'. One such 'truth' is expressed in Steiner's aphorism 'Die Wirklichkeit wohnt nur in den Rändern des Traums.'[1] That is to say, 'reality' is to be found at the boundaries between reflection and the unconscious.

Such boundaries can be transgressed, if not overcome, by developing the art of nuance. Steiner's entire poetic oeuvre amounts to a celebration of nuance in language. One of many examples is the title of his poem 'Über dem Tod'. Iris Murdoch remembers that Steiner explained to her the crucial difference between 'Über *den* Tod' (On Death) and 'Über *dem* Tod' (Above Death) during their last encounter before he died in November 1952 (Nachwort, AsP: 450). He had chosen the latter, thus suggesting that death should not be granted a final say. Steiner's differentiation between 'on death' and 'above death' is an expression of his subtle rebellion against the inevitable which he incidentally shared with Elias Canetti, although the latter was much more outspoken about his 'rebellion' against the 'tall order of death' than his friend. Death is not the ultimate end for Steiner, but a further boundary, another of those boundaries that run through both his poetical works and his anthropological studies. But the boundary also exemplifies a fundamental, if not existential, problem to Steiner: what was the boundary between his poetic and scientific work? Was it possible for both sides of his existence to interact across the borders of both 'disciplines'? And if so, how?

To begin with, one obvious border-oriented aspect of anthropology, especially given Steiner's concern with the study of taboo, was the issue of what constitutes a boundary or causes man to draw borderlines at all in terms of his

---

[1] Franz Baermann Steiner, *Fluchtvergnüglichkeiten. Feststellungen und Versuche*, ed. by Marion Hermann-Röttgen (Stuttgart: Flugasche, 1988), p. 17.

social behaviour, including his conception of the sacred. The study of taboo is *per se* an investigation into the nature of boundaries in any type of civilization. One classic boundary in Steiner's theory of taboo refers to the elementary constellation: that which is perceived by primitive society as 'sacred', and thus 'prohibited', must not be touched but must be separated from the sphere of impurity (SWI: 199). By examining taboo in scholarly terms Steiner was drawing boundaries of meaning both on philological and on empirical grounds. Much more so than Freud in *Totem and Taboo* (1913), Steiner was evidently preoccupied with the interconnection between taboo and danger. To him, taboo was mainly concerned with 'the protection of individuals who are in danger, and with the protection of society from those endangered' (SWI: 108).

The contiguity of danger, the divine, and salvation finds its classical expression in German literature in Hölderlin's famous lines: 'Wo aber Gefahr ist, wächst / Das Rettende auch' (Wherever there is danger, there grows / salvation too).[2] For Steiner, whose knowledge of Hölderlin was comprehensive, Hölderlin was like Steiner himself another 'wanderer', not least in the history of (German) poetry (Adler and Fardon, SWI: 82). To a certain extent, Steiner develops his thinking in introducing 'taboo' as a saving force in Hölderlin's sense of the word.

For Steiner, as for Hölderlin, danger may also provide a context for hope, as with those 'Gefahren' (dangers) named in the title of the first part of Steiner's third book of poems, *Sorge Bild Begegnen* (Anxiety, Image, Encounter), which provide hope in the shape of two silent mouths, a glowing image of peace in a bay, and the prospect of tents and houses promising 'Heimkehr' (homecoming; AsP: 219). Thus, hope may enable the poet to cross the boundary constituted by danger.

The interplay of defining and transgressing boundaries was not only an integral part of Steiner's work but an essential aspect of his own identity. After his stay in Palestine in 1930 and 1931 he saw himself, in contrast to his largely assimilated family background, as an 'Oriental in the West' with evident inclinations towards Zionism and, after 1938, as a refugee and a 'displaced person'. Although the life of the Gypsies interested him as much as the distinct social behaviour patterns and traditions of the Polynesians, the Papago or Bashkiri, the concept that, for better or worse, traditional ethnological and cultural boundaries were 'used up' had clearly entered his thoughts.

This thought may have been reinforced by the feeling that 'homelessness' had become his 'world', as Steiner put it in one of his aphorisms.[3] This implies

---

[2] Friedrich Hölderlin, *Sämtliche Werke und Briefe*, ed. by Jochen Schmidt, 3 vols (Frankfurt am Main: Deutscher Klassiker Verlag, 1992), I, 350 ('Patmos').

[3] Steiner, *Fluchtvergnüglichkeiten*, p. 17.

that cultural boundaries are meaningless. Indeed, he lived through a period in which the violation and destruction of social and political borders was commonplace. The individual, threatened by the onslaught of totalitarianism, could no longer rely on ethical norms, or on boundaries of any sort, as a form of protection. Yet, Steiner objected to the abandonment of boundaries as such. As a student of Hölderlin and Rilke he knew that civil society and culture itself can only be preserved if, at the end, a sense of measure, or 'Maß', prevails. This 'measure' or 'moderation' can be guaranteed only if newly defined boundaries are set in place and accepted. But defined and accepted by whom? What is the relationship between the collective and the individual in terms of setting norms and subscribing to the meaning of words? And what possible part can the scholarly minded poet, the *poeta doctus*, play in this process? Is he both an advocate of boundaries and of their potential transgression? This ambivalence towards borders and boundaries conditioned some of Steiner's finest poetry.

II.

Given the impact of Steiner's erudition in ethnology and anthropology upon his own poetry, the potential cross-over between his scholarship and his poetry needs to be considered in terms of his contribution to what has been called anthropological or, rather, ethnological poetology. Only a few German-speaking poets after Herder can claim to have made a similar contribution, yet even fewer have done so on the basis of actual ethnological research.

The conception 'ethnological poetology' was introduced, *inter alia*, by Hans-Jürgen Heinrichs with reference to Michel Leiris, and by Helmut Heißenbüttel in his discussion of Hubert Fichte's text *Xango*.[4] This form of poetics reflects the endeavour on part of the ethnologically minded poet to recognize himself in the sphere of Otherness, and to come to terms with the Other in himself; it further implies the concern of the poet to reorganize Otherness, in all its complexity and heterogeneity, on a poetic basis; or, more generally speaking, with literary terms of reference.[5] By contrast, though, Heinrich emphasizes that Leiris's main interest was to determine the 'myriad of his [Leiris's] own Selfs' (p. 80), through encountering Otherness.

---

[4] Another obvious reference in this context is Fichte's 'Geschichte der Empflindlichkeit' which ignores any boundaries between poetics and science. For some recent comment on Fichte's approach, see: Walter Grond, *Vom neuen Erzählen. Gipfelstürmer und Flachlandgeher* (Innsbruck: Haymon, 2001), pp. 18–27.
[5] Hans-Jürgen Heinrichs, *Ein Leben als Künstler und Ethnologe. Über Michel Leiris* (Frankfurt am Main: Fischer, 1992), p. 72.

In Steiner's case a different interest prevails. Judging from his ethnologically inspired cycle *Variationen* (Asp: 143–155) and *Fabeln* (Asp: 193–209) Steiner intended to retain a strong feeling of 'Otherness' in his lyrical adaptations of ethnic otherness by his specific choice of words and syntax. The poet's 'Self', although still present in the first two variations on Bashkiri songs ('Lied vom Gelbhaar' [Song of the Yellow Hair] and 'Lied vom Spiel der Lerchen am Morgen' [Song of the playing larks in the morning]) almost vanishes in the following fifteen songs. The most 'self'-revealing of these poetic variations is the 'Lied von den Meistern (Variationen auf drei tschetschenische Sprichwörter)' (Song of the Masters [Variations on three Chechen Sayings]). This raises the question of who is in charge of man and his language. The poet's answer leaves us in no doubt: 'Wie sehr du auch eilst, dich meistern die wege' (No matter how much you hurry, the paths will master you; Asp: 145). Whilst words belong to all of us, only the heart (one of Steiner's key-metaphors for self-contained identity) belongs to itself. This must be qualified by the statement that, as we know from other poems, Steiner saw this identity as an endangered quality. Eventually, the 'heart' turns into a wound as Jeremy Adler put it with reference to Steiner's elegaic poem 'Gebet im Garten' (Prayer in the Garden; Nachwort, AsP: 449). At a point like this, the poet's image is inspired by his ethnological expertise: 'Bei manchen Völkern wird das zu opfernde Tier besonders sorgfältig getötet, damit ja kein Blut vergossen wird' (In the case of some peoples, the animal intended for sacrifice is slaughtered with great care, so that no blood is spilt; Nachwort, AsP: 449). In a sense this was, as Adler quite rightly suggests, to some extent a self-referential comment; for someone with a weak heart (Steiner suffered from chronic heart-disease) can become a 'victim' of sacrifice 'without letting blood'. Yet how does the concept of the 'border' come into questions like this?

Ethno-poetics in Leiris's understanding is exposed to the problem of how to deal with two types of boundaries: the methodological and, in most instances, linguistic difference between ethnology and poetry. For instance, in *La Règle du jeu*, Leiris practises both a separation and a reshaping of both methods. This reshaping presupposes, of course, that the poet or ethnologist is in control of analysing and possibly re-defining existing boundaries. By contrast, Steiner, as a poet, could imagine a scenario in which Man was no longer in the position of drawing borderlines, since the boundaries were in command of Man.

There is another, and possibly more important, difference between these two ethnologically motivated writers. Leiris had belonged to the surrealist movement and published in *La Révolution surréaliste* alongside Breton, Éluard, Aragon, and Desnos. To a certain degree it was inevitable that Leris would, at least initially, view his ethnological research from the perspective of a surrealist. This is evidenced by two of Leiris's earlier publications in the periodical *Documents* (1930), one of which was devoted to 'L'Oeil de l'ethnographe' whilst the other investigates the 'Toiles récentes de Picasso'.[6] A careful reading of the first edition of *L'Afrique fantôme* (1934) will confirm Leiris's interrelating of his surrealist experience and his ethnological research which eventually led him to regard both as 'games' (*La Règle du jeu*).

By contrast, Steiner resisted the surrealist temptation even if he was, towards the end of his short life, occasionally overcome by a feeling of pointlessness ('Es ist alles so grotesk sinnlos... [It is all so grotesquely senseless...]; AsP: 450).

In summary, one could argue that Steiner's implicit ethno-poetology insisted on 'Otherness' being recognizable as a decidedly 'alien' entity. His adaptations of Indian and Persian fables were not intended to be documents of poetic assimilation; instead, they testify to Steiner's fundamental belief in accepting the Other on his/her own terms. As recent research has shown, the concept of the 'border' must be recognized as an integral part of Steiner's ethnological work in the sense that borders are necessary for the formation of identity both at an individual and collective level.[7]

III.

What is meant by 'accepting the Other'? Does such acceptance imply the ever continuing existence of borders between 'us' and 'the others'? Or can it be envisaged to *mutually* transgress this border – towards one another?

Border consciousness has been a key-motif in literature and, in particular, in poetry at least since Roman days.[8] Furthermore, with all its political, philosophical, and linguistic connotations, it can be regarded as a defining measure in the formation of cultures and civilizations.[9] The existential significance of border consciousness has, however, risen sharply during the twentieth century with its traumas of emigration, exile and, in some cases, remigration.[10]

---

[6] Both publications in: *Documents*, 2 (1930), 2/57–58 and 7/404–405.

[7] Nicolas J. Ziegler, 'Eroberungen. Das Hauptwerk der Dichtung von Franz Baermann Steiner' (unpublished doctoral dissertation, University of London, 2000), p. 154; see also SWII: 122.

[8] Dieter Lamping, *Über Grenzen. Eine literarische Topographie* (Göttingen: Vandenhoeck & Ruprecht, 2001).

[9] See *Nachdenken über Grenzen*, ed. by Rüdiger Görner and Suzanne Kirkbright (Munich: iudicium, 1999)

[10] See Marietta Krauss, *Heimkehr in ein fremdes Land. Geschichte der Remigration nach 1945* (Munich: Beck, 2001); see also her important essay 'Grenzen, die sich tief in die Seele graben. Ein unwiederbringlicher Verlust von Heimat: Das Trauma der Emigration, das auch nach der Rückkehr nicht heilen kann', *Süddeutsche Zeitung*, 259, 10–11 November 2001.

Poetry works with demarcations of language and meaning as one of its prime materials; it instrumentalizes lines of demarcation between a word and a 'blank' to use Wolfgang Iser's concept. By the same token, however, it can transform such borders of verbal experience into thresholds that may invite the reader to respect or transgress them.[11] As we have seen borders, boundaries, and lines of demarcation, with all their subtle semantic nuances,[12] have strong existential connotations. This is probably most explicit in Steiner's poem 'Spätere Jahre des Dichters' (Later Years of the Poet) which states: 'Was immer kommt: es trennt. / Und also kommt es, trennungen, durchs eigne wort' (Whatever will come divides / And so it comes: division, by my own hand; AsP: 230). The meaning of the last line is, and needs to be, ambivalent; for it can suggest that the divisions occur 'by my own word' as Hamburger's translation reads. But it is equally plausible to see these 'divisions' running through the poet's 'own word'. Both meanings highlight the existential quality of this (linguistic) border experience. Words can expose 'divisions', or lines of demarcation, in our perception of the world and, at the same time, they can become the object of dividing lines. This does not necessarily undermine their value. Steiner's poetry was not dominated by a sense of the early twentieth-century *Sprachkrise* (Crisis of language). Indeed, Steiner's poems display a fundamental belief in the communicative faculty of language, a belief which he shared, for instance, with his friend H. G. Adler but not with, say, Paul Celan.

Nowhere in Steiner's poetical works is the conception of 'Grenze' (border) more prominent than in his cycle *Eroberungen* (Conquests) which, if seen in the context of the twentieth-century extended poem, ranks beside Eliot's *The Waste Land*, Rilke's *Duineser Elegien*, and Octavio Paz's *Blanco*. Steiner's cycle *Eroberungen* refers from the outset to the experience of the lonely individual placed on, and living at, boundaries. In the course of the poem, the speaker seems to look for ways and means to overcome such boundaries and, with them, his own painful loneliness.

The main movement of the cycle begins, first of all, with the 'step' (part I) which turns out to be a step towards 'recollection' (part II); recollection or memory leads to the organic and spiritual centre of the human being, the 'heart' (part III) which endeavours to focus the act of remembering ('Ein Weniges zu behalten' [To Retain a Little], part IV); the poem then addresses the lonely individual (part V) who will meet his match in the shape of 'Der Sterbende' (The Dying Man, part VIII). There follows some elaborate reference to the 'Other' and to the

---

[11] See Rüdiger Görner, *Grenzen, Schwellen, Übergänge. Zur Poetik des Transhistorischen* (Göttingen: Vandenhoeck & Ruprecht, 2001). The following attempts to explore further what I have outlined in the chapter 'Grenzen der Bedrängten und Exilierten' (pp. 67–75).

[12] See Paul A. Chilton, 'Grenzsemantik', in *Nachdenken über Grenzen*, ed. by Görner and Kirkbright, pp. 19–32.

beloved ('Im Rücken die Schläferin' [With a Sleeping Woman at His Back], part VI) and to a symbol of nature ('Das Eschenblatt' [The Leaf of the Ash], part VII). What follows next is movement as a motif ('Die Räder' [The Wheels], part X). This seems to take up the initial motif ('steps'), transforming and accelerating them. Eventually, after a strong expression of melancholy ('Die Spinne und die Monde' [The Spider and the Moons], part XII), the movement comes to a halt ('Der Schritt hält an' [The Step ceases], part XIII).

The use of the term 'Eroberungen' is intriguing as it is not quite clear who is conquering what, or what is conquering whom. Be that as it may, 'conquests' raises the question of borders, their violation, and the possible need to restore them. To begin with, we are dealing with the borders of the 'heimat des herzens' (home of the heart; AsP: 354) or, more precisely, the foreign territory that borders the land to which the lonely person initially feels emotionally attached. This very border, however, appears to be 'uncertain' and difficult to define. We soon find, though, that this border is inhabitable to the extent that the lonely man has built himself into it, albeit he is still looking in both directions ('doppelgesichtig' [double-faced]; AsP: 355). The interplay between ambivalence and supposed certainty is a defining element not only of this fifth part of *Eroberungen* but of the entire cycle. The 'Einsame' (Lonely Man) desires openness on both sides of the border; and he is keen not to see the border as a demarcation line but as a mark of orientation:

Er duldet nicht trennung,
Hält hüben und drüben im liebenden aug, solang ers vermag.
Doch vermag ers nicht lange – (AsP: 355).

(He does not tolerate division. / He maintains both here and there in his loving eye. As long as he can, / But he is not able for long –)

The sobering fact is that the political circumstances do not allow, or cater for, the tolerant but lonely 'inhabitant' of the border. His destiny is to be displaced from the border area which he had tried to cultivate as a place for mediation. He becomes a refugee; but even as a displaced person he is sure 'Daß ich steh, wo ich stand, an der grenze [...] / Mein erschaffenes herz sagt es mit jedem schlag: / Bleib an der grenze' (That i stand where i stood, on the border, / [...] / My created heart says so with every beat: / Stay on the border; AsP: 357).

Such borders can emerge anywhere and at any time. In Steiner's great poem they even take the shape of a wall: 'mauer des erinnerns' (wall of remembrance; AsP: 348) which might suggest finality ('Hier ist das ende' [Here is the end]; AsP: 348). But the following stanza already questions this fearful assumption: 'Ist es ein ende?' (Is it an end?; AsP: 348). The definite article has turned into a indefinite one, thus easing the impact of the word 'end'.

In fact, the poetic usage of the word 'border' or 'boundary' often entails some reference to its counterpart. The threshold may figure as an object of philosophical reflection[13] or as a poetological issue.[14] In Steiner's *Eroberungen*, the threshold, like the border, is given an existential dimension:

Bin ich die schwelle
Niedrig noch nicht genug,
Daß du anhältst und innehältst,
Dich nur hinhältst,
Sieh, wie offen
Ist die rauschende nacht. (AsP: 352/53)

(Am i the threshold, / Not yet low enough, / That you stop and pause, / Yet only offer yourself and linger, / Look how open / The murmering night.)

The feeling is expressed in the form of a song which is seen as slowly branching out above the cliffs ('Über die klippen verzweigt sich langsam ein lied' [Over the cliffs a song slowly branches]; AsP: 352). That is to say, the cliffs, indicating natural borders, generate a song that represents transition and focuses on the symbol which the physicality of the cliffs has generated, that of the threshold.

In part VIII of *Eroberungen* the proximity of 'border' and 'threshold' is particularly striking for 'Der Sterbende' (The Dying Man) epitomizes just that – the inevitable interrelation between finality and transgression in the moment of dying. This is of course reflected in the style. Steiner employs the prefix 'über' in all possible connections which, at times, leads to the formation of neologisms. The very first line of 'Der Sterbende' indicates this verbal aspect of transition: 'Von verschwimmender farbe sind die *über*hängenden ränder, / Zerstückt und zerschlissen. // Saubere schranken kennen wir nicht' (The overhanging edges are hacked and shredded / by blurred colour / We do not recognize clean barriers; AsP: 364). In the following we see branches hanging over a 'nachbarland' (neighbouring land); streets and roof mingle. An overwhelming feeling of imprecision conditions our modes of perception. 'Übertanzt, übersponnen, überbrückt' (danced-over, spun-over, bridged) – these are the dominant verbs. The shapes, colours, and, finally, borders become blurred and the ability to discern is now so precious that the dying man cannot afford to exercise it any longer:

---

[13] Suzanne Kirkbright discusses this point with reference to Jaspers in 'Karl Jaspers on the Threshold Motif: A Biographical Encounter', in *Nachdenken über Grenzen*, ed. by Görner and Kirkbright, pp. 45–56.
[14] See Rüdiger Görner, *Grenzen, Schwellen, Übergänge* (op. cit.).

[...] so verschränken sich
Stunden der tage, stunden der nächte
In einander im unentschiedenen dämmer.
Ungenau sind die ränder, saubere schranken
Kennen wir nicht zwischen dingen,
Zwischen bereichen der welt. (AsP: 364)

([...] so they fold themselves / hours of the days, hours of the nights / Into one another in the indecisive twilight. / The edges are imprecise, clean barriers / we do not recognize between things, / between parts of the world.)

Shadows are cast over lines of demarcation and differentiation. It comes to light here that the 'mauer des erinnerns' (wall of remembrance) was, in fact, an assembly of tightly fitted shadows which are now dissolving. This said, 'der Sterbende' seems to take comfort from recollecting some images of the past with apparent precision. Finally, though, he cannot trust what he believes he has 'seen':

Das mädchen weinte.
Dies ist eins der erinnerten bilder ... aber geschah es einst?
[...]
Weinte das mädchen wirklich,
War es kein schluchzendes lied, für ein künftiges spiel, einen künstlichen abend,
Zur probe gesungen? (AsP: 370)

(The girl was crying. / This is one of the images remembered ... but did it happen once? / [...] / Was the girl really crying, / Was it not a sobbing song, for a future game, an imagined evening, / Sung in preparation?)

The boundary between recollection and imagination has become as blurred as the dividing line between life and death. 'Otherness' has ceased to have any ethnological quality; for it can now be associated with what emerges from the state of perpetual mingling and fusing, the mixing of different spheres of existence. Thus it is possible to argue that by means of his blurred phantasies the dying man generates a different world, which would have looked alien to him before. In this alien space the inner and outer world seem to merge.

In this poetic exploration of the unknown, Steiner's approach more resembles Levinas than Leiris, and in particular Levinas's conception of the Other as something that is conditioned by the *terra incognita* of the future and by death. In his 1946/47 lectures on *Le Temps et l'Autre*,[15] Levinas had defined Man's relationship with the Other as an expression of our attitude towards the future

---

[15] Emmanuel Levinas, *Le Temps et l'Autre* (Montpellier: Fata Morgana, 1979)

which includes the knowledge of our own limitations and finiteness. From Levinas's point of view this encounter with 'l'autre' takes place in the form of an 'event', 'l'évènement', that is to say, like a surprise for which we can never be sufficiently prepared.

In a certain sense, Steiner's poems, and *Eroberungen* in particular, attempt to prepare the reader for this inevitable 'event'. Having said that, Steiner's evocation of blurred poetic images does not only prepare us for the Other; it also has the effect, and here paradox comes full circle, that this 'blurredness' makes the reader long to turn the threshold back into a border and to re-draw the line. Steiner's poetry illustrates that the border experience as such can be an 'event' too, a kind of 'Grenzereignis' (border event), to quote Hans Blumenberg, from which the most genuine poetry derives.

Ultimately, we need to acknowledge that through our yearning to retain what we once strove to overcome, namely the differentiating powers of borders, to a remarkable extent we internalize a paradox. It is the very paradox that precariously underpins the meaning of 'Eroberungen'. For perhaps these 'conquests' ultimately refer to man conquering himself; and yet, it is typical of Steiner's position that such 'conquests' must also presuppose some form of self-defeat.

One of Steiner's challenging legacies as a poet consists in just this: his unremitting exploration of the paradoxes in the human condition. It is these which shape his poetry and his poetic language with its distinct use of contrasts and its deliberate contradictions in terms. As the shadows of time and exile began encroaching on his language, Steiner succeeded in turning them, too, into words with the effect that we can see in these verbalized shadows something boundlessly illuminating.

GUARDING THE MYTHS

Franz Baermann Steiner's *Conquests*

Katrin Kohl

Franz Baermann Steiner's extended poem *Eroberungen* (Conquests) was written in exile in Oxford mainly during the years 1940–1943, by a poet isolated from his family, his people, and his language, living as a Jew in a society which he experienced – and conceptualized – as culturally alien. The cycle was begun in 1940 and gradually expanded, with the final plan envisaging 13 parts, though parts IX and XI remained unwritten and part X incomplete. The work was only published posthumously – like most of his work – and reception is still in the early stages.[1]

The title of the work is both topical for the time of composition, and resonant of the conquests that extend back through history and into myth. Steiner's work as an anthropologist was driven by a 'deep aversion to the imposition of Western values on non-Western peoples' and a passionate 'concern for the right to self-determination of non-Western peoples, among whom he includes his own Jewish people' (Adler and Fardon, SWII: viii–ix).[2] An aware-

---

[1] For a critical edition with commentary see Franz Baermann Steiner, *Eroberungen. Ein lyrischer Zyklus*, ed. by H. G. Adler, Veröffentlichungen der Deutschen Akademie für Sprache und Dichtung, Darmstadt, 36 (Heidelberg, Darmstadt: Schneider, 1964). This is abbreviated below as E, and references to the cycle are normally given with the part and the line number. The text is reprinted with details of composition and notes by Steiner and H. G. Adler in AsP: 335–382 and 409–420. For a translation of parts I to VII see 'Conquests I-VII', translated by J. Adler, in SWII: 249–266. This is the translation used here, though short quotations are occasionally modified to help clarify a point. Unless otherwise stated, all other translations are the author's own. For an account of the extant corpus and the process of composition of *Eroberungen* see also Nicolas Julian Ziegler, 'Eroberungen. Das Hauptwerk der Dichtung von Franz Baermann Steiner' (unpublished doctoral dissertation, University of London, 2000), pp. 104–108. Ziegler's thesis offers a detailed account of the reception of Steiner's literary work – which was beset by misfortune – and an interpretation of *Eroberungen*. Quotations from this thesis are by kind permission of Dr Ziegler.

[2] Steiner came from an assimilated German-speaking Jewish family in Prague; see Alfons Fleischli, *Franz Baermann Steiner. Leben und Werk* (unpublished dissertation, University of Freiburg, Switzerland, 1970), p. 8. Steiner's commitment to Judaism and the creation of a Jewish state was inspired by his visit to Palestine in 1930–1931.

ness of the impact of historical conquests emerges in Steiner's vehement response to an attack by Mahatma Gandhi in 1946 on the establishment of a Jewish state in Palestine. Steiner sees the Jews as an Oriental people forcibly prevented from realizing their cultural identity in Europe, and invites Gandhi to see Jewish demands as part of a common cause against imperialist subjugation of non-European cultures:

> No non-European power has ever built a colonial empire. Do you regard the ceaseless encroachment on the life and lands of other races, that of Asia in particular as inconsistent with European civilisation? [...] Would you not say that European civilisation that does no more hold other cultures in tutelage or suppression ceases to be the Europe we know? And if they do so to Asiatic countries what they have done to yours, how must they treat an Oriental people which lives among them and is always at their mercy? (SWII: 132) [3]

Steiner's experience of being an outsider in an alien, 'other' culture is complemented by a religiously founded identification with collective humanity – a collectivity which manifests itself most intensely in suffering, as Steiner elaborates in a letter to his friend Georg Rapp:

> I have never moaned in your presence or complained about what the Germans are doing to my people. [...] Don't think that I have discovered some special comfort which enables me to keep silent when others complain. It is much rather the case that, for me, every horror which people perpetrate (against whomsoever) defines the nature of man. That man am I. If I refused to recognise that every, but really every abomination which so-called Germans, so-called English, Romanians, Poles perpetrate is simply the precise extension of obscure thoughts and feelings which I have had at one time or another, then everything that I believe about man, about creation, about sin, would become meaningless. [...] Here, humanity as a single whole is committing a crime, and the longer that continues, the less it can be seen how you, YOU, WE can be forgiven. The fact that the greater part of the Jewish people is undergoing destruction can only intensify our suffering into boundlessness. (SWII: 118–119)

Violence against the Jewish people is internalized to a point where the self becomes the locus of both infliction of suffering, and the suffering that ensues, while 'the power to overcome suffering only comes out of suffering itself' (SWII: 116). Perpetrator and victim, active and passive participant interact in a space that connects individual and collective experience, politics and history,

---

[3] On Steiner and Zionism see Adler and Fardon, SWII: 16–28.

myth and religion. These tensions sustain Steiner's poetry, with the individual and collective dimensions of suffering finding their most profound expression in the late poem 'Gebet im Garten' (Prayer in the Garden), written in 1947 on the birthday of Steiner's father.

Like the concept of 'suffering', that of 'conquest' is opened up to complex significations. In his essay 'Über den Prozeß der Zivilisierung' (On the Process of Civilisation) of 1944,[4] Steiner deconstructs the binary oppositions that inform Western identity. Proceeding from the 'normal' definition that 'European culture is [...] the culture characterised by the greatest and most extensive control over nature that is known to us', Steiner concludes: 'The process of civilisation is the conquest of man by the natural forces, the demons. It is the march of danger into the heart of creation' (SWII: 123 and 128). He reinterprets the conqueror as the object of conquest and inverts the notion that 'civilisation' conquers and supersedes the primeval demons, thereby undermining the very basis on which Western concepts of progress are founded. In his poetic cycle *Eroberungen*, traditional categories of 'conquest' are destabilized further through the voice of the poet as exile, and the power of myth.

Myth is key to Steiner's understanding of anthropology, and central to his poetic project.[5] Steiner's friend Elias Canetti finds his own conviction reflected in Steiner, that myths are the 'greatest and most precious things which humanity [has] produced', and holds that they embody 'the essential feature in a particular human group'.[6] Myth connects the individual to the collective, and provides a framework of narratives and rituals that extend through natural life into metaphysical beliefs. Crucially for Steiner, myth permits free exploration of other cultures without the structures of rational subjugation that obliterate alterity. Poetry, for him, is essentially mythical, and stands in opposition to the Western rationalist tradition extending back to Plato, as he elaborates in an extended note on the poet Friedrich Hölderlin:[7]

> Hölderlin – der einzige große Intellektuelle der Deutschen, der sich der Dichtung, der Verdichtung – ergeben hat. Man bedenke, was für eine entschiedene Ablehnung Platos darin liegt, und nicht bloß der berühmten Stelle des 'Staats', sondern des griechischen Versuches: der Einordnung des

---

[4] 'Über den Prozeß der Zivilisierung', in F. B. Steiner, 'Feststellungen und Versuche', ed. by J. Adler, *Akzente*, 42 (1995), 213–219; translation: 'On the Process of Civilisation', trsl. Michael Mack and J. Adler, in SWII: 123–128.

[5] On the role of myth in Steiner's thought see Adler and Fardon, SWI: 80–82.

[6] Elias Canetti, *Aufzeichnungen 1992–1993* (Munich, Vienna: Carl Hanser, 1996), pp. 18–19.

[7] Hölderlin is the only poet to whom Steiner directly addressed a poem ('An Hölderlin'; AsP: 81–83; see H. G. Adler, 'Das Hölderlinbild Franz Baermann Steiners', *Hölderlin Jahrbuch*, 9 (1955/56), 238–240 (p. 239)). See also Steiner's comments on Hölderlin's purely mythological use of the poetic word (ibid., p. 240).

Mythos in eine übergeordnete Harmonie der Vernunft (statt umgekehrt), nicht des 'Apollinischen' also, sondern des eigentlichen griechischen Humanismus.[8]

(Hölderlin – the only great intellectual among the Germans who devoted himself to poetry, to condensing. It is worth reflecting on the decisiveness of his rejection of Plato, not just of the famous passage in the 'Republic', but of the Greek project: the integration of myth into a superordinate harmony of reason (instead of the other way round), i. e. not of the 'Apollinian' but of true Greek humanism.)

Steiner's equation of 'Dichtung' (poetry) with 'Verdichtung' is significant, for it infuses poetry with the power of myth. The play on 'Dichtung' and 'dicht' (dense, tightly woven) implies a process of concentration and intensification, qualities which Wagner and Nietzsche had also associated with myth. In his extended treatise *Oper und Drama* Wagner sees myth as a process of 'Verdichten' and as 'das Gedicht einer gemeinsamen Lebensanschauung' (the poem of a shared philosophy of life),[9] while Nietzsche defines myth in *Die Geburt der Tragödie* (The Birth of Tragedy) as 'das zusammengezogene Weltbild' (the concentrated picture of the world) and the 'Abbreviatur der Erscheinung' (abbreviature of phenomena).[10]

'Verdichtung' is the guiding poetic principle of *Eroberungen*. It evidently governed the process of composition, with themes, figures, images, and words being repeated in different constellations and gradually accruing new significances as individual experiences develop into personal myths and connect with collective myths. The frame is already given in the earliest extant version of *Eroberungen* (December 1941), which consists of parts I, II, IV, and XIII in substantially complete form (E: 61–70).[11] This first version establishes the central figures: the striding man (I), the lonely man, and the dying man (II), with all three figures reemerging at the end (XIII). The final version develops these figures, gradually enriching their significance and introducing material from an immense diversity of cultures. The cycle in its final extant form was still 'Verdichtung' in progress: parts IX and XI remained at the planning stage, and part X unfinished. It cannot be assumed either that the completed parts had

---

[8] F. B. Steiner, 'Notizen über Hölderlin', *Hölderlin Jahrbuch*, 9 (1955/56), 235–237 (p. 235).

[9] Richard Wagner, *Oper und Drama* (1850/51), especially part II, section 2, in *Gesammelte Schriften und Dichtungen*, 10 vols (Leipzig: Fritzsch, 1871–1883), IV, 39–44 (pp. 43–44).

[10] Friedrich Nietzsche, *Die Geburt der Tragödie*, section 23, in Nietzsche, *Sämtliche Werke. Kritische Studienausgabe*, ed. by Giorgio Colli and Mazzino Montinari, 15 vols (Berlin, New York: de Gruyter, 1967–1977), I, 145–149 (p. 145). Translation: *The Complete Works of Friedrich Nietzsche*, ed. by Oscar Levy, 3 vols (Edinburgh, London: Foulis, 1909), III: *The Birth of Tragedy*, trsl. W. A. Haussmann, p. 174.

[11] The editor H. G. Adler regards this as the third version (E: 76); see also Ziegler, pp. 104–106.

attained a stable state. Comparison of the early and late extant versions shows that the (potentially complete) final part of the early version was expanded for the late version: the newly introduced lines in XIII take up themes and motifs of the new part III 'Das Herz' (The Heart), and incorporate three quotations from Jewish sources.[12] The process of mythic proliferation both enriches and deepens the mythic texture.

Significances of the title *Eroberungen* emerge only gradually for the reader, in a meditative process of engaging with the complex recollection of individual and collective experience through memory – the process by which the self asserts control over time.[13] 'Conquests' are introduced in part I in the form of a concrete image – they are 'treasures' being arranged by the central figure 'der schreitende' (the striding man, I, 15; AsP: 345) at the end of a day:

> Mit verscheidendem lächeln
> Ordnet seine schätze der schreitende,
> Verschliffene reste vom vergangenen her,
> Daß sie zusammengedrängt
> Auftun ersehnten glanz.
> Schwerlich gibts andren besitz als diese kleinode
> Gehäuft auf verdämmernde kante einer gegenwart,
> Eroberungen,
> Trümmer einst gerundeter seligkeiten. (I, 16–22; AsP: 345)

(With dying smiles, / The striding man orders his treasures, / Worn-out remnants from the past, / That they, compressed, / May open their desired glory. / There can scarcely be any possessions other than such jewels, / Heaped up on the fading edge of the present, / Conquests, / The debris of formerly perfected bliss.)

In contrast to the expectations raised by the heroic title, the 'conquests' are reduced to relics of the past, located precariously and in failing light in an

---

[12] XIII, 1–16 and 48–60 and 69–70 (AsP: 380–382) are not yet part of the early version. Steiner identifies the quotations in his notes (E: 131–133). XIII, 2–6 quotes I Enoch XL, 3–7: see *The Apocrypha and Pseudoepigraphica of the Old Testament in English*, ed. by R. H. Charles, 2 vols (Oxford: Clarendon, 1913), II, 211; He quotes from the German translation in *Altjüdisches Schrifttum außerhalb der Bibel*, ed. by Paul Rießler (Augsburg: Filser, 1928), pp. 378–379. XIII, 48–49 quotes the words 'Jichud we jarah' from a hymn that forms part of the Yom Kippur service, and Steiner comments critically on the translation by Gershom G. Sholem in *Major Trends in Jewish Mysticism* (New York: Schocken, 1995). XIII, 50–53 quotes from the *Paralipomena Jeremiae* or 'The rest of the Words of Baruch', chapters V–VI, Rießler, pp. 907–912.

[13] Jeremy Adler points out the affinity to T. S. Eliot's 'Only through time time is conquered' in *Burnt Norton*, which Steiner partially translated, and suggests that Steiner 'personalises the idea'; J. Adler, '"The Step Swings Away" and other poems by Franz Baermann Steiner', *Comparative Criticism*, 16 (1994), 139–168 (p. 150). See T. S. Eliot, *The Complete Poems and Plays* (London: Faber and Faber, 1969), p. 173.

undefined present, evoking lost bliss, and confined to an isolated individual. A gloss provided by Steiner on the occasion of a reading identifies these 'Eroberungen' as a metaphor for 'manche, beständige, unauflösliche Erinnerungsstücke' (certain enduring, indissoluble pieces of memory);[14] 'Erinnerungen' (Memories) is then the title of part II. The metaphor evokes the consciousness of transience captured in T. S. Eliot's 'fragments [...] shored against my ruins' from the end of *The Waste Land*,[15] and also the smooth, tactile physicality attributed to Rilke's symbol of archetypal suffering at the end of the *Duino Elegies*, 'ein Stück geschliffenes Ur-Leid' (a lump [...] of polished original pain).[16] Their imagined physicality gains significance from the challenge they pose to Western concepts of value: no other type of 'possession' is conceivable, and even these 'conquests' prove insubstantial at the end of the journey (XIII, 64–67; AsP: 382). The morphological reciprocity between 'Eroberungen' and 'Erinnerungen' – with 'oben' (above) corresponding to 'innen' (within) – suggests externalization of memories, and correspondence between the individual and the divine, which finds its fulfilment in union.

The significance of 'Eroberungen' is enriched by association with Daniel Defoe's *Robinson Crusoe*,[17] recalling the age of adventurous conquests while providing a story of cultural independence, mutual respect, and mutual salvation of the islander and the captain; by the themes of 'heimat' (home[land]) and boundaries, bridges and thresholds; and by the landscapes and peoples that evoke the cultural diversity suppressed by Western civilization. Memory allows the speaker to recollect and reflect personal experiences through different aspects of the self, which are shaped by myths and construct new myths. The role of memory for the individual consciousness elaborated in part I is complemented in part X by the memories of whole communities, here exemplifying the terrible human loss caused by the mass conquest that was destroying Steiner's world as he wrote. The poet poignantly laments the brutal annihilation of the 'geliebte leiber' (beloved bodies; X, 12) and the rich memories – 'schätze' (treasures; X, 14; AsP: 373) – that formed those bodies.

---

[14] This is one of the explanations Steiner provided in 1943 on the occasion of a reading of the eight-part version of the cycle of 1942 (see E: 86 and AsP: 387).
[15] *The Waste Land*, Part V, l. 430, in Eliot, *The Complete Poems and Plays*, p. 75.
[16] *Duineser Elegien*, X, l. 58, Rainer Maria Rilke, *Werke*, ed. by Manfred Engel, Ulrich Fülleborn et al., 4 vols (Frankfurt/M. and Leipzig: Insel, 1996), II, 199–234 (p. 232). In the following, the *Duineser Elegien* will be abbreviated DE. For a translation see R. M. Rilke, *Duino Elegies*, trsl. J. B. Leishman and Stephen Spender 4th ed. (London: Hogarth Press, 1968). Adler and Fardon refer to Rilke's image of 'Ur-Leid' in relation to Steiner's letter to Georg Rapp and comment that for Rilke, as later for Steiner, 'suffering provides the genuine measure of value' (SWII: 100).
[17] On the relationship with Defoe's text and Steiner's Robinson figure see Ziegler, pp. 126–128.

The apparently simple metaphoric substitution at the start of the cycle – 'conquests' for 'memories' – is thus modulated through individual consciousness of experience and collective consciousness of history, with images gaining new meanings as they recur and connect with each other. Patterns of repetition in themes, images, syntax, and vocabulary set up mythical resonances that draw on the Hebrew Bible, the *Gita*, the *Qur'an*, the *Tao Te Ching* and other texts,[18] ranging through many periods, cultures, and religions. Texts are quoted, alluded to, transformed, and amplified, and powerful myths gain concrete shape in the poem, notably the Way from Taoism. It connects the beginning and end of the cycle through the path of the striding man, and flows through the lovers' room in part VI:[19]

Weg ohne ende, wie unscheinbar
Fliesst er durchs zimmer, (VI, 68–69; AsP: 361)

(Way without end, how unassumingly / It flows through the room.)

Steiner's familiarity with myths from a diversity of peoples is often reflected in brief allusions that become recognizable only where he provides an elucidating comment, as with the menstruation mythology incorporated in part XII.[20] This process counteracts conquest in its every aspect and manifestation, moving towards dissolution: Steiner comments on the final part that once the protagonist has 'understood the conquests, *they scatter* and they too disintegrate' (E: 130–131). The cycle concludes as selfhood and time are relinquished:

Ganz übergeben
Sind die eroberungen:
Weggerollt, abgeglüht, fremd, verloren,
So ist die seele allein [...] (XIII, 64–67; AsP: 382)

(The conquests are / Quite relinquished: / Rolled away, burnt out, alien, lost, / So the soul is alone [...])

Individuation gives way to 'Einung ist das erschauern' (XIII, 43; AsP: 381), a quotation of 'Jichud we jarah' from the Yom Kippur service evoking human fear and awe before the sublimity of God in the process and state of union (E: 131). Exile, as the historical condition of the Jew, and the exemplary condition of mankind, is overcome only in union with the divine.[21]

---

[18] See Steiner's introductory remark (E: 78–79 and Adler and Fardon, SWII: 72).
[19] See Adler, '"The Step Swings Away"', p. 151.
[20] See XII, 86–91 (AsP: 379) and the associated comment, E: 128–129.
[21] H. G. Adler comments that the cycle centres on 'the fate of the wandering refugee and the fugitive wanderer who recognises the human condition in his personal situation'; he highlights the unifying force imparted to the work by the glorification of the one creator (E: 140). On the interrelation between exile and *jichud* see Ziegler, pp. 143–145.

Steiner referred to the work as 'in a sense autobiographical' and as 'a metaphysical autobiographical poem';[22] this – together with other affinities, notably the thirteen-part structure – has invited comparison with Wordsworth's *Prelude; or, Growth of a Poet's Mind*.[23] Like Wordsworth, Steiner introduces geographical locations that helped shape his life: a suburb of Prague, city of his childhood (II, 5; AsP: 346); Dalmatia and Palestine, which he visited in 1929 and 1930/31 respectively (IV); Carpathian Russia, visited in 1937 (IX); wartime London (X, 91–136; AsP: 375–376); Oxford (XI); and the literary location of Robinson Crusoe's island, the land of childhood reading that inspired a fascination with exotic cultures (II, 12–31; AsP: 346). Like Wordsworth's poem, *Eroberungen* begins with the grown man striding through a landscape, and a certain narrative progression suggests reflection on the course of an individual life: childhood and puberty (II), a sexual relationship in the city (VI), and life as an exiled intellectual in London (X), with part XIII returning to the striding man, the ceasing of his movement, and images of dissolution.

Nevertheless Steiner's comment that the work is a 'metaphysical autobiography' calls the very basis of Romantic autobiography into question, for his metaphysical beliefs reach for collectivity and the overcoming of self-centred Western individuation. While presupposing a development from 'Ich-Losigkeit' to 'Ich-Bewußtsein' in the development from childhood to manhood,[24] the cycle also holds these states in tension in a complex human consciousness that reflects through time and anticipates losing itself in God. Autobiographical elements are everywhere transmuted into myth.[25] Memories of reading Robinson Crusoe (II) are developed in the course of the cycle and prepare for the myths of the lonely man (V) and the dying man (VIII). Steiner's exile in London is read through the exile of the Jewish people in Babylon (X); and an outline for the unwritten eleventh part entitled 'Zur Zeit des Hochwassers' (At the time of the Flood) envisages the flooding of Port Meadow in Oxford

---

[22] 'Die "Eroberungen" sind ein umfangreiches, in gewissem Sinne autobiographisches Gedicht' (Steiner to Rudolf Hartung, 14 March 1952); '[ein] metaphysisches autobiographisches Gedicht' (Steiner to Rudolf Hartung, 5 April 1948). Quoted after Fleischli, p. 42.

[23] 'Steiner bases his poem around an original concept of the self, and it is not to be ruled out that Wordsworth's thirteen-part *Prelude* (1805) provided a precedent for his project' (Adler, '"The Step Swings Away"', p. 148). William Wordsworth, *The Prelude or Growth of the Poet's Mind*, ed. Ernest de Selincourt, 2nd ed. rev. Helen Darbishire (Oxford: Clarendon, 1959). This edition gives the 1805/06 version and the 1850 version in parallel. Further references will be to the 1850 version.

[24] Steiner comments on these concepts in a note relating to Part V, 'Der Einsame' (AsP: 412–413).

[25] Ziegler notes that in depicting autobiographical elements, Steiner takes concrete representation as the basis and then moves through various thematic levels and perspectives, finally relating them to a metaphysical frame of reference.

merging into Noah's Flood. Early sexual experiences are depicted in a series of episodes in part II, 'Erinnerungen', beginning with the boy witnessing two lovers, followed by a celebration of the beloved through song, and an evocation of her elusive identity: '[…] und wer kann sagen, / Ob sie mein war, ganz fremd, ob schwesterlich' (and who can say, / Whether she was mine, quite strange, whether sisterly; II, 64–65; AsP: 347). The imagery gradually introduces associations of death and culminates in images of closure, suggesting that Steiner may here be incorporating allusions to his beloved sister, whose early death broke his heart:[26]

> In silberkammern wächst die morgensonne,
> Ein weißes lachen löst sich aus dem traum.
> O langsame stunden, eingleiten sanft und reuelos
> In einen tag ohne schatten.
> Gelegt in die nähe, die nichts mehr verlieren läßt,
> Ruhte das bräutliche antlitz.
>
> Hier ist das ende. mauer des erinnerns.
> Eingesunkene straßen. (II, 70–77; AsP: 348)[27]

(In silvery rooms grows the morning sun, / A white laughter removes from the dream. / O slow hours, slipping gently and without regret / Into a day without shadows. / Placed into proximity, that permits no further loss, / Lay the bridal visage. // Here is the end. wall of remembrance. / Sunken roads.)

Pain is both externalized in the wall of remembrance – with the wall later gaining positive resonance in association with the Holy City (IV, 99; AsP: 353) – and internalized in the subsequent image of the closure of the heart, a leitmotif which becomes associated with the lonely man and the dying man and gains ambivalent significance in the course of the cycle, recurring finally at the hypothetical threshold of eternal marital union (XIII, 24–26;

---

[26] According to Canetti, 'all women whom [Steiner] later courted with indescribable patience resembled this sister' (Canetti, *Aufzeichnungen 1992–1993*, p. 19). See also Adler and Fardon, SWI: 29 and p. 254 in the current volume.

[27] Ziegler reads these lines as unambiguously depicting the first sexual encounter, and he supports this with reference to the 'Nachlaß' (pp. 129–131). However, it is perhaps significant that Steiner's poem in memory of his sister, 'Erinnerung an den Neusiedler See' (Memories of the Neusiedler Lake), links the image of her 'versargtes gesicht' (coffined face) with dreams, sunrise, and laughter (AsP: 160–1, ll. 27–29). The quoted lines with their colour and dream imagery and the motifs of the wall and roads are resonant of the poetry of Georg Trakl, in which death is a central theme, and the figure of the sister a recurrent motif; see Georg Trakl, *Dichtungen und Briefe. Historisch-kritische Ausgabe*, ed. by Walter Killy and Hans Szklenar, 2nd ed., 2 vols (Salzburg: Müller, 1987), e. g. 'Helian', 'Passion' and 'Grodek' (I, 69–73, 125, 167).

AsP: 380–1). In this way personal experiences are explored in ever-changing constellations, drawing the reader into the process of reflection and intensification through the recurrence of themes and key words, motifs and images. The reader thereby participates in the process of myth-making that constitutes the cycle.

Where the speaker in Wordsworth's *Prelude* is the actual author, and the poem has the dual purpose of enabling him 'To understand myself', and his friend Coleridge 'to know / With better knowledge how the heart was framed / Of him thou lovest',[28] *Eroberungen* has neither a stable speaker/protagonist nor a stable addressee. In an explanatory note on the first part of the cycle, Steiner refers to the 'Ichperson' (I persona) walking through the evening landscape and reflecting on life and the nature of memory,[29] but this masks the instability and elusiveness of the first-person pronoun and its complex relationship with the figures introduced in the course of the cycle. The depicted wanderer is not the coherent, centred 'I' of the *Prelude*, in control of his own striding body – 'I paced on / With brisk and eager steps' – and experiencing joyful reciprocity between inner and outer world: 'For I, methought, while the sweet breath of heaven / Was blowing on my body, felt within / A correspondent breeze'.[30] The figure at the centre of the first part is introduced in the third person and attains a presence that seems to exceed normal human dimensions with its dynamic movement. The components of the body are referred to with definite articles rather than first-person possessive pronouns that would connect them to the reflecting self:

Der schritt schwingt hin,
Den abend durcheilt der leib,
Gedehnte brust achtet nicht der arme,
Leicht und hilflos sind die arme angehängt … (I, 8–11; AsP: 345)

(The step swings away, / The body hurries through the evening, / The stretched breast does not heed the arms, / The arms are loosely attached and helpless …)

This figure is particular, but in consisting solely of body parts it is devoid of subjectivity. The third-person perspective marks it out as a creation of the speaker, in accordance with a quotation from Montaigne that constitutes the first in a series of texts introducing the cycle:

---

[28] *The Prelude*, Book I, ll. 627–629.
[29] With reference to Part I, where the central figure is portrayed only in the third person and the pronoun is not used (see E: 86), and with reference to Part V (E: 92) and Part XIII (E: 130).
[30] *The Prelude*, Book I, ll. 60–61 and 33–35.

Andre formen den Menschen; ich beschreib ihn und bilde einen Besondern ab, einen schlechtgebauten, der, hätt ich ihn neu zu schaffen, wahrlich sehr verschieden von dem sein würde, der er ist. (E: 8)[31]

(Others form man; I describe him and depict a particular one, a badly built one who, if I had to create him anew, would truly be very different from the one he is.)

The utopian dimension in the Montaigne quotation is developed in the course of the cycle. The striding man's 'inner life' forms the subject of 'Das Herz' (III), and in the fourth part, imagery of closure gives way to the images of a threshold (IV, 87; AsP: 352) and openness (IV, 91; AsP: 353) as he attains unity of body, movement, thoughts, and emotions in his spiritual homecoming to the Holy City:

Es glaubt dieser eilende,
Abendmütige, mit tief schöpfender brust:
Daß er vor jahren stand vor der Heiligen Stadt; (IV, 93–95; AsP: 353)

(This hurrying man in an evening mood / And with a heaving breast believes: / That long ago he stood before the Holy City;)

Unity of the self is not a given – it recalls and prefigures union with the divine. The figures of the 'lonely man' and the 'dying man' mythically embody aspects of the self through space and time. The self is thus explored not through concepts of inwardness and individuality, as in Romanticism, but through processes of externalization and increasingly collective significance.

While the ultimate orientation of the 'ich' in the cycle is metaphysical, there is nevertheless a strongly developed social dimension that emerges through different figures and perspectives. In order to locate Steiner's view of the self, Jeremy Adler and Richard Fardon point both to the German Modernist deconstruction of the self in the wake of Ernst Mach's psychology and physiology of sensation, and to Steiner's anthropological frame of reference, which yields an early structuralist conception of the self as defined by its social role. Compellingly, they suggest that the perspectives developed in *Eroberungen* can be seen as 'indebted to [Georg] Simmel's notions of "concentric" and "overlapping" circles which meet in any given subject'; the subject forms the point of intersection between many conflicting cultural and social circles – most ambitiously, between religions – and 'is actually enriched and strengthened by the dualisms it has to bear' (SWII: 77–78).

---

[31] Michel de Montaigne, 'Du repentir', in *Les Essais*, ed. by Pierre Villey, 2nd ed. 3 vols (Paris: Quadrige/PUF, 1992), III, 804–817 (p. 804).

The tensions between different perspectives are played out in the voices of
the cycle, with intertextual dialogue being indicated in a variety of ways, often
by quotation marks or indentation. In the second poem, there is the beginning
of an unidentified song (II, 60–61; AsP: 347), the adapted *Robinson Crusoe* narrative framed by references to an 'open book' (II, 12–29; AsP: 346), and
snatches of utterances from the islander and the captain. Part IX – which did
not get beyond the planning stage – was to have combined a Walachian and a
Yiddish song in a wild medley conjuring up the magic of Carpathian Russia
with its ethnic diversity, against the backdrop of a history of conquest by Magyar hordes (E: 102–104). Part X, with its London setting, incorporates an allusion to Louis MacNeice's poem 'The British Museum Reading Room' – quoted
in an explanatory note by Steiner – and mediates it through a voice Steiner has
added:

> Und der vorbeigeht, mit tiefer lippe spricht er, mit schwerer zunge:
> 'gurgelnde klage, habichtgesicht –
> Unsrer sippe ähneln sie nicht.' (X, 124–126; AsP: 376)[32]

> (And he who walks past, with low lip he speaks, with heavy tongue:
> 'guttural lament, hawk-like face –
> They do not resemble our kin.')

Steiner admired T. S. Eliot[33] and acknowledged that he learnt much from the
way 'the master' used quotations in *The Waste Land*, though in 1948 he comments critically on his emulation of Eliot's montage techniques in *Eroberungen*,
now rejecting them in favour of more refined integration of quoted material.[34]
In fact, contrast of voice and register is far less pronounced in *Eroberungen* than
in *The Waste Land*, and unlike Eliot, who incorporates non-English material,

[32] For the note, see E: 111. The quoted lines read: 'Between the enormous fluted Ionic col-
umns / There seeps from heavily jowled or hawk-like foreign faces / The guttural sorrow
of the refugees.' See Louis MacNeice, *The Collected Poems*, ed. by E. R. Dodds (London:
Faber and Faber, 1966), pp. 160–161 (p. 161).

[33] For Steiner's reception of Eliot and especially the relationship between *Eroberungen* and
Four Quartets see Adler and Fardon, SWII: 68–73, and Ziegler, pp. 116–118.

[34] Steiner to Rudolf Hartung, 30 May 1948, quoted after Ziegler, p. 117. A critical response to
Eliot is evident in Steiner's poem 'Von Schlafmitteln oder Traummitteln' (On the Means to
Sleep or to Dream) of the same year (AsP: 228). While working extensively with quotations
and allusions, Steiner was acutely concerned to preempt any accusations of plagiarism. With
reference to his textual methods of distinguishing quotations and his scholarly annotations
identifying extraneous material, he comments: 'I would a hundred times rather be accused
not unjustly of pedantry, than be accused even once without justification of plagiarism'
(Steiner to Rudolf Hartung, 30 January 1950, quoted after Ziegler, p. 118). As regards the
poetic text itself, he stresses in 1948 that the full meaning of a passage including a quotation
should be accessible irrespective of whether the reader recognizes the presence of a quotation (Steiner to Rudolf Hartung, 30 May 1948, quoted by Ziegler, p. 144). This view stands in
tension with the prominent presentation of certain quotations in *Eroberungen*.

Steiner assimilates quotations linguistically, rendering them all in German. The register is generally anti-prosaic and colloquial vocabulary is avoided; there is only sparing use of colloquial forms, for example in the condensed exclamation 'achgott, achgott' ('o-god, o-god'; VI, 62; AsP: 361) or the elliptic 'Gibt wohl kein andres' ('There's probably no other'; VI, 101; AsP: 362). But it is evident here that the central voice is unstable. Multiplicity of voices is then thematized in the final part of the cycle, in a passage based on a vision from the First Book of Enoch:[35]

> Wer hält die tönenden stimmen zusammen?
> Preisen muß die eine, die andre verweisen,
> Anschlag verwehren;
> Fleht für des tales geschöpfe die dritte,
> Kündet die vierte die einkehr ins tal. (XIII, 2–6; AsP: 380)
>
> (Who holds the resounding voices together? / The one must praise, the other rebuke, / Ward off an attack; / The third intercedes for the valley's creatures / The fourth heralds entry into the valley.)

In an explanatory note, Steiner quotes the passage from Enoch, which consists of first-person narrative and gives the four voices in different order; Steiner's rendering in the poem concludes with the voice that promises union with God. The apocalyptic vision in the Book of Enoch evokes the revelation of all names and all hidden things, and the four voices encompass the roles of voice in eternity. The poet's voice now opens out to the archetypal voices of the metaphysical realm as the journey ends and the self yields up all forms of human identity in this final part of the 'metaphysical autobiography'.

The Hebrew text does not yet form part of the extant early version of the cycle. The incorporation of this and other texts from the Jewish tradition may be seen as part of a process that is fundamental to Steiner's conception of the poetic task: that of preserving myths. He elaborates on this in a comment on the unwritten eleventh part of the cycle, which extends into a polemic on the 'pseudo-mythologies' and 'intellectual somersaults' of Romantic German philosophy. For Steiner, myths are rooted in a people's shared rituals and beliefs, and the poet's enterprise must be determined by religious values:

> das Maß, das [der Dichter], der einzige Hüter der Mythen aller Völker, besitzen muß, das moralische Maß, die Verantwortung für die Auswahl und die Wirkung seiner Vision, kommt aus einer religiösen Bindung. Vom allgemein Menschlichen abgesehen, ist der 'atheistische' Dichter [...] ein Unding. (E: 125)

---

[35] For the source, see above, note 12.

(the standard which [the poet], the only guardian of the myths of every people, must possess, the moral standard, the responsibility for the selection and the effect of his vision, derives from a religious bond. Setting aside the universal human dimension, the 'atheistic' poet [...] is an absurdity.)

Steiner's friend Elias Canetti, while sharing his deep and enduring concern with myth,[36] comments on Steiner's diverging view of the role of religion. Emphasizing his own need for 'freedom', Canetti perceives in Steiner two opposing impulses: on the one hand a 'free' exploration of myths based on a respect for myths as they have been transmitted, and on the other hand an ever more strictly observed commitment to the Law of Judaism.[37] Steiner's rejection of the 'atheistic poet' may be directed against Nietzsche and the effect of his work in the age of National Socialism. In *Die Geburt der Tragödie*, while acknowledging religion as part of myth, Nietzsche posits that the 'true aesthetic hearer' is best equipped to appreciate myth, and that myth both gives access to a 'glorious, intrinsically healthy, primeval power', and itself regulates and reins in the artistic imagination.[38] For Steiner, the religious Law must guide the poet's vision and provide the moral standard by which he judges the effect of his writing.

Steiner's selection of Jewish texts incorporated in his poem aims to confirm and preserve the religious identity of his people at a time when it was suffering the most violent persecution.[39] The personal myth of the lonely man is connected with Joseph, the archetypal Jewish slave and exile. His story is established in the Torah: he is 'Der erste von uns, der die heimat verlor' (The first one among us, who lost his home; V, 153; AsP: 358).[40] In his rendering of the story, Steiner introduces an important detail that endows the myth of Joseph with equivalent value to the founding myth of Christianity: Joseph's interpretation of Pharaoh's dream, in which he recommends storing corn and food for the years of famine,[41] is reinterpreted as Joseph's conversing with Pharaoh about 'brot und wein' (bread and wine; V, 166; AsP: 358). The poem thus counters the Christian appropriation of this most fundamental of human symbols, and further enriches the fusion of Greek and Christian myth previously

[36] Myth is central to Canetti's key work *Masse und Macht* (Hamburg: Claasen, 1960; *Crowds and Power* [London, Gollancz, 1962]); see Adler and Fardon, SWI: 80.
[37] Canetti, *Aufzeichnungen 1992–1993*, pp. 18–19.
[38] Nietzsche, *Die Geburt der Tragödie*, section 23, pp. 145–146. (Translation Haussmann, pp. 173 and 176).
[39] The central role of Jewish mysticism for the cycle forms the focus of Ziegler's interpretation (pp. 96–221), with reference especially to the Hebrew Kabbalah as interpreted by Gershom Scholem.
[40] Exile of the Jewish people is then central to the text quoted in Part XIII (50–53; AsP: 381) from the 'The Rest of the Words of Baruch'; see E: 132–133.
[41] Gen. 41.14–36.

achieved in Hölderlin's celebration of Dionysus and Christ in the elegy 'Brot und Wein'.[42]

The trajectory of Steiner's 'metaphysical autobiography' corresponds to his definition of the 'mythical' in the work of Hölderlin – the poet who for Steiner above all exemplified the mythical possibilities of poetry: 'das Mythische ist [...] bei Hölderlin das Vehikel einer [...] Zuordnung, die von einem privaten Zustand zu einem der allgemeinen Giltigkeit vordringt' (the mythical in Hölderlin is the vehicle of an assignment that advances from a private state to one of general validity).[43] The process is evident in the role of the speaker in part I of the cycle (AsP: 345). The voice of the implicit 'I' is detached from the striding figure not only by the impersonal perspective, but also by a progression in attitude from individual emotion, implied by the introductory exclamation 'Wie hoffnunglos [...]' (How hopelessly [...]; I, 1), to increasingly general utterance. While the first three sections of this part are mainly narrative and focus on the striding man in a small-scale landscape, the final section moves the gaze up to mountains, storms, and stars, imbuing the image of 'conquest' with the qualities of the sublime as it is re-interpreted to signify the 'conquest' of mountain summits, only to become detached from any active or passive force – 'Eroberungen, keiner hat teil daran' (Conquests, shared by none; I, 27). The final lines of part I evoke the hypothetical song of an inspired poet – 'ein trunkener [...] / Mit singender stimme' (an inspired drunk [...] / with singing voice; I, 30f.) – and culminate in gnomic confirmation that this is appropriate to 'dem gange des menschen' (the gait of man; I, 36). The depiction of a particular striding man has transformed into an all-encompassing myth of mankind on the journey of life. Moreover, the figure of the striding man here recalls both the inspired poet figure and the gnomic voice of the speaker: together, they embody the ancient myth of the *poeta vates*, for according to Hölderlin – himself a 'wanderer'[44] – poets are 'wie des Weingotts heilige Priester, / Welche von Lande zu Land zogen in heiliger Nacht' (like holy priests of the wine-gods, / Who from land to land used to travel in holy night).[45]

For Hölderlin, the role of 'Dichter in dürftiger Zeit' (poets in desolate times)[46] is to keep awake the memory of the gods, so that mankind may be

---

[42] Friedrich Hölderlin, *Sämtliche Werke und Briefe*, ed. by Jochen Schmidt, 3 vols (Frankfurt/ M.: Deutscher Klassiker Verlag, 1992–1994), I, 285–291.

[43] 'Notizen über Hölderlin', p. 235. Hölderlin's central role for *Eroberungen* is evident especially in the versions of part X (see E: 114–115 and 118–120).

[44] See 'An Hölderlin' (AsP: 81–83, l. 11). This poem emerged out of Steiner's work on part X of *Eroberungen* (see E: 115). Ziegler (p. 184) comments that in this poem Hölderlin, like the 'I' in *Eroberungen*, is understood as the wanderer and representative of man in exile.

[45] 'Brot und Wein' (Bread and Wine), ll. 123–124; for a translation see *Poems of Hölderlin*, ed. and trsl. by Michael Hamburger (London: Nicholson and Watson, 1943), p. 170.

[46] 'Brot und Wein', l. 122.

prepared for the return of the golden age. In Steiner's cycle, the wandering poet-priest becomes the exile. Towards the end of part V, 'Der Einsame', the striding figure merges into the 'lonely man', who is celebrated as 'der hüter der heimat, hüter der zeit' (the guardian of home, guardian of time; V, 183; AsP: 358)[47] – echoing Steiner's definition of the role of the poet as 'guardian of myths'. The wandering exile enriches the community he comes to inhabit, in accordance with Simmel's theory of the wandering 'Stranger', who 'imports qualities into [the group], which do not and cannot stem from the group it-self'.[48] The myth of Joseph, the 'Increaser', establishes a foundation myth for the exiled Jewish poet's contribution to the eternal world:

Ist es die mehrung, die dich bedrückt?
Fragst du, nun ohne heimat, und doch ihr wächter.
Was gab ich der ewigen welt, wie habe ich sie vermehrt?
Ach sei nicht befangen, gedenk jenes Mehrers,
Des ersten von uns, der die heimat verlor: (V, 149–153; AsP: 358)

(Is it the increase which oppresses you? / Do you ask, who now have no home, and are yet its guardian? / What did i give the eternal world? How have i increased it? / Oh do not be shy, remember the Increaser, / The first one among us, who lost his home:)

The role of the poet as exile is exemplified above all in the fact that Steiner works with the language and poetic tradition of the very people who were, at the time of writing, seeking to annihilate his own people. This tension is fundamental to Steiner's project: as H. G. Adler comments, Steiner not only remained loyal to the German language during the years of Nazism, but 'preserved, guarded and elevated it' and 'became a poet of the German tradition' (E: 138–139). Commenting on Simmel, who as a German Jew 'had the experience of being a member of a society and confronting it from the outside' and whose university career was negatively affected, Steiner highlights his capability of 'transforming the disabilities under which he labours into something that enriches others' (SWII: 211). Steiner works with the poetic tradition of the most violent of conquering peoples to project a vision of cultural diversity, sustaining the tensions that characterize the role of the poet 'in desolate times'. The paradox is captured in 'An Hölderlin': 'Deutschland sogar, das grauen.

---

[47] The 'debris of formerly perfected bliss' is here attributed to the 'lonely man' (V, 186–187; AsP: 359).

[48] Georg Simmel, 'Exkurs über den Fremden' (Excursus on the Stranger), in *Soziologie*, 3rd rev. ed. (Munich and Leipzig: Duncker und Humboldt, 1923), Chapter 9, Note; quoted by Steiner in an Oxford lecture on Simmel in 1952, 'Some Problems in Simmel', SWII: 208–226 (see 211 and 225, note 5). Steiner interprets Simmel's comments as a reflection of his German Jewish identity (p. 211).

[...] Deutschland sogar, deine heimat.' (Germany even, the horror. [...] Germany even, your home; AsP: 81).

The mythical suggestiveness of *Eroberungen* depends on processes of linguistic 'Verdichtung' that are characteristic of the tradition of German classical poetry. Steiner works with the richly varied anti-prosaic diction of Klopstock, Hölderlin, and Rilke.[49] Brevity and concision complement intensifying repetition as key words and images are modulated in ever-changing constellations across different parts of the poem. 'Verdichtung' can be followed into the individual words and sentences of *Eroberungen*, as is evident in a comparison between the early and final versions of the first few lines:

Early version, 1941:

Wie hoffnungslos trinkt sich die brust
Satt an dem abend
Und die abendluft
Ist zwischen den bäumen, unter den wolken,
Das klare zwischen den ruhenden körpern
Und auch ewig bereit und verloren, (E: 62)

(How hopelessly the breast drinks / its fill of the evening / And the evening air / Is between the trees, beneath the clouds, / The clarity between the resting bodies / And also eternally prepared and lost,)

Final version:

Wie hoffnunglos die brust sich satt trinkt an dem abend ...
Abendluft zwischen bäumen,
Abendluft unter wolken:
Zwischen ruhenden körpern das klare, doch ewig bereit und auch verloren,
(I, 1–4; AsP: 345)

(How hopelessly the breast drinks its fill of the evening ... / Evening air between trees, / Evening air beneath clouds: / Between resting bodies the clarity, eternally prepared but also lost,)

---

[49] In the eighteenth century Klopstock advocated emulation of classical poetry in order to spur German writers on to compete with the greatest classical and contemporary poets. His poetic practice in classical odes and the epic *Der Messias* was complemented by a series of essays commending such techniques as inversion, concision, and intensifying repetition. See esp. 'Von der Sprache der Poesie' (On the Language of Poetry), in Friedrich Gottlieb Klopstock, *Ausgewählte Werke*, ed. by K. A. Schleiden, 4th ed. 2 vols (Munich, Vienna: Carl Hanser, 1981), II, 1016–1026, and Karl Ludwig Schneider, *Klopstock und die Erneuerung der Dichtersprache im achtzehnten Jahrhundert* (Heidelberg: Carl Winter, 1960). See also H. G. Adler's comments on Steiner's use of language (E: 147–148).

The revision has slowed down the pace and strengthened the rhythmic structure. Each line is end-stopped, with a parallel structure defining the short second and third lines in contrast with the long lines. Inversion and elimination of semantically weak words (articles, conjunction 'and', verb 'to be') add expressive force. The language is thereby distinguished more clearly from prosaic diction, an effect also achieved by defamiliarization: the standard form 'hoffnungslos' (hopeless(ly)) is modified to 'hoffnunglos', in line with standard morphological formations used in part II ('atemlos', II, 42 and 'namenlos', II, 66; AsP: 347). Subtly, the linguistic form of this word in the first line alerts the reader to the theme of hope, which gains prominence in parts VII and VIII. Steiner uses the German language not as a given, but moulds it into a dynamic medium that involves the reader in the process of 'Verdichtung'.

Similarly, the verse form of *Eroberungen* is rooted in the German tradition of classical metres. Steiner worked with this intensively, as is evident from his comments on a series of odes in which he develops Klopstock's adaptations of classical forms: 'Wirklich gefügte freie Rhythmen, die Abwechslung und Strenge haben, [stammen] nur von Dichtern [...], die sich der Disziplin der Ode unterzogen haben.' (Truly formed free rhythms, endowed with variation and rigour, originate only from poets who have subjected themselves to the discipline of the ode; Anmerkungen, AsP: 390). Klopstock's use of classical forms had been characterized by varied experimentation, including combinations of ode forms, the hexameter and the distich both in strophic and in stichic poems. Crucially, he also developed free verse in a fusion of the biblical and the classical traditions, using parallelism as a structural principle with varying groups of lines. Steiner will have been well aware of these possibilities, and the tradition had meanwhile been enriched by the odes, elegies, and free verse of Hölderlin, by Rilke's *Duino Elegies*, and by the weighty, sonorous lines of Trakl's 'Helian'.[50] Rilke's *Duino Elegies* provided a model for an extended poem in free verse characterized by long lines, predominantly but by no

---

[50] Trakl, *Dichtungen und Briefe*; a number of motifs in *Eroberungen* recall Trakl's poetry, notably the figure of the lonely man (e. g. Trakl's 'Verklärter Herbst' (Autumn Transformed), l. 5, p. 37; 'Nachtlied' (Night Song), l. 9, p. 68); 'Brot und Wein' in V, 166 [AsP: 358] (e. g. Trakl's 'Gesang des Abgeschiedenen' (Song of the Departed), l. 10, p. 144; 'Helian', l. 19, p. 69) and the unusual adjective 'monden' (moonly) in XII, 92 [AsP: 379] (e. g. Trakl's 'Gesang des Abgeschiedenen', l. 21, p. 144; 'Grodek', l. 10, p. 167). The last line of the cycle, 'Rieseln die sterne über den schwarzen see' (The stars trickle down over the black lake; XIII, 47; AsP: 382) similarly suggest Trakl resonances, e. g. 'Elis. 3. Fassung' (Elis Version 3), ll. 26–27: 'Zeichen und Sterne versinken leise im Abendweiher' (Signs and stars sink quietly in the evening pond; p. 86).

means exclusively dactylic.[51] In Steiner's cycle, as in Rilke's, hexameter cadences are frequent, and used for expressive effect. It is thus entirely characteristic that a reference to Genesis should be embodied in a complete hexameter:

–　v　v　–　v　–　v　–　v　v　–　v　v　–　v

Denn seinen stand verglich er mit dem berichte des werdens. (V, 141; AsP: 357)[52]

(For his stand he compared with the report of becoming.)

Correspondingly, the quotation from the First Book of Enoch is given rhythmic definition by hexameter cadences and a concluding pentameter cadence:

–　v　v　–　v　v　–　v　v　–　v

Wer hält die tönenden stimmen zusammen?

–　v　–　v　–　v　v　–　v　v　–　v

Preisen muß die eine, die andre verweisen,

–　v　v　–　v

Anschlag verwehren;

–　v　v　–　v　v　–　v　v　–　v

Fleht für des tales geschöpfe die dritte,

–　v　v　–　v　v　–　v　v　–

Kündet die vierte die einkehr ins tal. (XIII, 2–6; AsP: 380)[53]

Steiner looks above all to the tradition of the classical elegy with its ancient tradition of transmitting myths. He exploits its thematic diversity to encompass the universal poetic themes of transience and hope, death, love, and war. Reflection on man's relationship with the metaphysical realm both in temporal and spatial terms is typical of the German elegiac tradition as defined by Schiller in 'Über naive und sentimentalische Dichtung' (1795). For Schiller, the 'sentimental' is epitomized by Klopstock, whom he identifies particularly with the elegiac mode: the disposition of the elegiac poet is characterized by

---

[51] H. G. Adler comments that in *Eroberungen* 'the dactyl, sometimes approaching the hexameter, is predominant, but by no means determines the rhythm of the entire poem' (E: 144). Jeremy Adler states categorically that 'for the verse form, Steiner is largely indebted to the T. S. Eliot of "Ash Wednesday" and after' ('"The Step Swings Away"', p. 150), and 'the verse form breaks away from the metric structure of Klopstock and distances itself from Hölderlin's free verse and its tradition, instead building on Eliot's free verse' (Nachwort, AsP: 456). This is not persuasive. While it is not possible to draw an absolute distinction between the German classical tradition of free verse and Eliot's free verse, Steiner's verse form is characterized above all by the sustained use of the dactylic sequences and hexameter cadences typical of the German tradition.

[52] Steiner refers to Genesis in a note (E: 97).

[53] Translation see above, p. 174.

the interaction of feeling and reflection, and by a constant tension (immer-währende Spannung des Gemüths)[54] that stands in contrast to poetry in the 'naïve' mode; it is this tradition which Hölderlin and Rilke build on.

Rilke's *Duino Elegies* are likely to have formed an important if not the main model for Steiner's project, and they certainly played a crucial role for the structure of the cycle.[55] Rilke had originated from the Prague community in which Steiner grew up, and Steiner comments in 1949 that 'reading Rilke is a prerequisite for reading my poems'.[56] H. G. Adler, friend from Prague, compares Steiner's cycle to Rilke's when he states that 'aside from the *Duino Elegies*', *Eroberungen* even in its fragmentary state is 'the most powerful and unified cyclical poem in the German language in this century' (E: 139). Steiner was evidently both conscious of emulating Rilke's work, and concerned to avoid it. In 1943, when his cycle had potentially attained a ten-part structure, he comments: 'That must be avoided at all costs, because of the [10] Commandments. […] On no account 10 parts! After all, that would also be bad because of the D[uino] Elegies' (E: 99). The comment implies an 'anxiety of influence' which is also evident in a comment of 1948:[57] 'With *Eroberungen* I had finally said goodbye to Rilkean language and thereby simultaneously overcome the indirect influence of Hölderlin.'[58] In fact, the reception process is more complex and productive than this would suggest, as is evident from Steiner's solution to the structural problem – though it is not inconceivable that a sense of not having freed himself sufficiently from his poetic ancestors contributed to the eventual abandonment of the cycle.

Steiner avoids a ten-part structure by planning two new parts, IX and XI – never written – and by splitting up 'Der Sterbende' into part VIII with that title, and part VII, 'Das Eschenblatt' (The Leaf of the Ash). Significantly, 'Das Eschenblatt' places a symbol at the centre of Steiner's cycle which recalls the concluding symbol of the *Duino Elegies*. The focal theme of Rilke's cycle is

---

[54] Friedrich Schiller, *Werke. Nationalausgabe*, ed. by Norbert Oellers and Siegfried Seidel (Weimer: Böhlaus Nachfolger, 1943-), XX: *Philosophische Schriften* ('Über naive und sentimentalische Dichtung' [On naive and sentimental poetry]), ed. by Benno von Wiese (1962), pp. 413–503 (p. 457).

[55] Steiner's reception of Rilke – on whom he gave a lecture, 'Rilkes Weg zur Beschwörung' (Rilke's Path to Incantation; Oxford Refugee Club/University German Literary Society, Oxford 1943, *Nachlaß*) – will need to be evaluated in detail, as will his reception of Alfred Mombert (see Adler and Fardon, SWI: 35; also Ziegler, pp. 110–115).

[56] Steiner to R. Hartung, 4 January 1949, quoted after Ziegler, p. 112.

[57] See Harold Bloom, *The Anxiety of Influence. A Theory of Poetry* 2nd ed. (New York, Oxford: Oxford University Press, 1997).

[58] 'Mit den "Eroberungen" hatte ich mich endgiltig von der Rilkesche[n] Sprache verabschiedet und damit gleichzeitig den indirekten Einfluß Hölderlins überwunden' (Steiner to Rudolf Hartung, 5 April 1948, quoted after Ziegler, p. 104). This view is echoed by Ziegler (p. 104).

the poet's exploration of the relationship between life and death, with the poet searching for a role in a transient world that has been divested of its objective metaphysical framework. The cycle ends with the poignant image of catkins and spring rain symbolizing union between life and death – symbols of a force that may give life not through upward movement, but in falling.[59] Steiner develops the equivalent symbol of the 'knospe tödlicher / Trüber schwärze' (bud of deadly / Dull blackness; VII, 29–30; AsP: 363) in the midst of life-giving spring. As in Rilke, this is held up for contemplation with the biblical apostrophe 'siehe'.[60] Steiner modulates its significance to focus on the theme of hope that is fundamental to part VIII – 'Wie alle farben der hoffnung / Gedrängt sind in eine' (How all the colours of hope / Are crammed into one, VII, 27–28), using the verb 'drängen' that Rilke employs in connection with the fig tree, symbol of transience overcome.[61] Steiner's symbol of the bud of hope prepares for the exploration of death in part VIII, 'Der Sterbende'.

The corresponding fifth part, 'The Lonely Man', focuses particularly on consciousness of transience, and here Steiner evokes a childhood space similar to Rilke's concept of a timeless, unified, inner 'pure space' (der reine Raum[62]) inhabited by the pre-conscious child or non-conscious animal:

Unbereut blättert die zeit ab für sie,
In ihrer welt ist nicht fremde von heimat geschieden,
Vögel durchschweben,
Puppen durchschlummern,
Glänzende käfer, bewaffnete heere
Durchziehen gleich und gleich den einzigen raum, (V, 28–33; AsP: 354)

(Unrepented, time peels off for them, / In their world, alterity is undivided from home; / Birds soar through, / Pupae sleep through, / Shining beetles, girded armies, / Like among like migrate through the single space,)

---

[59] DE, X, ll. 106–113. Rilke's symbol can be seen as a response to the Christian tradition celebrated in Klopstock's *Der Messias*, which culminates in the life-giving Resurrection; see Katrin Kohl, '"Ruf-Stufen hinan": Rilkes Auseinandersetzung mit dem Erhabenen im Kontext der deutschen Moderne', in *Rilke und die Moderne* (Munich: iudicium, 2000), pp. 165–180 (pp. 178–180).
[60] DE, X, l. 107; Steiner: VII, 24 (AsP: 363).
[61] DE, VI, l. 4.
[62] DE VIII, l. 15. Steiner later in this part refers to an 'innerer raum' (inner space; V, 139; AsP: 357), which again suggests a connection with Rilke's concept of the 'Weltinnenraum'. See Rilke's poem 'Es winkt zu Fühlung fast aus allen Dingen': 'Durch alle Wesen reicht der *eine* Raum: / Weltinnenraum. Die Vögel fliegen still / durch uns hindurch [...]' (*One* space reaches through all beings: / Inner space of the world. The birds fly silently / right through us [...]; Rilke, *Werke*, II, 113, ll. 13–15).

While Rilke laments the early force exerted on the child to change its perspective and turn its back on 'das Offene' (the open),[63] Steiner has childhood ending with the intrusion of measurement and names, a process culminating in closure of the heart (V, 55; AsP: 355). Whereas the process of reversal for Rilke's 'early child' (das frühe Kind[64]) is entirely negative, Steiner suggests a positive transitional phase for 'the early lonely man' (der frühe einsame; V, 65; AsP: 355), who is temporarily able to retain a double perspective, conceived in terms of the theme of 'heimat'. The myth of the lonely man then connects up with the figure of Joseph, who is understood as the guarantor of the objectively founded eternal world. Steiner's project thus diverges crucially from Rilke's: a collective religious framework imparts pre-existent meaning to the poet's role, which is to endow individual experience of time and space with collective significance.

Where Rilke develops elegiac tension in the development of the poet's role, Steiner invests such tension in the movement from individuation to collectivity. His project is thus more akin to the mythic project of Hölderlin, and it is above all Hölderlin's elegies that Steiner works with in *Eroberungen*. The first part resonates with motifs from the beginning of 'Brot und Wein': the evening setting with gardens, bells, wind and mountains, satiation (satt), hope, the heart in the breast, inspired singing, the lonely man, the role of memory, the journey.[65] At the end of Hölderlin's elegy, the poet extols the 'exact' (genau[66]) fulfilment of old prophesy – exactness becomes a leitmotif in 'Der Sterbende' (VIII). The elegy 'Der Gang aufs Land' (Walk into the Countryside), celebrating a country walk with a friend, provides a foil for Steiner's lone striding man and the leitmotif of the closed heart: It opens with the apostrophe 'Komm! ins Offene, Freund!' (Come! Into the open, friend!), and evokes inspiration with reference to an open heart – 'aufgegangen das Herz ist' (the heart has opened).[67] The final lines of part I gain their vatic power from the title 'Der Gang aufs Land', from the motifs of inspiration ('trunken') and appropriateness ('dem Geiste gemäß') against the backdrop of a mountain landscape, and from the hexameter cadences in the two final lines:[68]

Dies, einmal dem leben gemäß, ist nicht verwerflich,
Ist dem trunke gemäß, der höhe der gipfel
Und dem gange des menschen. (I, 37–39; AsP: 345)

---

[63] DE VIII, l. 2. For Rilke, the child is forced to adopt the adult perspective early on (DE VIII, 6–9).

[64] DE VIII, l. 6.

[65] 'Brot und Wein', parts 1–3, ll. 1–54, in Hölderlin, *Sämtliche Werke und Briefe*, I, 285–291.

[66] 'Brot und Wein', part 9, l. 151.

[67] 'Der Gang aufs Land', in Hölderlin, *Sämtliche Werke und Briefe*, I, 276f.; see ll. 1 and 15.

[68] See 'Der Gang aufs Land', ll. 16 and 26.

(This, once appropriate to life, is not objectionable, / It is appropriate to the cup, to the height of the summits, / And to the gait of man.)

In part II, Hölderlin's simile comparing the lovers to swans in his elegy 'Menons Klagen um Diotima' (Menon's lament for Diotima)[69] becomes part of the evocation of the lovers in the second part (II, 46–57; AsP: 347),[70] with lament being conveyed in the image of the sobbing drunk who kneels before the 'house of the swans'; the swans have long gone to sleep, and the voices of the lovers are now in the past.

Rilke's and Hölderlin's elegies form part of the tradition of the threnodic elegy, which is the dominant sub-genre in modern European poetry, and according to Horace the oldest.[71] But Steiner also incorporates other strands of the tradition in his cycle: the erotic elegy, exemplified by Goethe's *Roman Elegies* or *Erotica Romana*, and the paraenetic elegy with its potential for political condemnation and exhortation.[72] Part VI, entitled 'Im Rücken die Schläferin' (With a Sleeping Woman at his Back), depicts a lover reflecting on an encounter with a woman who is sleeping in the same room. A multitude of motifs connect the beginning of Steiner's poem with the first of Goethe's elegies: the man at the centre, initially isolated; the cityscape with churches and pillars; the window, though Goethe associates this with the woman, Steiner with the man; the reference to time.[73] Steiner's poem then moves into the interior and thematizes the clothes of the beloved and the bed – motifs central to Goethe's original second elegy, which he excised for the printed version.[74] Goethe's famous fifth elegy, in which the poet compares his sleeping beloved to a classical sculpture, is alluded to in Steiner's image of her 'saubergemeißelter leib' (neatly sculpted body; VI, 38; AsP: 361).[75] Steiner ironically weaves the famous source into his text, in order then to introduce the Taoist concept of the Way (VI, 61 and 67–69; AsP: 361), and the theme of death which interlocks

---

[69] Hölderlin, *Sämtliche Werke und Briefe*, I, 267–272, ll. 43–47; (Translation Hamburger, pp. 137–151).

[70] The fragment of part X that gave rise to the poem 'An Hölderlin' includes the statement 'DENN DIOTIMA LEBT' ('FOR DIOTIMA LIVES'), see E: 115.

[71] *Ars poetica*, l. 75; see Friedrich Beißner, *Geschichte der deutschen Elegie* (Berlin: de Gruyter, 1941), p. 2.

[72] See Beißner, pp. 1–12.

[73] Johann Wolfgang von Goethe, *Sämtliche Werke, Briefe, Tagebücher und Gespräche*, ed. by Friedmar Apel, Hendrik Birus et al., 40 vols (Frankfurt/M.: Deutscher Klassiker Verlag, 1985-), I, 392–441; first elegy, printed version, p. 393.

[74] Goethe, *Sämtliche Werke*, I, second elegy, manuscript version, pp. 392–394; Steiner: VI, 20–23; AsP: 360.

[75] Goethe, *Sämtliche Werke*, I, fifth elegy, printed version, pp. 405–407; Adler and Fardon note this allusion in SWII: 77. Steiner's neologistic pun 'mein schläfchen' (my little sleep; VI, 74; AsP: 362) may allude to the manuscript version of Goethe's fifth elegy, in which the poet refers to his sleeping beloved as 'mein Schätzchen' (l. 14, p. 406).

with the theme of love in the line 'Von der bettstatt zum grab' (From the bed to the grave; VI, 99; AsP: 362), culminating in the image of the feathered tree, which bears no fruits of temptation (VI, 90–93; AsP: 362) and may symbolize a return to Paradise.[76]

The emotive force of the paraenetic elegy is brought to bear on the horror of war in the tenth part, 'Die Räder' (The Wheels). It is a genre revived by Klopstock in a series of elegies condemning the 'wars of conquest' that succeeded the French Revolution,[77] and Steiner foregrounds the power of the word to judge, admonish, and condemn through paradox, in the first line: 'Vom kriege schweig, doch verschweig ihn nicht.' (Remain silent about the war, but do not conceal it; X, 1; AsP: 373). Strong dactylic rhythms celebrate the beauty and value of living creatures in the process of depicting their destruction, with selective use of complete hexameters strengthening the utterance of eternal truth (X, 12, 16, 20):

> Wenn die gemeinsamen straßen der schönen erde
> Voll sind der fliehnden, schwarzer donner
> Kindlein und schreie verschlingt, die geliebten leiber der menschen
> (jeder das rätselgeschäft von selig verädertem blut,
> Von besungenen, keinmal geborgenen schätzen)
> Frevlich zerhaun, verwesen auf offnem feld,
> Daß verwandtes getier und vögel der zeiten und lüfte
> Lumpen verschleppen, gefetzt aus trautem gewand,
> Zerren und sammeln der mädchen gepriesenes haar
> Für den in erdgang und wipfel klügeren bau;
> Wenn dies alles so ist, wie aber und aber geweissagt:
> Schweige. (X, 10–21; AsP: 373)

(When the communal roads of the beautiful earth / Are full of fleeing people, black thunder / devours screams and children, the beloved bodies of humans / (each one the mysterious concern of blissfully veined blood, / of sung and never salvaged treasures) / Viciously smashed, decay in open fields, / That related creatures and birds of times and skies / Carry off rags, torn from familiar clothes / Pulling and gathering the girls' praised hair /

---

[76] See Ziegler, p. 161.
[77] E. g. 'An La Rochefoucaulds Schatten' (To La Rochefoucaulds Shadow) and 'Der Eroberungskrieg' (The War of Conquest), Klopstock, *Ausgewählte Werke*, I, 146–147 and 150–151. For a discussion of these poems as examples of the paraenetic elegy see Ingrid Strohschneider-Kohrs, 'Bilderlogik und Sprachintensität in Klopstocks paraenetischen Elegien der Spätzeit', in *Klopstock an der Grenze der Epochen* ed. by Kevin Hilliard and Katrin Kohl (Berlin, New York: de Gruyter, 1995), pp. 46–67.

for the more prudent structure in earth passage and treetop; / If all this is as it has been prophesied again and again: / Be silent.)

In this part of the cycle, Steiner realizes the full potential for pathos that the German classical tradition had evolved for the language of poetry. The poet's voice thereby gains the power to counteract the trivializing response of the passive onlookers: '"wir bedauern dies unglück"' (We regret this misfortune; X, 70; AsP: 374). Sustained dactylic sequences are complemented by ever more insistent repetition of the words 'Alles versinkt' (All sinks down) and 'Alles verstummt' (All is silent) to reinforce an emotional commitment that impels the reader to understand the boundless suffering inflicted on mankind. Steiner here engages with the immediate present, in a concrete geographical space, to address the issue of conquest as a social and political force. Language, the medium through which cultures transmit their values, is pressed to its limits.

In *Eroberungen*, Steiner exploits the range of possibilities offered by German classical poetry, enriching that tradition with a vastly expanded cultural frame of reference. Where Rilke's *Duino Elegies* take the elegiac genre into an 'inverted' aesthetic space independent of time and untouched by human forces, Steiner's project engages the reader in complex interaction with the concrete empirical world. Consciousness of time is pursued through individual and collective memories rooted in immediate experience, while consciousness of space is explored through individual and collective awareness of 'home' and 'boundaries'. Diverse models of time and different geographical spaces are brought into contact in a process of mythic 'Verdichtung'. The themes of transience and 'Heimat', so central to the German elegiac tradition, connect up both with age-old spiritual beliefs established in enduring ritual, and with the pressures of the modern world. In the archetypal role of the 'wanderer', the poet re-enacts the exile that constitutes the historical identity of his people, becoming the 'guardian of the myths of every people'.

'TO FIND A LANGUAGE WHERE NO NEIGHBOURS CALL'

Reflections on the Reception of Franz Baermann Steiner's Poetry[1]

Nicolas J. Ziegler

Several poets, critics, and philosophers have considered Franz Baermann Steiner to be one of the most important poets in mid-twentieth-century German literature. At the same time, though, until recently Steiner's oeuvre remained practically unknown to a wider audience. For some years, there have been different attempts to explain this situation. However, the reception of Steiner's poems has never been thoroughly contextualized or interpreted.

This essay primarily focuses on Steiner's relationship with his would-be publisher, the Weismann-Verlag, Munich, which tried to publish a selection of Steiner's poems under the title *In Babylons Nischen* (In the Niches of Babylon) between 1948 and 1950 but went into bankruptcy before the book was printed. In more than one hundred letters, the editor Rudolf Hartung discusses Steiner's verse in great detail and also considers his place in post-war German poetry. The correspondence provides some essential insights into Steiner's success and failure, at a time when, generally speaking the time and the climate were right for his introduction to the literary world. The discussion of this correspondence supports the view of Michael Hamburger, that 'if his own selection of poems had not failed to appear in 1949, it seems most probable that it would have established his reputation as securely as Celan's was established by the publication of his first collection in Germany three years later.'[2]

When Steiner left Prague for good at the age of 28, he had already written a substantial body of work, including an estimated 800 poems, not to mention several fragments, stories, and an unfinished novel. Nevertheless, the public

---

[1] Based on Nicolas Ziegler, 'Eroberungen. Das Hauptwerk der Dichtung von Franz Baermann Steiner' (unpublished doctoral dissertation, University of London, 2000).

[2] *Franz Baermann Steiner*, Modern Poetry in Translation, New Series 2, with translations and an introduction by Michael Hamburger (London: King's College, 1992), p. 11

reception of his work was very limited at that time. He published only three poems in the *Prager Tagblatt* in 1932 and 1933. He also promoted his writing by giving away copies of his poems, and by holding public readings. One of his dance-poems was read in 1929 at a reading at the *Prager Gewerkschaftshaus* (Prague Union Building). This was positively received by the press (Doku-mente, AsP: 428). Two years later, he again gave a public recital together with the poet and future literary critic Heinz Politzer where he read from his poems and prose. Again, the reviews in the daily newspapers were positive.[3] According-ing to Suse Tieze, one of his close friends, there may well have been other public readings.[4] In 1935 the well-known Orbis Verlag in Prague published Steiner's translation of a book of poetry by the Czech poet Emanuel Lešehrad.[5] However, when Steiner finally left his hometown in 1938 he had not yet suc-ceeded in presenting his poetry to a wider audience.

At the time of the Munich Agreement Steiner became a refugee and with-drew into intense isolation. At the same time, he had a prolific creative output. However, when in 1944 Steiner succeeded in publishing various poems in *Po-etry London*, the success as a poet rather upset him, in that he found the choice of his poems and the translation unsatisfactory, and felt that the limited re-sponse was an affront.[6] He even considered taking legal action against the publishers. His attitude seemed extravagant, not least since the poems had met with a positive response in an article in the *Sunday Times* on 4 March 1944, the first and only review of Steiner's poetry in England during his lifetime, which was written by Stephen Spender in 1944. He referred to Steiner's poems in a particularly positive way: 'The poet who is really a revelation to me in this collection is a German, Franz B. Steiner'. He praised Steiner's poetic expres-sion and regarded him as a 'master of rhythms'. This appraisal was even weightier given the political background. He was simply seen as a promising young poet. Steiner was similarly upset about two BBC broadcasts, which Erich Fried had arranged in the spring of 1947. He did not even listen to the reading of his poem 'Vor dem Aufbruch' (Before Setting out). His friends were puzzled and concerned. One commented: 'I can't understand that you didn't listen to the radio. Do you feel bitter? Or is it apathy? Or hatred?'[7] But Steiner wrote: 'I am not a young poet and know my work. As my work has been ex-tensively discussed among [my friends], I am not interested in another valua-

[3] Marcel Atze, *Ortlose Botschaft. Der Freundeskreis H. G. Adler, Elias Canetti und Franz Baer-mann Steiner im englischen Exil, Marbacher Magazin* 84 (Marbach am Neckar: Deutsche Schiller Gesellschaft, 1998), pp. 16–17.
[4] Interview with Suse Tieze, 13 November 1996.
[5] See also Robert Pynsent in the current volume.
[6] Steiner to Lore Salzburger, 8 January and 8 July 1945.
[7] Hedwig Bischoff to Steiner, 31 March 1945.

tion.'[8] The statement is somehow representative of his attitude towards his work. Steiner had a strikingly unbalanced view, taking too much interest in the private reception of his poetry, and almost no interest in its possible commercial success.

From his many letters we learn that in exile he also gave away copies of his poems to some of his friends, and read the texts to them without any commentary. With others, e. g. Lore Salzberger, Esther Frank, Josef Hahn, Hans and Henriette Werner, Willi Schenk, Hans Kaiser and Eithne Wilkins, Tom and Pat Evors, and above all Elias Canetti, he discussed his poetry in great detail.

Steiner had a close and important but controversial relationship with Canetti. They often met in the Student Movement House in London where topics such as myths, foreign culture, and literature were discussed at great length. Canetti also supported Steiner's work and persuaded his own publishers to print Steiner's poems (Dokumente, AsP: 429). Others, too, such as the young poet Georg Rapp tried to help him but without much success. Erich Fried was more successful. He formed a group of exile-poets in 1946.[9] This group was loosely organized and existed for three to four years. Apart from Fried and Steiner other members were H. G. Adler, Hans Cohn, Hans Eichner, and Georg Rapp. Fried was the organizer, Steiner the intellectual authority and a role model for the younger poets. Hans Eichner has noted that Steiner was much better educated and wrote better poetry then the rest of them. Fried also thought highly of Steiner's lyric poetry, hence the group's first publication in 1947 was dedicated to Steiner's poetry alone, the pamphlet *Gestade* (Shores). Two years later the group prepared another slim volume of *Gedichte* (Poems), which included four texts by each member. However they failed to make any significant impression on the public, and Steiner, disappointed, distanced himself from the group as early as the summer of 1949.

In August 1947, the Insel Verlag showed an interest in publishing Steiner's lyric poetry but failed him in the spring of 1948. However the influential cultural magazine *Literarische Revue* printed two of his poems. This was Steiner's first publication in Germany. Including publications in the *Literarische Revue* of the Willi-Weismann-Verlag, Munich, Steiner managed to have another ten poems published in 1948–49. However, his collection *In Babylons Nischen. Ausgewählte Gedichte 1930–1946* (In the Niches of Babylon. Selected Poems 1930–1946) which had initially been accepted by Weismann had to be abandoned after they went out of business, largely because of the financial problems of the

---

[8] Steiner to Richard Rosenthal (*Neue Rundschau*), 2 July 1947.
[9] See Jeremy Adler, 'Erich Fried, F. B. Steiner and an Unknown Group of Exile Poets in London', in, *Literatur und Kultur des Exils in Großbritannien*, ed. by Siglinde Bolbecher, Zwischenwelt 4 (Vienna: Theodor Kramer Gesellschaft, 1995), pp. 163–192.

post-war period. With that, Steiner's poetry fell into almost complete oblivion. Nevertheless, these few successful years with publications in Great Britain and above all in Germany itself showed the possibilities which might have developed under more positive circumstances.

Rudolf Hartung, who was an editor at the Weismann-Verlag, took a keen personal and professional interest in Steiner's poetry. Steiner's five-year correspondence with Hartung provides an invaluable insight into Steiner's creative work and into the reception of his poems in post-war Germany. Rudolf Hartung (1914–1985) was a literary critic, a publisher's editor, and a writer. His correspondence with Franz Baermann Steiner began in the spring of 1948 and ended with Steiner's death in 1952. It is made up of approximately two hundred letters, almost all of which are preserved in Steiner's literary estate thanks to Steiner's habit of keeping a carbon copy of his own business letters.

Hartung thought that Steiner's poems were the first convincing attempt since the war to express what he regarded as the fundamentally changed basis of human existence in the post-war era. He thus recognized Steiner's centrality in modern German poetry. As the most educated critic of the *Literarische Revue*, Hartung was an influential voice in literary Germany, whose significance lay in his call for a new literary beginning, which was to confront a changed reality with new a aesthetics, whilst yet keeping within tradition. He thought it necessary to find a combination of concrete and abstract elements in verse, which would make things 'visible'. He further called for truthfulness in literature in order to depict fundamental social developments accurately. He was not interested in a possibly amusing depiction of the 'old' world, but, instead, in a truly creative view of a newly emerging world. Like many others, Hartung was asking himself on what kind of values the recreation of the human subject should be based after the traditional faith in science had collapsed, and after the incomprehensible horror behind the broken facade of the 'Greater German Reich' had been revealed. Furthermore, what kind of language and form should the poet use? The rhetoric of dehumanized man had rendered the idiom of a historical national literature meaningless and unusable.

As early as May 1948, Hartung saw a 'new world' with 'forms' (Gestalten) 'of a truly legitimate existence' in Steiner's poetry.[10] He wrote to Steiner, telling him of his admiration for the extraordinary compelling force of his later poetry, i. e., that written after 1945, in which things seem to take on actual shape and life. He found that Steiner was able to portray the 'new world' adequately. However, he also had some critical objections, comparable to those which the scholar Hugo Friedrich later applied to modernist verse in general,

---

[10] Rudolf Hartung to Steiner, 16 May 1948.

namely that the new poetry needed some getting used to, that it required a 'willingness on the part of the reader to descend into its own darkness'.[11] This willingness was, however, almost non-existent among German readers and editors of Steiner's day. The Insel Verlag's refusal in 1948 was typical: the editor, Friedrich Michael, wrote that 'there is a certain violence and darkness [in Steiner's poems] with which my colleagues and I cannot make friends.'[12]

In retrospect, Steiner's poetic approach may have suited the circumstances of the time better than his lack of success might suggest. The construction of a caesura in the history of literature was a problematic undertaking. Indeed, the whole concept of a 'new beginning' after 8 May 1945 is still replete with difficulties, and may be no more than a rhetorical device hiding the deeper question concerning a potential historic continuity. It is, of course, exaggerated to argue that the literature of the early post-war years was, in Hermann Korte's words, dominated by 'old Nazis' in the Western occupied zones.[13] On the other hand, it is true that most of those writers who succeeded had already had a readership before and during the war. Hence, works of exiled poets were generally published in the Soviet Zone or in foreign countries and not, initially, in West Germany. The critics and their bourgeois readership viewed the times as a tragedy and demanded tragic poetry with a stress on humanity, resurrection, and solace. As early as 1947, as Köpke has noted,[14] there was a reluctance among the readership to accept any writing that could remotely be construed as 're-educative' or as displaying anything other than a German viewpoint. The Expressionist, Alfred Döblin, for example, had his work rejected by one reviewer in 1947 on account of its 'Yiddish' tone! The Germany of this time, clearly not yet over its prejudices from the 1930s and 1940s, was the Germany Steiner tried to address through his poetry with its many references to the Old Testament, and its leaning towards literary modernism, including Expressionism and Surrealism.

Steiner sought to go beyond Rilke's pictorial poetry in the *Neue Gedichte* (New Poems) in favour of a poetry devoted to metaphysical truth, and Hartung recognized that he had succeeded in combining 'realist' concreteness with an 'existential' message. Indeed, he fully understood Steiner's visionary quality. However, although he was enthusiastic and convinced of Steiner's potential to tackle the problems of lyric poetry at that time, he also had a clear sense of the reality of the situation when it came to the choice of Steiner's poetry for publication. He doubted that the reader would be interested in

---

[11] Hugo Friedrich, *Die Struktur der modernen Lyrik* (Hamburg: Rowohlt, 1956), p. 16.
[12] Friedrich Michael (Insel Verlag) to C. M. Schröder, 2 March 1948.
[13] Hermann Korte, *Geschichte der deutschen Lyrik nach 1945* (Stuttgart: Metzler, 1989), p. 24.
[14] Wulf Köpke, 'Exilliteratur in der Sicht der deutschen Kritik', in *Rückkehr aus dem Exil*, ed. by Thomas Koebner (Marburg: Wenzel, 1990), p. 130.

Steiner's early work or in his odes. But even concerning the remainder of Steiner's lyric poetry, which he considered suitable for publication, he misjudged the literary public, which proved indifferent to Steiner's concerns.

Steiner's synthesis of tradition, mysticism, and avant-gardism occupy a special place in the German literature of the first post-war years, alongside the early work of Paul Celan and Nelly Sachs, which was, like Steiner's own work, unknown at the time. It was only later, in 1957, that the public took note of Nelly Sachs's poetry, and that Paul Celan achieved recognition as a major poet. Unfortunately by that time the Weismann-Verlag itself had collapsed, and Steiner had died.

Hartung occasionally criticized Steiner for what he regarded as the inaccessible and Jewish character of some of his poems, notably 'Gebet im Garten' (Prayer in the Garden). Nonetheless, Steiner's trust in, and evolving friendship with Hartung was based on the latter's profound understanding of Steiner's poetry. As a result, Steiner opened his heart to Hartung and wrote to him at great length on many topics, such as his own poetry, his relationship to art, the political ideals of his youth, and his views on psychology, as well as his opinions of German and foreign authors and his exile in England.

There are several important theoretical ideas treated in the correspondence which have a bearing on Steiner's poetry. Steiner explains that painting and sculpture had always interested him deeply, and that his poetry was influenced by form and abstraction in art, and by its sense of colour.[15] In his poem 'Traum von einem Abschied' (Dream of a Farewell), for instance, it emerges that the composition is comparable to Matisse's vivid use of colour in his paintings. In 'Fern von Ithaka' (Far from Ithaka, 1943), the inspiration may derive from Claude Lorrain's painting 'Pastoral Landscape with Shepherd' (c. 1646). This influence is reflected in Steiner's imagery, such as 'die buschigen dämmerbäume' (bushy trees in half light; AsP: 175), 'der schäfer' (the shepherd), and so on, as well as in its geometrical structure and the sense of space. Typical of Lorrain are the peaceful trees, the gnarled roots, the hopping children, and the shepherd walking under an infinite Mediterranean sky. Despite such borrowings, Steiner created a true and independent sense of actuality. While in 1943 Europe was laid to ruin and its peoples were driven from their homelands ('sklavenwehmut der augen' [sadness of slaves in his eyes]), the exiled poet was looking for refuge, not unlike the wanderer in the poem and the one in Lorrain's Arcadian vision.

Steiner's artistic interest also extended to the Dutch painters, such as Jan van Eyck and Jan Vermeer. He was inspired by the latter's symbolism, his

---

[15] Steiner to Rudolf Hartung, 30 May 1948.

meditative quality, and his individualist world-view. Steiner may also have seen parallels to his own life in that he had only been known to, and highly appreciated by, an elite circle of cognoscenti during his lifetime, not to a wider public. Similarly, Vermeer was largely unknown in his lifetime, and was only accepted as one of the great masters at the turn of the nineteenth century. Steiner may have derived some comfort from his belief that he might share a similar fate.

In some of his letters, Steiner described his political past in Prague and his early work, most of which was lost during the war.[16] These early motivations, like his early involvement with Communism on the one hand and his religious faith on the other, reappear in his later work.

Steiner thought that the religious poets of his time were lacking in seriousness and did not have the precision which he himself demanded. He was particularly harsh and even hasty in his judgement of poets who tried to capture metaphysical and religious themes in their poetry by applying psychology to metaphysics. Steiner even judged his friends and the London circle of poets with the same severity, and this was the reason why he eventually distanced himself from the group in the summer of 1949. He wrote that he was very disappointed with the 'young people', and felt that he had wasted a lot of time in acting as their editor.[17] The separation from the group was not difficult for him because at that time he was already somewhat optimistically planning the publication of his poetry in five volumes. In addition, Steiner sketched out an astonishing publishing plan. He planned an edition of his collected works comprising a total of 26 separate volumes of poems, essays and prose – a plan that would have taken him through to 1963 on his own reckoning! For the end of his career, he even envisaged an edition of his complete works in 25 volumes. Clearly, in his extreme isolation, he comforted himself with fantasies about becoming a classic, with an oeuvre almost approaching that of Goethe, whose own edition of his collected works amounted to around 40 volumes. This fantasy is all the sadder given Steiner's chronic inability to finish any major project.

In contrast to the over-optimistic evaluation of his own work was his critical attitude towards his exiled colleagues in London and, in particular, towards Thomas Mann, whom he accused of having achieved nothing through his emigration to the States, and of lacking humility with regard to his fate.[18] By contrast, Steiner was plagued by guilt in connection with his

---

[16] Alfons Fleischli, 'Franz Baermann Steiner. Leben und Werk' (dissertation, University of Freiburg, Switzerland, 1970).
[17] Steiner to Rudolf Hartung, 4 August, 1949.
[18] Steiner to Rudolf Hartung, 4 January 1949.

friend H. G. Adler, writing to Hartung in the summer of 1948 about his bad conscience because he had not assisted Adler when the latter was persecuted by the Nazis. He blamed his own inefficiency and his unpractical nature which, he believed, had hindered him from helping Adler to emigrate before the war.

This despair and guilt went hand in hand with constantly growing responsibilities at university. In the summer of 1949 Steiner's correspondence with Hartung almost ceased. His dissertation was still not quite finished, and his academic work was becoming too much for him. His last letters emphasize his increasing isolation and the stress he felt at a time when, in fact, happier circumstances, academically as well as privately, prevailed. He also expended his energy to the detriment of his health. He saw himself as a devout and secluded poet, who, at the end of his life, found support in his remembrance of Prague, and in the intellectual world of the Old Testament.[19] When, in 1950, Steiner's health was to some extent restored, their correspondence was taken up again. He wrote that, after a crisis 'one saw things in a different light, and one reached for the things that could justify the strain of recovery, and then I found – my poems'.[20] Looking death in the face, Steiner reached for his poetry to overcome his suffering and to justify his survival. Sadly, this was not enough. Alongside his anthropology, his correspondence with his friend and editor Rudolf Hartung stands as a cultural historical document of a lifelong dream, an intense literary friendship, and the failure of an editorial project.

After Steiner's death in 1952, the public reception of his work began. Evans-Pritchard in his obituary of the poet was the first to emphasize his importance for literature and scholarship.[21] Evans-Pritchard also mentioned his sad fate, which had hindered his development as a poet and scholar. A few months later, Rudolf Hartung's article appeared in which he praised Steiner's work and described the difficulty of its publication because the reading public sought to forget the 'guilt, pain and tears of the past' and was not ready for the lament of the isolated poet and his sad destiny.[22] H. G. Adler wrote several articles, among them, in 1954, the first introduction to Steiner's life and work.[23] His edition of a collection of 80 poems by Steiner, *Unruhe ohne Uhr* (Unrest without an Hour), was also published that year, and other poems, such as 'Das Blei' (The plummet) followed. Commentaries and critiques were written in various newspapers and magazines, where Steiner's links with

[19] Steiner to Rudolf Hartung, 18 June 1949.
[20] Steiner to Rudolf Hartung, 30 January 1950.
[21] *Man*, 52/264 (1952), 161
[22] Rudolf Hartung, 'Der Dichter im Exil', *Eckart*, 22 (1953), 250–251.
[23] H. G. Adler, 'Ecca poeta', *Neue Wege*, 9/94 (1954), 4–5.

Hölderlin, Rilke, and Trakl were recognized.[24] In a major article, too, Peter Michelsen emphasized his progressiveness.[25] Some years later, in 1970, the Swiss scholar Alfons Fleischli completed a doctoral dissertation on Steiner, and this provided the first comprehensive study of Steiner's life and work.[26] Fleischli's thesis is based on detailed research, as well as on conversations with Steiner's friends, including conversations with H. G. Adler and Canetti. It is still an essential text.

In Britain, Hans Eichner, one of Steiner's friends from the former group of exiles, published an article on Steiner's poetry in *German Life and Letters* in 1954. He praised Steiner's personal vision, which, according to Eichner, Steiner unfolded within a traditional framework. He also singled out his temporality, his immediacy, his mystery, and the beauty of his work. However, he noted: 'difficulties are raised for the reader by Steiner's making full use of his wide learning whenever this aids his poetic purpose.'[27] More articles followed. In 1956, *The Times Literary Supplement* included a piece on his poems, and in 1958 Michael Hamburger published his anthology *Nine Modern German Poets* in the United States where Steiner is ranked alongside Eich, Benn, and Brecht.[28] In C. M. Bowra's book *Poetry and Politics 1900–1960*, Steiner is seen in a more critical light.[29] His poem '8. Mai 1945' is compared with T. S. Eliot's poetry and found lacking in political character. However, interest in Steiner tended to subside in Britain and America towards the end of the 1960s, and eventually died down. When Steiner's cycle *Eroberungen* was finally published in 1964, it received little notice in Germany, and there was no reaction to it in Britain either. Only one significant critic in Italy took note.[30] This was the lowest point of Steiner's reputation.

The late 1980s and early 1990s brought about a turning point in Steiner's acceptance, and now scholarship found a new basis for the understanding of his work. Of particular interest were the studies by Jürgen Serke, Michael

[24] For example, H. G. Adler, 'Das Hölderlinbild Franz Baermann Steiners', *Hölderlin Jahrbuch*, 9 (1955/6), 259–280.
[25] Peter Michelsen, 'Die Fremdheit der Sprache', *Deutsche Universitätszeitung*, 10, 12, 22 June 1955; reprinted in extended form in Peter Michelsen, *Zeit und Binding. Studien zur deutschen Literaturgeschichte* (Göttingen: Vandenhoeck & Ruprecht, 1974), pp. 170–172.
[26] See note 16 above.
[27] Hans Eichner, 'The Poetry of Franz Baermann Steiner, 1909–1950 [*sic*]', *German Life and Letters*, New series, 7/3 (1954), 180–184.
[28] This collection was also later published in Great Britain: *Modern German Poetry 1910–1962. An Anthology with Verse Translations*, ed. by Michael Hamburger & Christopher Middleton (London: MacGobbon & Kee, 1962).
[29] C. M. Bowra, *Poetry and Politics 1900–1960*, Wiles Lectures 1965 (Cambridge: CUP, 1966).
[30] See Guido Ludovico Luzzatto, 'Un grande poeta del dolore: Franz Baermann Steiner,' *La rassegna mensile di Israel*, 53/8 (1967), 323–333.

Hamburger, and Volker Kaukoreit.[31] In these years, too, Jeremy Adler, H. G. Adler's son, was instrumental in furthering Steiner's oeuvre, helping it to take its proper place in the history of contemporary literature. A major exhibition about H. G. Adler, Elias Canetti, and Franz Baermann Steiner, *Ortlose Botschaft*, which covered their English exile, their work, and their friendship, was shown in Marbach and Berlin in 1998, in Vienna in 1999, and in Prague in 2000 as part of the prestigious *Praha 2000* festival.[32] The exhibition received major critical notices in the press, including the *Frankfurter Allgemeine Zeitung*, *Neue Zürcher Zeitung*, and *Lidove Noviny*. The success of this exhibition has greatly fostered the establishment of Steiner's reputation. The recent critical appraisals have appeared in more accessible places than their predecessors, such as *Akzente*, *Sirene*, *The Times Literary Supplement*, *Marbacher Magazin*, and *Literatur und Kritik*. Around forty percent of all the articles written about Steiner have appeared since 1998. Thus Steiner's reputation at last seems secure, as evidenced by his inclusion in standard reference works like the *Lexikon deutschsprachiger Schriftsteller* and the *Literatur Brockhaus*, which now contain essays on Steiner.

Paul Celan regarded Steiner as one of the most important German-speaking poets of the mid-twentieth century. From Gottfried Benn to Stephen Spender, his readers were united in their praise of Steiner's literary quality which, according to Theodor W. Adorno was of a kind that is 'very rare'.[33] The beauty and power of his poetry is finally being discovered. But why had he been neglected for so many years? As elaborated, it was obviously very difficult in the 1940s and 1950s to publish difficult religious German poetry in Britain or Germany. Nor was Steiner – as his friend and editor Rudolf Hartung pointed out – endowed with the skills required for self-publicity, which might have helped him to further his work. However, at a more general level, the misfortune that befell Europe also prevented the full development of his oeuvre and its reception – and even contributed to his death. As his friend Iris Murdoch wrote: 'Franz was certainly one of Hitler's victims.'[34]

---

[31] Jürgen Serke, *Böhmische Dörfer. Wanderungen durch eine verlassene literarische Landschaft* (Vienna & Hamburg: Zsolnay, 1987), pp. 300–313; Michael Hamburger, 'Franz Baermann Steiner', *Akzente*, 30 (1992), 429–445; Volker Kaukoreit, *Vom Exil bis zum Protest gegen den Krieg in Vietnam. Frühe Stationen des Lyrikers Erich Fried. Werk und Biographie 1938–1966* (Darmstadt: Häusser, 1991).

[32] Marcel Atze, *Ortlose Botschaft. Der Freundeskreis H. G. Adler, Elias Canetti und Franz Baermann Steiner im englischen Exil*, Marbacher Magazin 84 (Marbach am Neckar: Deutsche Schiller-Gesellschaft, 1998).

[33] Theodor W. Adorno, '[Franz Baermann Steiner]', *Akzente*, 39/5 (1992), 29.

[34] Iris Murdoch in 'You', *Mail on Sunday*, 5 June 1988, p. 18.

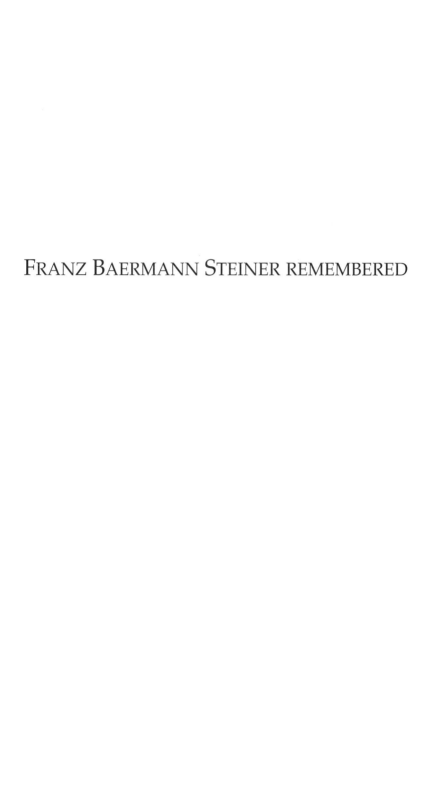

FRANZ BAERMANN STEINER REMEMBERED

LETTER FROM H. G. ADLER
TO CHAIM RABIN

H. G. Adler
96, Dalgarno Gdns. W10

17.3.1953

Dear Dr Rabin,

Thank you very much for your kind letter. I am writing in haste – so please excuse the rather untidy format – to provide you with some details about Franz. As much as it pleases me to be able to get to know you better in this way, I am nevertheless somewhat surprised that Professor Bergmann did not contact me directly.[1] I did after all contact him to suggest the article and he knows perfectly well that I have been a friend of Franz since childhood. Oh well, never mind.

Franz Baermann Steiner was born on 12th October 1909 in Prague. His father's family originated from Tachau in the Bohemian forest. They were down-to-earth, stubborn, and tenacious people who were used to hard work and displayed notable wit. Franz resembled his father and throughout his life displayed the same stoic character and unerring sense of humour. Heinrich Steiner was a salesman by profession, who, having endured many twists of fate and terrible experiences in the First World War (Isonzo Front), eventually became quite prosperous. Heinrich Steiner was an insatiable reader of good books, which he loved with as much passion as he did his wife, Marta, née Gross. His [Franz's] mother came from a large Prague family. The siblings were very different, something which manifested itself in both character and approach to work. Marta Steiner was a gentle but nevertheless determined woman. During the war and also just afterwards, when her husband devel-

---

[1] H. G. Adler's letter to Rabin appears to have been written at the prompting of the Jewish philosopher Hugo Bergmann, with whom Steiner had stayed in Jerusalem, and who, as a leading figure in the Hebrew University, had invited Steiner to lecture there. This came to nothing, as did Steiner's dream of taking up a post in Social Anthropology at the University on Mount Scopus. Bergmann thought highly of the mature Steiner as both a poet and an anthropologist, and presumably requested the biographical information for a publication, possibly an obituary. Adler's introductory remarks express surprise at the roundabout route Bergmann appears to have taken to elicit this information, since it would have been simplest for Bergmann, with whom Adler was on good terms, to write directly to him.

oped a severe heart condition following an attack of scarlet fever, Marta not only looked after the running of the house but also the business and was the focal point of a loving and harmonious family life. It is to her credit that her chronically ill husband survived into his seventies, although he himself succeeded in maintaining a surprising level of vitality. Only when Hitler ordered a massacre in the area around Minsk in October 1942 did the life of this noble and brave man come to a sad end. Heinrich was 73, his wife Marta around 57 years old. Franz never recovered from the loss of his parents. In June 1913 Franz's sister Suse was born. He was deeply devoted to her. Suse was delicate and frail from childhood and greatly resembled Franz in many ways. (Their handwriting could easily be confused.) Suse's development was difficult. Despite being brought up in a good-natured atmosphere with many talents and everything she could wish for, she seemed generally dissatisfied and only found happiness after devoting herself to the care of mentally handicapped children in 1932. All at once she bloomed and surprised everyone with her almost frightening intellectual and emotional maturity. On 22 November 1932 at the age of only 19, after only a few days of illness, Suse fell victim to a streptococcal infection. This unfortunate event – only one of far too many to afflict particularly the many branches on the maternal side of the family almost annually – merely succeeded in deepening the already close family ties. Although there was no outpouring of sentimental grief, this insurmountable suffering had a continuing impact on both parents and brother. The exceptional transformation in Suse, particularly in her last weeks, and her sudden death affected Franz's character for ever. The death also had the side effect that the family, and Franz in particular, benefited financially from an insurance payout.

Franz was a somewhat stocky, strong, and for the most part healthy child. He had a distant, often dreamy disposition – something which he shared with his mother – which did not deter a liking for daring, boyish games and even sporting achievement. Franz had great stamina, even in later years, and was a competent boxer and wrestler. Unfortunately, even as a child he had a tendency to overreach himself. He did not possess his ailing father's ability to control himself and as a result there were many often harmless but sometimes quite serious accidents which could quite easily have had a tragic outcome. Franz was the same when it came to intellectual matters: he took many things to the very limit, pleasure and denial alike, but everything was fine as long as his caring mother was able to protect him. His eventual separation from the parental home following the occupation of Prague and then the war meant that Franz found himself without this protection and was never to find it again as long as he lived. Yet, whenever a helping hand was offered, he felt unable to accept it. The same helping hand was, often in tragic circumstances, not recognized as such and refused. When, in his last year of his life, he finally found the woman who could really have made a difference in this respect, it was already too late. In terms of character, Franz always remained a child, cared for at first and then alone, and his personal tragedy was that of a child robbed of its sister and orphaned too early. But I am getting ahead of myself here. Franz was an alert child with really very little interest in children's games unless they involved the rough and tumble of playing soldiers or robbers. This meant that until he was around ten years old he always sought the company of his elders, yet not of adults. An enthusiasm for reading soon developed. Texts of a more gentle nature were less popular than exciting stories for boys and there was already an early interest in natural history, zoology, and botany in particular, with an early grasp of biological problems. There was also an early interest in collecting which lasted longer than usual and which bore quite astonishing fruits. He was particularly fascinated by caterpillars, butterflies, beetles, other insects, and mosses and lichen. He needed ever more equipment to serve his collecting needs, for even at the age of ten or twelve he went about his tasks with almost scientific enthusiasm, something which pointed to a future career as a naturalist. That is indeed what Franz wanted to be and it was not until an optician said that Franz would never be able to work with a microscope because of his weak eyes (he was consulted because Franz was unhappy with his own microscope work) that these plans were abandoned. Franz's room was packed full of collections, preparations, and equipment, especially as there were few natural objects which he had not managed to bring home. Moreover, Franz and I regarded our collections as mutual property (my room was also full to bursting) and even when walking together as adolescents we would fill our rucksacks with stones, bark, fungi, and other things, until we could no longer carry them. Then, perhaps in a post office in the Bohemian forest, we would package them up in large parcels and send them home.

Franz's school results at primary and later at grammar school were, with the exception of biological subjects, not outstanding. He was not particularly enamoured of the school way of life and showed little respect for the teachers. Franz attended German schools all the way through. He was generally popular with his classmates, even admired, particularly in later years. If one was nice to him, he could be a great friend, but one dared not mock or tease him. Then he could become quite nasty and as he had all kinds of moves and remarkable agility at his disposal, he could be a formidable opponent. Those who liked him were particularly taken by his sense of humour, his knowledge, and the countless weird and wonderful ideas at which everyone marvelled. There was just a glimmer of the versatility of his later years. Yet he displayed a versatility of a more youthful nature which was a mixture of great, sometimes extreme earnestness and energetic high spirits. It was really quite odd to observe him during serious discussions outside, where all at once some natural object would attract his attention. He would constantly and yet always unexpectedly spit out of the corner of his mouth and in so doing hit distant yet precisely chosen targets. This continual spitting (fortunately only when outside) was something he found it hard to give up and earned him the nickname 'Spucki' (Spitty), which did not perturb him in the least at grammar school, amongst friends or at *Pfadfinder*[2] gatherings (he even signed himself as such occasionally and as a poet wanted to be known as Benjamin Skutty, for Czechs had altered the name to Skutty – not Schkutty – being unaware of its simple 'etymology'), yet once at university he could become quite annoyed if one persisted in addressing him thus. Up until his second year at grammar school Franz displayed no particular interest in anything other than nature and voiced no particular opinions on any of the great issues in life. Details of the social and intellectual life of German-speaking Jews in Bohemia and especially Prague at the turn of the century are by now widely known thanks to the story of Franz Kafka's life. Little had changed for the majority of the Jewish population by 1930. For the generally culturally inactive petit-bourgeoisie, usually shopkeepers or artisans, things were much as they had been in Kafka's parents' day. One went to the synagogue on holidays and paid sentimental allegiance to a little known, but therefore more small-minded (in no way precise) understanding of what it was to be Jewish. Those better off – and amongst them especially the educated – were often only Jewish in name and saw themselves even more than in Kafka's youth as liberal, sometimes even social-democrat Germans, which is how they were perceived for the most part by the German Christians in Prague. The Jews could take heart from this, for anti-Semitism was very rare amongst the Germans in Prague, whilst in wider Czech circles, Jews and Germans were simply seen as one in the same, and the more anti-German they were, then the more anti-Semitic too. During the First World War and in the years following, German-speaking children and even adults were verbally abused as Jews on a surprisingly regular basis by Czech schoolchildren and even adults – and the true Germans in Prague had to put up with this too. Apart from these Jewish circles, whose views displayed the many facets of an attitude intent on assimilation, there was a numerically small core of orthodox Jews (who nevertheless sometimes saw themselves as German) and a steadily increasing number of Zionists, who, up until the demise of the Bohemian Jewry, nevertheless formed a minority in comparison to the aforementioned groups, as well as to the Czech Jews of Prague, and out-

---

[2] In Steiner's day, the *Pfadfinder* were a German youth movement similar to the Boy Scouts, but less organized, and with no uniforms.

numbered only the communist group, which had formed amongst the youth in the 1920s and particularly in the years immediately before the war.

Steiner's parental home was German and mildly social democrat (reading the *Prager Tagblatt* and the *Sozialdemokrat*), but no great emphasis was laid on either, particularly not the former. Assimilation was a matter of course: the maternal side of the family had held these views for at least a generation and the father, with his mild progressive views, his quiet atheism, and his lack of interest in things Jewish, saw the unity of mother tongue and a discreet embracing of Germanness as natural. Steiner senior did not alter his views in later life either but never made a fuss of them and was, in spite of everything, far more Jewish in character than his wife, who showed far more interest in the matter. She gave in to a vague sense of religiosity and, under Franz's influence, became far more thoughtful on the matter, moving closer to a more conscious but not prescribed idea of Jewishness. It is therefore no surprise that Franz had very little contact with Jewish culture as a child. He did attend religious education classes and subsequently entered the synagogue, but as his parents did not support this and did not attend the synagogue, Franz increasingly lost contact with it from the beginning of his grammar school years; a quite different development began. Nevertheless, the influence of Jewish culture remained and was not fully honoured until later in life. A Catholic priest taught at the grammar school, a weak and defenceless man who was cruelly mocked by the children. Once, during the break, Franz was at the centre of this gruesome game. Suddenly he was pulled away from behind. It was the hand of the Jewish religious education teacher Professor Lieben. Franz received a clout on the ear and the warning: 'I will not have you tease the Galoch! He is your teacher.'

German and German-Jewish Prague had, at least in the last fifty years of its history, far less in common with Austria and Vienna than with Germany and Berlin. Whatever was emerging on the intellectual scene in the empire, the German Jewry included, usually arrived in Prague some 20 or 30 years later, where it would be altered and often weakened in order to suit traditional Austrian or Bohemian taste. Ideas took on new form as they were combined with the spirit of a bilingual city, in which, it must be said, German and Czech tended to maintain a distance from each other rather than proving mutually beneficial. Consequently, German was the sole language of the Steiner household (except that the maids were always Czech), although both parents and children were familiar with and halfway competent in Czech. One of the many things adopted from German culture was the German-inspired youth movement. This took on the liberal form essential in Prague, as seen in the Prague *Pfadfinder*, which were already functioning during the war (in the militaristic Viennese style) and which only later became a true youth association in the imperial German style, reaching its peak between 1920 and 1926. Almost the entire German-speaking youth of Prague, unless they belonged to Zionist or German nationalist and other splinter groups, were drawn to the apolitical and effusive, emotionally charged, if rather boyishly rough *Pfadfinder* trend, which promoted a natural life intended to serve goodness and beauty and oppose bourgeois barrenness. Franz joined the *Pfadfinder* in the autumn of 1921and remained a member until Spring 1926. He took the ideals very seriously and developed them according to his own ideas, sometimes taking them too far. A 'natural life' was what he wanted. He combined the opportunities which walking and summer camps afforded with his own interests in natural history and in this way became an eccentric, distinctive member of the association. Social and at times even socialist hyperbole, which maintained a careful distance from all emotive tendencies, ruled his life and the future which he was mapping out for himself. He even went so far as to refuse to use mass produced products. He wanted to make his own equipment from natural materials and almost went to the extent of only writing on beech bark and no longer on paper. At this time Franz began in earnest to study the major works of natural history, something which soon intensified a gradually developing atheism, but which also diverted him from his idealistic social games, at which point his enthusiasm for the *Pfadfinder* also began to wane markedly. The natural and necessary in life, which it was now his aim to pursue, could no longer be a childish, naive youth association, which, if one stopped to consider it closely, was really far more bourgeois than Franz had previously been prepared to admit. It was his aim to confront this bourgeoisie.

At first Franz still thought it would be possible to realize these new ideals from within the organization, particularly given that some older members and even more of his own age group felt the same and were under the influence from outside of individual young communists (the majority of which were Jews, just as in the *Pfadfinder*, where there was one German for every four Jews). All his life Franz was someone who held extreme or at least well-defined views and struggled in later years to bring himself to be more moderate. The *Pfadfinder* trend could not be combined with passionate communist beliefs for long, the latter seeming both mature and very much of its time, whereas the former appeared both childish and reactionary. In 1926 Franz joined the Red Student association and later joined other communist organizations – I think it was the Communist youth or the party itself. Franz was deeply involved for exactly two years, until, in the summer of 1928, he formally withdrew. This did not come about suddenly nor was it the result of any rash decision. It was a difficult thing for him and also involved some personal connections which meant he ended up still paying his membership fee until the summer of 1930. Then Franz went to Palestine for a year, allowed his old associations to dissolve, and avoided his old friends when he came back from the East. It was typical of Franz's conscientious precision, which he had already proven with his interest in natural history, that he now took communism very seriously, both as a social programme and as a philosophy. Socially, his understanding of it was not free of certain romantic, immature notions, similar to the adolescent ideals current in the wider circles of Jewish intellectual youth in Central Europe. This image [of communism], carefully created by those fighting for the cause, was determined by idealized misrepresentations of life in Russia in the years following the Revolution. Free love, communal property rights, abolition of money, social justice, and other wonderful things tempted, just as Bucharin had described them in his ABC of Communism. The childish thoughts about a natural life which Franz had harboured during his years with the *Pfadfinder* found their [natural] progression here. These dreams, the empty and untenable nature of which Franz soon learned to acknowledge, were superseded by other things: the company of older people, of idealists, dreamers, and hypocrites, of foreigners and simple people from the populace. He sometimes sought the company of Czech workers, as he has done on a casual basis when taking part in the *Pfadfinder* activities of walking, camping, and such like. Of utmost importance, however, was the study of Marxism, during which Franz read almost all the important works, ranging from early Marxism and its precursors to Lenin and Trotsky. Autocracy was not a defining characteristic of the party at that time and certainly not obvious to Franz, so he was easily able to incorporate everything which was not specifically included in the prescribed party line. Soon the split between Stalin and Trotsky became clear, and Franz, despite now being less involved at heart, was more inclined towards the Internationalism of Trotsky. This did not have a practical impact on Franz's life in any significant way. It was not this which was important for Franz's future development but rather the beginnings of a sociological education, which despite its one-sided nature, did open his eyes to the possibility of wide and far-reaching connections and also made him aware of distant peoples, especially China, whose civil war he studied in detail, but also Mexico, India, colonial politics, the issue of the black population etc. At this time Franz began several Marxist studies, one dealing with the Chinese situation, but none of them have survived.

My own development, which will only be alluded to here, because it was to be important for Franz, was moving in a quite different direction at this time. As different as we always were as human beings, our childhood and early youth ran in parallel in large part, even if the emphasis of our moods was always basically different.[3] I did not, to be more precise, get involved in

---

[3] Translator's note: The syntax in the original seems to have gone awry in this sentence, and so it has been adjusted to capture the underlying sense.

Franz's socialist-communist episode, observing it from outside to begin with, rejecting it completely later. My heart was drawn to religious, or more accurately mystical speculation, a great enthusiasm for all the arts, especially literature – all things which Franz did not know at this time or towards which he displayed open distrust or even disgust. (I probably identified with Jewishness even less than Franz did, I felt far more German, something which, as far as I know, Franz never made much of.) In the summer of 1927 the two of us set off with our tent and wandered here and there through the Bohemian forest. During this holiday, it became clear that we held incompatible points of view. Were I to compare the countryside with the perception of an artist, then my love for nature would be called into question; if I dared to praise the beauty and atmosphere of a lowly hut, then I was subjected to a lecture on misery which dwelt there. Once the walking holiday was over, we had become so distant from one another that we hardly saw each other for almost a year, although the relationship was never broken off (I agreed to his mother's request to prepare Franz for the history examination before sitting his *Abitur* [school leaving certificate] with a notoriously impossible teacher). In September 1928 things culminated in a discussion which lasted for hours in which I revealed a great deal of my rather extravagant mystical speculations, and surprisingly this time, whereas a year before he had been horrified by far less daring suggestions, he was deeply moved and during the next two years followed my lead, at first hesitantly, then with more conviction, but without ever giving up anything of his own thought and research, or, above all, of his level-headed approach, influenced by Marxism, which he even tried to reconcile with mystical currents for a while. Franz began to read or even study the medieval German mystics, Jakob Böhme, Angelus, Silisius, Lao Tzu, Liehtzu, Chuang Tzu and Indian holy writings, especially the Bhagavadgita. He loved this last work very much and still valued it in his last years as the text which had opened his mind to religion and indeed given him his first access to the Bible. He began reading the Bible with some hesitancy, prepared at first to acknowledge the New Testament as well, at least the Evangelists, even although he had by then, with the exception of some Mystics, already begun to strongly reject Christianity (including the figure of Jesus) and would do so with increasing vehemence in later years, something which could, particularly with regard to Protestants, verge on intolerance. In this year Franz also began to display an interest in artistic things. He was almost equally fascinated by poetry, drama, and prose but also began to develop an interest in the plastic arts. He was particularly inspired by the literature of the fantastic (i. e. E. T. A. Hoffmann) and Russian psychological novels. He became acquainted with the work of Kafka and, from the new poets, read Rilke and Mombert. Franz had been keeping a strictly secret diary written in a secret language for years but had written little else apart from the Marxist essays mentioned above and had certainly not produced anything literary. Now – it was the 10 November 1928 – he surprised me with his first poem, having only recently declared that he would certainly never write poetry. The first stanzas were haphazard, on a fantastic theme, half Hoffmann, half inspired by the nocturnal magic of Prague, and relatively self-contained in format, if rather undemanding in form. They were partly influenced by Mombert's free verse, partly by a variety of Eastern role models as Franz had come to know them through German translations. Later, when he also tried several times to write in rhyme, Rilke's influence became apparent. The output was not great but brought Franz great joy and gave him the opportunity to meet other young authors who were experimenting with German poetry in Prague. Soon the choice of theme became more varied; religious and erotic problems alternated or appeared together in poems. This first period of creativity, which Franz later rejected outright and of which nothing original survives, only a fraction in fundamentally altered form, at first changed and eventually determined his personality and his attitude to the world. Whatever changes of direction or intensification took place in his development, the basis for Franz's individuality as a person, artist, and scholar was already in place by then, apart from reception of Judaism, which would soon follow and which altered and completed the whole structure. He owed the precision, love of detail, reliability, and self-control in his work and poetry, and the cool criticism of both his own achievements and those of others to the natural sciences. Despite having first extended and then broken through its ideals before giving them up altogether as unworkable, he had Marxism to thank for his understanding of social, historical and philosophical connections in a universal matrix, which he was more conscious of on an intellectual level, rather than developing it systematically. His deep mistrust of anything systematic prevented him from doing so. He also had [Marxism] to thank for his interest in people and human relationships and in almost all peoples of the world. He did not want to evaluate or compare them with one another, but rather understand and explain their individuality. Finally, he had it to thank for the unprejudiced freedom with which he carefully observed both indigenous peoples and Eastern and Western high culture. He owed a debt to mysticism and religion for his personal relationship to all phenomena, their imaginative comprehension and study, the true essence of his artistic creativity, which he always wanted to be understood as a religious achievement, even when dealing with what were actually non-religious reproaches. The more mature Franz became, the more these elements fused together and were combined in his most successful creations. Franz also made great efforts to found his relations with women on this basis but, due to many unfortunate events and frequent over-sensitivity, he remained unsuccessful throughout his life. This, along with the aforementioned childishness, which Franz never grew out of, is the second tragic character trait which, in a similar fashion to the other, and indeed, under the influence of the same woman, seemed to climb promisingly towards temporal relief just before his death.

After the decision had been made that Franz could not study biology, he and his family were undecided for some time as to what he should do after grammar school but it was, peculiarly, quite clear that he should take up an academic course, as he and everyone else could see that he was quite unsuited to a practical subject. The family did not consider him able to cope with life and saw an academic career as the right path. In his last year at grammar school his love for Greek grew and this perhaps provided the impetus to pursue a linguistic career, yet it was to be neither classical nor modern languages, of which he knew nothing with the exception of Czech. The love of India made Indian Studies attractive but when it came to registration, Franz opted for Semitic languages as his main subject, with Indian Studies or Comparative Linguistics as a supplementary subject. Franz soon lost interest in these supplementary subjects and became interested in Anthropology. First of all Franz devoted himself to old and new Arabic and in addition had to learn Ethiopian, which he always hated. Nevertheless, during his university years from 1928 to 1935, he attended a number of courses, some extramural, including some as an unofficial candidate at the Czech university, where he studied a number of other languages in depth, such as Hebrew, Turkish, Armenian, Persian, Malayan, English, French, and Russian, but also other things and general linguistics. Franz attended lectures on many other subjects at university too, even some on musical theory. Upon his return from his trip to Palestine, which I will discuss presently, Franz concentrated ever more on the study of ethnology, to which, however, following the advice of his teachers, he did not fully devote himself to until his doctorate. His studies dragged on longer than they should have, both practically and in terms of knowledge, something which had two causes: the almost insurmountable fear of examinations, which had already manifested itself at grammar school, and the disproportionate distrust of the value of his own achievements. The fear of examinations threw Franz into great confusion and as a result his *viva-voce* was the scene of embarrassing and delightful scenes which Franz enjoyed talking about. His main examiner was the Ethiopian specialist Grohmann, who Franz disliked. He put Franz off to such an extent that the well-meaning second examiner, the linguist and Indo-Germanist Slotty, first had to calm Franz down and in the middle of the examination offered him a cigarette with the words: 'Right Steiner, have a smoke and everything will be fine.' But then it was the turn of the Ethnologist Paudler to examine Franz. Paudler, much loved by Franz, was a sweet, somewhat chaotic man who was even more afraid of the examination than Franz himself. Paudler wanted to know something about Sachalin but Franz remained silent. Even Slotty's mediating intervention did not illicit a response. Then Paudler, highly nervous, blurted out: 'So, something about the fauna. You must know something about the animals on Sachalin.' Franz remained silent. Paudler went on, almost pleading: 'So tell us, Mr Steiner, what kind of animals live on Sachalin?' Finally, Franz's response came: 'Camels!' Paudler threw up his hands in horror: 'Sachalin and camels!' After many somersaults, the examination finally came to a successful conclusion. The doubt surrounding his own achievements prevented Franz from working up a final version of his dissertation 'Studies on the History of Arabic Roots', for which he had spent years gathering material and writing drafts. The feeling that he was producing something not quite perfect, not solid enough, tormented Franz in his scientific studies (and to a lesser extent in his art) until the end of his life, and is the reason, along with a premature decline in his health, that despite his many ingenious ideas, tireless work, and endless conscientious study, none of his many learned works reached a point at which he considered them ready for publication so that only the posthumous editing of the unpublished works will make the publication of books and longer studies possible. During his lifetime only a few incredibly meticulous yet short pieces were published. Franz even tormented himself in this way for almost three years with his short dissertation (only 35 typed pages).

In the late summer of 1930 Franz went to Jerusalem for a year to learn modern Arabic in a practical setting. At first he lodged with a Christian Arab but after a while the English authorities made this impossible for him at which point Hugo Bergmann took him in. Franz got to know the land and its people well – Arabs, Jews, other people, the Zionist structure – and the linguistic gain was also great. Whilst in Palestine he briefly visited Egypt and spent quite some time in Greece, something which he never forgot. In poetic terms too, he was able to exploit this year to the full; more in terms of influences than the finished pieces he brought back with him. Indeed, influences were the main riches gathered at this time, which was undoubtedly the happiest of Franz's life, something which he always acknowledged. It would remain his greatest wish to live in Palestine for a longer period or forever, or at least to be able to visit the country once more. Plans to emigrate or visit the country busied him right up to his last days but such unfulfilled, often also impossible wishes are a further characteristic of the many futilities which Franz was destined to encounter in life and which he regarded with a degree of pain, but also wise resignation, as being typical for him. – Anyway, Franz returned from Jerusalem a changed and very happy man. He returned an enthusiastic Jew and Zionist and also, of equal importance, as a convinced Oriental. Something of this had made its mark on his outward appearance and remained forever visible, especially when he was sun-tanned, which he never missed an opportunity to be. Contained in his views on the Asiatic, the Oriental, and the collective-social, for which the way had already been paved through other non-Jewish studies and passions prior to his visit to Palestine and even before his time at university, were also to be found his views on Judaism and the Jewish people, and on his own position through descent and religion as member of this people, in which he not only fought against general assimilative tendencies but also against every form of Westernization, even – or especially – when it manifested itself amongst Zionists or other practising Jews. Even then, Franz's vision could barely reconcile the notion Erez Israel being governed by a European power – least of all England – and towards America (or what he took it to be) he always displayed an abhorrence, a sentiment already expressed by his father. Franz now laid great emphasis on his Jewishness, yet it took him a long time before he was able to bring his new thinking and sensitivities in to line with the actual disposition and general outlook which formed the framework of his personality. At first the contradiction between his origins and previous views and his newly acquired intellectual stance was apparent and occasionally manifested itself in inconsistent behaviour and also impatience towards those who held different views, Jews or non-Jews. Gradually, however, he arrived at a highly individual synthesis of his own private peculiarity and an adapted Judaism. Franz's sympathies lay with a strictly traditional interpretation of the Jewish religion. More liberal currents were an anathema to him, or at least suspicious, although in practical terms he only observed a few commandments, often only for brief periods. Yet he never tried to disguise this, viewing it instead as a shortcoming, which he felt unable to eradicate forever. He never attended synagogue with any regularity, something which he first felt to be of importance during his time in Oxford (from 1939), yet in later years he would recite the daily prayers and numerous blessings (more quietly to himself than in a resounding voice). Franz always felt his Jewish education to be unsatisfactory, although he would frequently set about expanding his knowledge. I find it hard to describe Franz's attitude towards Zionist politics. He was certainly always very interested in it. He was always informed about all important developments but on many occasions he limited himself to a more critical evaluation of them, rather than wishing to become actively involved. Even when he did intervene – and that almost always took place in the background, be it through intermediaries, the discreet exertion of influence or in an advisory role providing expertise for leading figures (if I am not mistaken he undertook just such a role in the years immediately after the war, either directly or through a third party, for Mosche Schertok) – even when he did intervene, these were more or less unofficial actions. As far as I know,

Franz never came out in favour of any specific direction or party, but had, if anything, a tendency towards a socialist but in no way a Marxist current. Franz's overview of world politics and Zionist relations and developments was admirable and enabled him to have an insight and make predictions which were mostly proved right. As previously mentioned, he was deeply suspicious of westernizing tendencies in Zionism and had little time for a number of politicians from Russia, as well as for the leaders of Histadruth and the founding principles of the union movement in Palestine. As for the future of Israel, Franz expected most from Oriental and north African immigration, which would sooner or later surely wipe out the European and Western influences, although he was well aware of the difficulties here too and did not expect any beneficial results for some time. There exist probably only two literary documents which testify to Franz's Zionist work: an article from 1936 entitled 'Orientpolitik' written for the Prague periodical *Selbstwehr* (Self-defence) and a 25 page long letter to Ghandi from 1946. This letter was in response to a quote from an article by Ghandi in *Harijan* which appeared in the *Jewish Chronicle*. In it Ghandi expressed opposition to the Jewish terror and a Jewish political stance which he attacked as an exponent of Anglo-American imperialism. Franz now tried to explain to Ghandi that the Jews were an oriental people, that their claim to Palestine was in many ways justified, that they were just as much victims of European oppression – indeed the first – as the Indians and other Asian peoples and for which empirical reasons a policy of passive resistance like the one Ghandi had in mind for India did not come into question for the Jews. During his time at Oxford, Franz maintained friendly contact with Orientals and particularly Indians living there. In this way, and not by post, he was actually able to ensure his letter reached the hands of Ghandi and Nehru, with the success that the attitude of India towards the Jewish people was mollified and that more reserve was shown in the face of the blandishments of the Islamic block.

I am getting well ahead of myself here biographically. During his last years in Prague from 1931–39 [sic] he became very involved in literature. Franz wrote many poems, in which, amongst other things, his individuality was already developing even more. Sharply contoured images, the relinquishment of romantic formulae, the rejection of optimistic clauses, the contemplation of detail, sharp rhythmic profiling of the individual verse. Mystical elements still appear but no longer form the nerve centre of the poems. As such the symbol is no longer intended to capture a subjective experience but rather depict an evocative relationship with objective cultural content which demands insight and knowledge from the reader rather than appealing to his emotion, although the poems are intended, by means of a variety of techniques, to evoke atmosphere and indeed even a wide range of atmospheres. Poetry and specifically the lyric were understood by Franz in his mature years as an invocation and a form of communication with God, a form of a prayer. In those years, Franz was not yet sure whether his main achievement was to be poetry. He was forever changing his mind – and this continued into his final years – as to whether he should devote himself to literature or to science. His intensive, self-neglecting lifestyle simultaneously demanded ultimate achievement and tireless hard work and also sought to experience all manner of pleasures in the extreme. This undoubtedly damaged his health, which was naturally solid but nevertheless in need of care and which he endangered increasingly. When his watchful, caring mother was no longer there to take care of him, he neglected it altogether, to such an extent that with time he simply could not rise to the many demands he made of himself and allowed to be made of him and therefore the dilemma as to whether to choose art or science or pleasure became one he could not solve. Franz suffered a great deal as a result, but in the years before the war this was still not all that obvious. All of Franz's poems were the result of a process of much repeated refinement. There was always something to improve, to reject, to change round, to re-include and renew altogether. Nothing ever came easily to Franz and if it did he regarded it as suspicious and lacking in seriousness, even possibly as immoral and without conscience. For him art was never just inspiration and a game of imagination, but instead always a hard, conscientious task, which, once finished, seldom brought him any long term satisfaction or freedom from deep-rooted doubt, no matter how confident he tried to appear in his environment or how superior he felt himself to be in comparison to his poetic contemporaries, particularly in German literary circles. The contradiction between these demands and the self-confessed incompetence, real or imagined, often weighed greatly on his mind and often led to him giving an inconsistent impression of himself amongst literati or admirers: on the one hand he seemed self-assured to the point of arrogance, on the other modest to the point of timidity. Some statements and the diaries, of which only a fraction have survived, show, however, that nothing was as important to Franz as his poetry. He took refuge in it, especially in times of outer and inner turmoil, to the point of complete rejection of the by now increasingly threatening catastrophic world events, as if there were nothing else in the world. To be able to write ten, fifteen perfect poems: that seemed the highest achievable aim and could justify a whole lifetime. This threatened Franz's otherwise highly developed sense of proportion and he battled to complete his work and gain recognition as a poet with a naivety which was sometimes moving. It is most tragic that he was denied a greater public acclaim for his work in this area during his lifetime and that he had to be content with the approving acknowledgement of a few friends. Even then, in the Prague years, Franz left nothing untried and sought outlets for his art through private and public readings or by giving away copies of his poems. A great deal of what Franz wrote before the war has been lost because it was destroyed with his parents' possessions in Prague or later, as the result of the tragic loss of luggage during a journey from Oxford to London in 1942. Apart from purely lyrical poems, Franz experimented with translations of Czech and English poetry (a slim volume of poems in translation from the Czech Lešehrad appeared in 1935 with the Orbis publishing house in Prague but there does not appear to be surviving copy in Franz's papers). In addition he tried to come up with a contemporary form of the ballad – but here too no attempt has survived. Similarly, there are no surviving examples of attempts at dramatic writing, of which a play 'Raimundus Lullus' (circa 1931–32) was the most advanced. From 1932 onwards there were also a number of short prose pieces – short stories, novellas etc. – but as of 1938 Franz made no new attempts at writing prose and after1943, when he rewrote two old pieces, he did not even make any more plans to write anything of a narrative nature. He no longer acknowledged the existing attempts although a few are doubtless worthy of attention. Here are the titles of the surviving pieces: 'Der Garten der Liebe' [The Garden of Love], 'Sporner' [Spurs], 'Fabel vom Intellektuellen' [The Fable of the Intellectual], 'Die Einweihung des Lieblosen' [The Inauguration of the Loveless] (end lost), 'Der Knabe und die Schlangen' [The Boy and the Snakes] (also an older version: 'Seidene Schlipse' [Silk Ties]), 'Ein Frühstück' [A Breakfast], 'Betrachtungen beim Erwachen eines Schiffes' [Observations on the Waking of a Ship], and 'Die Verlobung' [The Engagement]. Franz devoted most attention to the plan for a novel, 'Der Friedhof von Turschau' [The Cemetery at Turschau], of which only fragments were written from 1933/36. They have survived. Turschau was to represent a tiny town in the Bohemian forest, the cemetery was to be an old Jewish cemetery but also symbolize the Jewish communities in the mountains which were gradually dying out due to death and emigration to the large cities. The declining but nevertheless still active Jewish individuality still to be found in a few families and in Stifter's landscape (Franz always had a particular love of Stifter) was to be placed in juxtaposition with the Jews in the city, weak intellectuals, assimilated Jews, communists, but also with strong characters from the East, as well as the German population of the country, who for the most part were shy of, if not actually anti-Semitic towards the remaining Jews, as was typical of the twentieth century. The main protagonists were to be a charming, conscientious Jewish girl and a fine young German forester between whom a beautiful love story developed. It is truly a shame that this story did not make it beyond the beginning and a few drafted scenes.

In those final Prague years, which were followed after 1935 by several shorter or longer holidays – Franz was in Prague for the last time in the winter of 1937/38 and never saw it again after 20 January 1938 – Franz had many friends, mostly Jews, who came from Prague or from abroad, but also Prague Germans and Czechs. For the most part, he kept quiet about his fairly numerous relationships with women, but even his male friends, whether it be individuals or groups, were mostly kept well apart. In Prague it was not yet as obvious as it would be later in England, that a deep shyness, even possibly a fear, held him back from telling friends and acquaintances who his other friends were. Franz was so intensely aware of the differences between people that it was a torture for him to have to put up with the contradictions in their individual traits. This meant that he never tried to bring people together but rather to keep them apart, whereby all things which might be considered opposites were emphasized as incompatibilities. In later years this became so pronounced that it almost became impossible for him to even mention some acquaintances in front of others. It was therefore far less the result of jealousy towards friends than an oppressive inability to coordinate what were for him disparate social provinces. At the same time he often suffered from the feeling that he was misunderstood and was overcome by an agonizing loneliness. For this reason it will always be difficult to provide an account of Franz's surprisingly wide-ranging contacts. This could only be obtained from many sources and by later summarizing the information gathered. Childhood friends, those from the *Pfadfinder* and from the communist movement, as well as those from grammar school for the most part lost touch with Franz after his year in Palestine and his only close friendship from the 1920s (if I exclude myself), perhaps the most intimate he shared with a man, was terminated by letter from Jerusalem. There was a problem with a woman (the close friend was Wolf Salus, the only son of the poet Hugo Salus. He can be named here because I was able to mediate between the two after the war and because Wolf is now dead; he died on 3/3/1953 in Munich, on the very same day as the memorial service for Franz in London). That was a great loss which was followed two years later by an even greater loss, the death of his sister Suse. I will now list at least some of the people and circles which were important for Franz between 1931 and 1939. In the first years after Palestine, Franz belonged to the circle around the Czech Fráňs Drtikol, to whom Czechs and some Jews, if they were interested in mysticism in all its manifestations, flocked every week to exchange information on reading and experiences. Then for a few years Franz regularly visited the Czech poet, translator and collector Emanuel von Lešehrad, an odd elderly gentleman who through a combination of immense pathos and moving childishness sought to represent the stereotypical esoteric poet and man of the world; one had to address him as 'master'. Through the 'master' Franz got to know a few mostly worthless young Czech writers and critics. For a few years there was a friendship with the well-to-do couple Arnold and Grete Schück, who associated with some artists, amongst them the painter Maxim Kopf and his then wife, the sculptress Mary Duras. In the Karolinenthal area of Prague, in which Franz (and I) was born and where his parents lived until autumn 1934 (they then moved to a far nicer apartment in Prague's Old Town in the top floor of the so-called Suschitzky Palace in the Langen Gasse, which offered a fine view over the Hradschin), a circle of young writers and literati developed around Frau Bergmann, an aesthetic lady who was around fifty years old at that time. Debates were held and clever and humourous parlour games played, at which Franz excelled. Here he read some of his own work and that of others including Kafka. A figure who could perhaps only have existed in Prague was the lame private tutor Fritz Baum who offered courses and lectures to the knowledge-hungry wives and daughters of the Jewish middle-classes to teach them poetry, philosophy, good Jewish-Zionist consciousness, and a not quite genuine humanity. For about two years Franz thought a great deal of Baum, in whose company the emotional, sentimental Viennese poet Heinz Politzer (a relation of Otto Weininger) was also often to be found and with whom Franz had a brief close friendship, which later turned into irresolvable enmity, when Politzer found ill-deserved fame amongst Prague society and was much supported by Max Brod. Through Baum, Franz came into contact with Paul Leppin, a German poet from the Prague of Kafka's generation and for whom Franz always had the utmost respect, something which this fine mind deserved. To a far lesser extent than Rilke and above all Kafka, but typical nonetheless, this German represented that twisted stubborn German-Jewish cultural mix in the Czech lands from 1890 to 1940 which gave it its European reputation. Leppin's son, who died young and was also a gifted poet, was also quite close to Franz. In 1933 Fritz Baum put on a reading in the 'Bücherstube' [Book Lounge] of poems by Franz and Heinz Politzer which marked the beginning of the quarrel with Baum and to a greater extent with Politzer. The son of the blind Prague poet Oskar Baum (a friend of Kafka) knew Franz from school and was therefore often in the house but without the relationship becoming particularly close. Franz's personal and intellectual contacts with the older generation of Prague Jewish-German writers were anyway often loose and more often unfriendly than friendly. Sometimes he did not value the people, sometimes he complained about and criticized their manner, which he regarded as frivolous, of questionable humanity, and merely seeking attention. Personally, apart from Leppin, he was most fond of the ageing and blind Oskar Wiener, a very unassuming talented man, whom he liked to visit and to whom he also read his new poems. He only had a very few conversations with Max Brod. Franz felt Brod did not understand him and that he undervalued, even looked down on him. Given that Brod is still alive, I will refrain from giving Franz's opinion on Brod

– which was undoubtedly never quite justified and factually often unfettered – even although it is illuminating in terms of Franz's relationship to literature and its role in society. Otherwise, Franz only knew Ludwig Winder personally. Werfel, whom he despised as a person and as an author, he never met. We formed a small group in opposition to what we considered to be the public literature business sometime in 1933, which quietly dissolved in 1938. The driving force for this was myself. The other members were Franz and two Prague Germans of the same age, the highly gifted poet Helmut Spiesmayr, a particularly likeable and humorous chap (he went missing in the last months of the war in East Prussia) and the much more difficult young musician and composer Peter Brömse, a son of the painter August Brömse and the singer Else Brömse-Schünemann (Peter, who against better family traditions, became a Nazi in 1938, was also lost towards the end of the war somewhere in the East). This league of friends, which others joined loosely, was set up according to principles which the composer Weber had established years earlier for a similar group: to fight for good and against evil in life and in art, unstinting mutual openness, especially in relation to the evaluation of each other's artistic efforts, bold intervention on behalf of that acknowledged as good and right, and the fight against all types of protectionist economy in cultural and artistic matters, in particular the views put forward by a corrupt press. Our group rarely appeared as such in public. That was already no longer possible given the unfortunate general situation but we were inspired by one another. We did not only get to know each other's work but also each of us shared whatever we had seen, read or heard which was of a stimulating nature. However different our opinions might have been, everything which could be defended as honest and fair was appreciated. We were not an esoteric society but instead good friends with a liking for bold humour and grotesque pranks, to which each of us contributed in our own way. Perhaps this was the only form which a group of young intellectual people could take, as yet unburdened by the terrible events of the time. – A quite different but no less significant group for Franz was the circle which formed around the couple from Leitmeritz, Karl and Dr Edith Vogl, where art received a degree of attention but the main focus was on philosophical, psychological, and sociological issues. This circle included between 20 to 30 people aged between 20 and 40. The minority were natives of Prague, the majority were Jews from the Bohemian provinces (in particular Leitmeritz) and one or two fine minds from Germany, – the first emigrés from Hitler's Reich – amongst them the leading mind of the group, the German from Frankfurt Dr Willi Strzelewicz (I am not too sure about the spelling). They met usually once a week and listened to a lecture setting out a problem which presented the opportunity for endless debate. This circle disbanded in 1938 as a result of the political situation. Of the many people with whom Franz had close contact in those days (I am overlooking above all numerous friends from Vienna about whom I mostly know very little) I will only mention two men: the Czernowitz-born sculptor Bernhard Reder, who lived in Prague from 1932 to 1937, and the poet Elias Canetti, who was living in Vienna at that time and who had chosen the city as his new home but was a Bulgarian Sephardic Jew. Through Reder, Franz sharpened his understanding of the formal in art, for the abstract technical composition and its clear separation from the thematic, which does not by its nature contribute directly to the essence of art. Franz lost touch with Reder when he moved away from Prague whilst the difficult and chequered friendship with Canetti, whom he met in 1937 in Vienna, lasted, with some occasional interruptions, until Franz's death. Canetti lived in England from the beginning of 1939. This writer was and remained Franz's most important literary friendship, to whom in his own opinion he owed more than to any other contemporary he knew either personally or through their work. Franz developed himself as an artist and to a similar extent as an intellectual through endless conversations with the versatile Canetti, who understood probably better than most how to scatter stimuli with an abundance of never-ending insights and ideas. Apart from his parents, there was perhaps no other person of such importance to Franz as Canetti, who, with his explosive, endlessly generous vitality, had the effect of a refreshing spring on the very different Franz. Canetti did a lot for Franz but also often harassed and pressured him, but without really being guilty because Franz's over sensitive nature and the sparing manner with which he carefully rationed his emotions made it impossible for him to return Canetti's generosity, the whirlwind vivacity of which sometimes quite terrified Franz. Wherever Canetti was, there was an all consuming fire whereas Franz's great human value lay in silence, in contemplative insistence, which was not to everyone's taste and in weaker moments caused Franz worry and annoyance, because his inner loneliness, which lacked the outwardly satisfying circumstance of loving protection, sometimes resulted in difficult conflicts in which the most precious elements of his own being could be darkened, forcing him to be untrue to himself in tortured and self-torturing outbursts. This caused him (and others) suffering, which he then always had to resolve in isolation. The means to this were, on the one hand, the many humanely moving and almost childlike characteristics with which he reconciled himself to the outside world, and, on the other, his deep piety and his poetry and scholarship, in which he overcame all perceived and regretted failings through devotion to his achievement.

Franz had a great love of walking and travelling which stemmed from his childhood spent observing nature and his days in the *Pfadfinder*. During the holidays and often at weekends he would travel out to the environs of Prague.

He knew the Bohemian forest and other Bohemian landscapes very well, but he was also able to take other trips and journeys, whereby he usually avoided the more comfortable routes, engaged in disputes, and did not shy away from little adventures. As an adolescent, he had already been excited by explorers such as Nansen and Hedin, in whose footsteps he later wanted to follow, in as much as he thought about joining exotic expeditions as a zoologist or botanist. This tendency also influenced his later ethnological intentions and it caused Franz great pain that first the war and then his poor health prevented him from undertaking any research trips, for which he kept preparing himself and which continued to occupy his thoughts in the last weeks of his life. Amongst these were plans to travel to the Arctic and the Orient, whilst in later years, apart from a plan to travel to Ceylon, he only made plans to travel to Africa. These intentions were further fuelled during the year in Palestine and immediately afterwards on his trip through Greece, but Franz would not be able to leave European soil again after this. In the years before the war Franz visited the following countries: Yugoslavia, Austria several times, Switzerland, Northern Italy, and France. Franz barely knew Germany, only having visited the eastern coast as a child and Passau and its environs in 1932. In the summer of 1938 he visited Copenhagen too [illegible annotation] to attend an ethnology congress. I want to add here also that during his years in England Franz visited large areas of England, Scotland, and Wales, sometimes on foot. After the war he visited Belgium to attend an ethnology congress in Brussels and in the years 1951 and 1952 he embarked upon two pleasurable trips through which he came to know large areas of Spain, a country where he felt particularly happy. After successful completion of his PhD Franz wanted to train as a pure ethnologist and for this reason attended the university in Vienna from the following autumn of 1935 for a year to in order to study under Kopperl, Pater Schmidt, and Heine-Geldern and in the autumn of 1936 he went to London where he studied under Malinowski. In both places he wanted to gain the theoretical background and assistance to introduce him to research circles and prepare him for an academic teaching career. Franz owed a lot to both institutions even if his subsequent development had little to do with either school and was nearer the trends current in Oxford and in the work of a number individual Americans: a comparative empirical ethnology which is based on careful research on location and which neither acquires nor seeks to understand or claim to explain its material by means of a predetermined social theory or the notion of a specific civilization or social group. According to this school of thought, the social teaching and psychology through which the Western society of yesterday and today tries to understand not only itself but also other societies should not be allowed to lay a foundation unchallenged; they ought to be abandoned. Franz, who to some extent did not see himself as an entirely voluntary guest in the Western world and was therefore very critical of it, found it easy to adopt an unprejudiced stance. The East could recognize itself in this, but so could that other culture in which he immersed himself, reflected once more in the mirror of the Western world, which no longer had to provide a model or a philosophy for life or, even with its Christianity, the inviolably right religion, but instead the technical tools, and they too were to be used with care and critical consideration. I will now try as well as time and my limited knowledge permits to outline briefly Franz's scholarly efforts and more or less completed works from 1935 to 1952. In so doing, the path he chose, which led from pure casuistic studies in the manner of the best central European tradition of ethnology to wide-ranging achievements in comparative sociology, will become clear. During his time in Vienna and London Franz dealt mostly with arctic ethnology (namely with Eskimos, of whom he was very fond), cradle forms, arrow-heads, and skin boats. In these studies he was chiefly interested in researching a thorough comparative topography of the history and development of the objects, their usage and purpose. Franz did not succeed in producing a study of the Eskimos or other arctic peoples but his knowledge in this area was highly regarded. Nothing remains either of his work on cradles for which, as with all his studies, he gathered together material with unflagging enthusiasm (he produced numerous detailed sketches). On the other hand there remains, as well as a large quantity of material, a short unpublished study on arrows and, the result of his work on skin boats, an essay 'Skin boats and the Yakut "xayik"' printed in *Ethnos* in Stockholm 1940. A lecture for the Copenhagen ethnology congress of 1938 was worked up in similar fashion: 'Dog sacrifice and parturition confession, their relationship to North Eurasian reincarnation beliefs' – a brief excerpt of the lecture exists in printed form. Franz's only research trips, if one wishes to call them that, took him for a few summer months in 1937 to the Carpathian region of Russia, where he studied the land and people from the Hungarian towns to the isolated meadows of the uplands with the same devotion as the far-flung Jewish communities and nomadic gypsies. Franz was deeply moved by the life and bustle there and brought home many drawings (now unfortunately lost) and a rich booty of outstanding photographs. Despite his poor eyesight Franz made great progress with his photography, which is most surprising given that he was unable to use the viewfinder properly. He was equally able to produce good photographs of landscape, typical portraits of friends and strangers, scenes, and animals; they were always pertinent, revealing of character, and, what is more, aesthetically pleasing and often almost works of art. Before he went to Palestine, he took introductory lessons from a professional photographer especially for the trip and then brought home photographs of Greece and Palestine which were worth looking at. In England, Franz gave up on photography as he did with many of his old joys – these denials functioned as a kind of penance during the war years – and although he took more photographs in his later years, these were mostly portraits, which often brought out the old characteristic flair, but he never quite reached his old heights again. – The pictures from Carpathian Russia contained everything which was special about his images, and were to be used as illustrations for a book about the country. For this he hoped for the support of the Czech authorities, who eventually let him down and so this pet project, which Franz wanted to write in English in order to introduce himself in the Western world as a serious travel writer, was abandoned. What was completed, this time in German, was only an essay 'The Gypsies of Carpathian Russia', the English translation of which appeared in the *Central European Observer* in London in February or March 1938. Franz also gave one or more lectures on Carpathian Russia in England, for which he had slides made. Another plan for a description of ethnology for young people, which had been suggested in Vienna, did not develop beyond its very early stages. In autumn 1937, Franz delivered a series of impressive lectures 'The Art of the Primitive Peoples'. The manuscript still exists. The final pieces of work from this period are published and are a discussion of the work edited by Koppers, 'The Indo-German and German question' (*Zeitschrift für Sozialforschung*, New York, 1938) and a short study 'Some parallel developments of the Semilunar Knife' (*Man*, No. 3, London 1941).

The more important works of the later period all remain unpublished and in their current state were never considered by Franz to be finished, complete, sufficient or printable, even although he valued them – and quite rightly so. I need not repeat the explanation I have already put forward for this and would simply like to highlight that a crucial external reason was the loss of his luggage in 1942, as a result of which the almost completed manuscript of his main work, the major study of slavery, with almost all the material gathered including the bibliographical notes, went missing. Next to the death of his sister and the separation from his parents, who were in no condition to emigrate, as a result of the war, this was probably the most tragic of the many strokes of fate which befell Franz. It caused a decline in his health and undoubtedly shortened his life. Franz began this work, the extant version of which was completed in 1949, 'A Comparative Study of the Forms of Slavery', in 1939. This topic, with which he distanced himself from his previous ethnological approach, was chosen because, considering himself incapable of direct or indirect war service and not wishing to opt for a current topic which could be open to misinterpretation, he nevertheless wanted to begin work on something which was factually and emotionally linked to Hitler's genocide and the eradication campaign against the Jews. Franz summoned all the strength he had for this project to the point of exhaustion. The outward aim of this book was

to gain an Oxford doctorate, a PhD, which was to open further doors for
Franz. The loss broke Franz and almost paralysed him for a long time when it
came to research. It took a great effort on his part to begin work on the project
again and I regard it as one of his greatest achievements that he finally overcame this. He did of course complain that he later only reassembled a fraction
of the material gathered, some of which simply could not be found again having been destroyed in the British Museum. The views in the new version were,
however, far more mature. Franz kept having to interrupt his work on health,
professional, and other grounds. This was compounded by growing insecu-
rity as to the value of the work and had friends and teachers and colleagues at
the university not continually encouraged and inspired him, then, in spite of
everything, the work would have probably never have been completed. He
eventually wrote his final manuscript of 390 pages under duress in only a few
months, leaving out a lot of information which he intended to include in a
later, more comprehensive version, and was able to submit the text as a thesis
in spring 1949, thus gaining the long-deserved academic title from Oxford. As
I said, Franz did not see the book as being complete, he saw it as a fragment
which he intended to build into a far wider framework in which it would be
published alongside the description of other institutions as part of a sociology
of work. The amount of material gathered (excerpts, evidence etc.) on the subject area of slavery and sociology is immense. Belonging to this area are the
'Lectures on the Division and Organisation of Labour' of 1951, in which there
are several pages taken directly from the book on slavery, similarly a synoptic
draft of a 'Study of the Types of Slavery'. The 'Lectures on Taboo', which constitute a short volume, were first able to be published from his estate. Franz
seems to have delivered his lectures on slavery fairly freely, but here too there
exists a fascicle which, particularly in its presentation, highlights partially new
information. I mention shorter works in passing: 'Joseph – Slavery and Hebrew Lineage' (lecture delivered at a conference in Brussels in 1948, of which
Franz was particularly proud – Joseph was Franz's favourite character from
Genesis, if not from the Bible as a whole, to whom he often referred in his
poetry), a most probably unpublished discussion 'Colson-Gluckman: Seven
Tribes of British Central Africa', a critical study 'On Gutmann's Das Recht der
Dschagga', 'Notes on Comparative Economics' (on animals as barter objects),
a sketch on both the 'Sociology of Aristotle' and 'Kinship and Nuclear Family',
and the unfinished 'Lectures on Simmel', the development and delivery of
which Franz was working on when he died. He valued Simmel especially
highly in his final years, during which he was also concerned with the sociological views of older thinkers, of whom Aristotle was already one example.
Even although he had not taken Hegel's philosophy, which he knew very well,
to his heart, he found Hegel's observations and views on sociology far more

refined and deep than those of the French thinkers from Montesquieu to Comte or those of Marx and his successors. He also intended to lecture on Max Weber, the only other of the Germans he valued, albeit far behind Simmel. I must also add an admirable draft lecture from 1944, 'How to Define Superstition', and the short pieces published in Franz's last years. These are the short articles with the headings 'Amhar', 'Danikal', 'Gala', and 'Somal' in *Chambers Encyclopaedia* (The people of Abyssinia, Somalia, and Eritrea were another favourite topic of Franz's) and the books reviews: 'J. P. Murdock: Social Structure' (*The British Journal of Sociology*, II, 4, London 1951), 'E. S. Pankhurst: Ex-Italian Somaliland' (dto., III, London 1952), and 'A. M. Hershman: The Code of Maimonides, The Book of Judges' (*Man*, LII, 191, London 1952). My list will be complete if I mention a plan for the 'Sociology of Elephants', which did not extend beyond the collation of some material. This very plan was one of the reasons that Franz went to England and was probably put to one side when Franz decided to research into slavery.

The time in London was intended as a research trip but what was planned as a temporary measure finally became a permanent arrangement. On the one hand it was love, on the other hate which bound Franz to England, very contradictory emotions which the phrase love-hate does not really convey with any accuracy. He certainly did not see it as his home, but Prague and Bohemia were not home either, but rather Palestine alone, but yet for all the complaints and mockery he directed at England and the English, he could no longer do without either of them, even if he could never or only half admit this to himself. Franz forced his way deep into the English character but was and remained a foreigner, the German-speaking Jew from Prague and the Bohemian forest (where he had spent a few months with relatives or such almost every year), but he belonged to England and England belonged to him; his being and the host country touched and penetrated one another. The laconic, the stoic, the restrained conciseness, the pointed, cool humour, the reserved treatment of friends and strangers, the apparently unmoved long silence and observation, the reticence and refusal to express an opinion – these were all characteristics which had been established in Franz from childhood, partly inherited from his father, but all became more marked in England and had much in common with the English national character. When Franz occasionally rebelled against this tendency amongst the English, then it was undoubtedly also directed, albeit unconsciously, against his own nature. Franz did not of course assimilate himself in England beyond the natural and inevitable minimum and rejected every attempt to curry favour, he found the gulf between them too deep; his mind and his will remained diametrically opposed to the English way. He found English individualism divisive, and he criticized it severely in theory, although he himself was in practical terms in his own way no less high-profile an individualist and only thought collectively if asked or per-suaded to, yet in truth it was other, quite different characteristics which set him apart from the English way, such as the actual or apparent thoughtless-ness, the Protestant optimism and opportunism, the thinking and judging ac-cording to mercantile categories, the typical English relationship to life, vic-tims, illness, and death, also English patience, the usual lack of sensitivity and imagination, the relationship to sport with its 'team spirit', the dedication to chance which the English express with 'happiness', 'prosperity', and 'don't worry' – all of this remained alien and repugnant to Franz, it irritated him and could make him furious if he detected it in even English or recently-arrived Jewish emigrés. In some respects, Franz's attitude to the English reminded one of that of the Scots, Irish, Welsh or members of the Commonwealth, who are always critical and hostile towards the English, but cannot bear to live in any other country for any length of time, and enjoy uniting with other intimate opponents of England, but when faced with outsiders who voice the same opinions, almost feel themselves insulted as English and begin to defend the English position. One must not misinterpret this to mean that Franz would ever have identified himself with England or even its politics in his dealings with Jews, Orientals or other foreigners, he never did that, he was also always in agreement with the notion of the English people, and it was only in his personal reaction that he displayed the behaviour described, which was cer-tainly more marked and more true than that of all other continental Jews known to me in the country, who consciously want to appear more or less English. Franz was particularly critical of contemporary England; he loved the common people but not the educated. He also loved the old poets, whom he knew very well, but he held little store by contemporary literature, in as far as it was written by native English writers and not by the great Irish poets. He basically felt much the same about the cultural state of the other western peo-ples as he did about England, whose dominant role was in his view almost over in the long term. He saw Protestantism as the beginning of this decline, from the Hussites to the French Revolution, which he also regarded as a Prot-estant phenomenon, as he did all kinds of Enlightenment, progressive beliefs, and that which he described as heathen Western optimism. In his eyes all of these were stages in the secularization process, which of course revealed the true face of the West, which had already been apparent in ancient Rome. It is therefore understandable that Franz, albeit in a reserved manner, should view Catholicism and some strict sects with more sympathy than most Protestant or agnostic strains as they seemed to him to display Eastern characteristics – like Zinzendorf's *Herrnhuter*. On a practical level, this meant that he was far more likely to agree with Catholic scholars in discussion than with most oth-ers, whose sociology, psychology, and systematic he more or less sharply rejected and sometimes heartlessly mocked. Perhaps it should be mentioned here too, how Franz saw the Germans. He saw in them a half-individualistic and half-collective people and it was in this intermediate position that he saw their tragedy.

The first years in England were difficult for Franz, he was in a deep crisis, which was clearly only overcome during the war. He even took the first steps towards emigration to the United States. Up until the Munich crisis of 1938 he was kept afloat by the loving care of his parents. Afterwards, all at once he was an emigrant, a social and intellectual situation to which Franz was particularly unsuited. The events, above all the worry over his parents, paralysed him. In this respect, he was not a fighter. Relations, friends, and acquaintances pressured him to do this and that for them, and above all to help them to enter the country. He was himself without the means. For him, it was just as impossible to establish ways of doing things, make contacts or facilitate entrance to the country as it was to find even the most modest employment for himself. He might go somewhere for help, where everything seemed hopeless and where he would allow himself to be sent away or superficially comforted (he saw through it straight away, of course), and then he became absorbed in observing the officials and petitioners, until he finally left having achieved nothing and with a heavy heart. He was bombarded with letters which he answered conscientiously and with a troubled mind: there is nothing to be done. He was left in this torturous and hopeless state, alone in his powerlessness, to await, even hope for the outbreak of war. With the little strength he still had, Franz took refuge in relationships with various women and became engaged to a woman from New Zealand who worked caring for refugees. This engagement was later broken off, as was sooner or later the case with all his more serious relationships with women, past and future. Franz often maintained several serious relationships at once, he could hardly decide and there were also brief but often passionate affairs, which would flare up from time to time. For the most part, the women were non-Jewish, sometimes married or otherwise unattainable, and clearly always unhappy creatures with almost morbid melancholic characters. Franz never managed to establish a happy relationship with women, let alone break it off in the long run, but the women too, and there were many fine people amongst them, did not understand how to really help him. At that difficult time it was particularly unfortunate and Franz exhausted himself boundlessly. Apart from the failed attempts to seek refuge with women, he threw himself into his poetry. The world was threatening to go up in flames, Franz was tormented and compelled and...... wrote verses, perfected them, thought about them; for days he forced his whole being into this artistic retreat, in which he put together so many mostly unrealized plans, more than ever before and more than he ever would again. Franz was badly damaged at this time, something from which he would never recover, and which contributed to his endless tragedy. He is one of the most tragic figures I have ever come across, disaster pursued him relentlessly, he was almost always powerless, could almost never break free, he suffered endlessly and was steadfast and brave in his pain, but yet unhappiness burned and killed him: he could not grow old. When I put all of this into words, it is not intended to be heartless, but if one wants to know Franz, if one wants to understand his individual nature and achievements, one must know of this and take it into account. He was a broken man, persecuted and mistreated, and few have suffered more intellectually or physically, to come to terms with themselves, not to despair completely of themselves and the world, to muster their talents over and over again despite all the obstacles, and to remain true to the end to their own values in the face of such discord. That he was able to achieve this does not simply absolve him of any harsh judgements, but instead underlines his greatness as a human being.

His situation was made even worse in the last months before the war in that he simply could not afford to stay in London, the one place where he could have, theoretically at least, carried out the demands made upon him. In Autumn 1938 Franz ended up in some home for intellectual refugees near Oxford and there he met the old Oxford Don, the 78 year-old classical philologist Christopher Cookson who invited Franz to stay for a month in his comfortable bachelor residence, which was in a villa. That month lasted the best part of ten years, for Franz lived in the home of this dear old man beyond the latter's death in April 1948, until the house was broken up in the late summer of the same year. In many respects, Franz benefited from living with the old gentleman, whom he loved very much and who did a lot for him; he had been saved but yet he was not really in the best place; living together presented many problems, for which neither party was to blame in the usual way and yet to which both nevertheless contributed. The mutual sensitivities, the complex game of often neglected consideration, the role of duty-bound recipient and that of benefactor always creates problems which can never be solved completely, and never for the long term. Franz occupied two rooms in Mr Cookson's home, was allowed to use the whole house and the garden, shared the old man's company at mealtimes and on long evenings, received gifts of money from him, imparted with the most elaborate excuses, and many things besides. The sense of dependence was a burden in spite of everything, the hospitality never really changed from a temporary to a more permanent situation and was more or less extended in silence; dealings with the housekeeper were never easy for the sensitive Franz, something which, in the days when rationing restrictions were becoming ever more stringent, meant that on the occasions when he was out of the house or when he was in London, Cambridge, and other places, Franz did not have enough to eat, because he did not request the ration card or food. Franz was undoubtedly undernourished during the war and even afterwards, a factor which, combined with agitation and a lifestyle which one could not describe as sensible, heightened his natural nervousness and undermined his health. Fortunately, the financial dependence on Mr Cookson lessened shortly after the outbreak of the war because Franz received weekly subventions for a few years from the Czechoslovak government in exile from which he was able to fund his studies, short trips, the most necessary acquisitions, and even the purchase of books. Franz took a generally passive approach to his current and future economic situation despite isolated ventures in search of protection and attempts at establishing important connections. In the same way he let things take their course in the Cookson house, so he did in other matters too. He was and remained a cause for concern, who, despite his ceaseless activity, had to be relieved of the vital existential problems. He undoubtedly often felt the unworthiness of his position and thought long and hard about it or debated with himself, and when Franz finally did gather himself and even achieved some acclaim, this was really due more to an objective but definitely not a subjective contribution on his part. Things always had to happen to him, he never took any decisions himself. Whenever he did try something, it came to nothing or it took a wrong turn. The only thing that was clear to him was that he must stay true to his scholarship and as a result he got in touch with the Institute of Social Anthropology shortly after his arrival in Oxford, where he was warmly received and soon highly valued. Professor Radcliffe-Brown, the professor of the faculty showed great interest and advised Franz to work towards a doctorate from Oxford. This was undoubtedly well-intentioned but definitely not the right thing for Franz, for to become a student, and a permanent student at that, did not suit Franz at all. If the completion of his studies in Prague had already cost him seven years, then his time at Oxford would take another ten. His status as a student was at times humiliating, something which annoyed him and which stood in no relation to his actual position and the recognition he received from scholars and colleagues. Franz himself was always very fond of Radcliffe-Brown as a person and displayed at times a preference for his successor Evans-Pritchard, who he valued more highly as a scholar. In latter years this relationship was often strained, something which was unfortunately mainly Franz's doing, for Evans-Pritchard had done a great deal for Franz and had spoken of his achievements and knowledge with great respect, something which assured Franz an unusual role which no one ever questioned. The only regrettable thing is that Franz was not given a permanent position at the Institute straightaway, something which he could never achieve through his own efforts and which was eventually only realized after an insistent campaign which at times resembled a siege and depended upon the completion of Franz's work on slavery and a much feared but in actual fact farcical examination. It was unfortunately already too late for Franz.

Franz was very fond of Oxford as a place. Of course, it was a contradictory and crisis-ridden affection, as was always the case with him, but it was no less of an affection for that. He emphasized over and over again, that there were three towns which meant everything to him and which had shaped his character: Prague, Jerusalem, and Oxford. With the help of Mr Cookson Franz was affiliated to Magdalen College, on the subject of which he would later have little positive to say, and expressed a similar disdain too towards the college system and the whole academic business in Oxford, from which he increasingly distanced himself. Nevertheless, he was, during the war at least, to one extent or another in close contact with several well-known individuals and there were always scholars and students whom he valued and liked. In the last twelve years of his life, however, Franz does not seem to have formed any intimate friendships, be it in Oxford, London or anywhere else. He was not drawn to any type of war service. All he did was perform watch duties for the civilian air-raid protection for a few years (He was allocated the area around The Church of Our Lady). When the London Czech government stopped its support towards the end of the war, a post was found for him, by Radcliffe-Brown I think, at the International Africa Institute in London, where Franz was paid an ongoing salary for certain scholarly bibliographical tasks. There were no great advances to be made with this. At first Franz was glad to be occupied, later less so. It demanded too much of his time and anything which hemmed Franz in, which meant keeping to deadlines, was almost too much for him. Eventually he was really unable to fulfil what was required of him due to ill health, which is why he felt relieved when he no longer needed this post having been appointed a Lecturer of Social Anthropology from Autumn 1949. Franz's teaching career only lasted for three years; it brought with it a degree of trouble, far too much strain, some recognition, and great joy. His lectures were well-prepared, solid, clear, and accessible (even if they did demand quite a lot) and were valued by those who attended them. His students found his personal tutorials far more important and preferable. Franz was an outstanding teacher, who very much inspired his students and guided them forwards with great prudence. His experiences and knowledge were seen to be inexhaustible, which is why even in seminars people waited to find out 'Now, what will Steiner say?' Yet, it often took a lot of encouragement to tempt him to speak.

Franz's rise as a poet took place during the Oxford years, more precisely in the period between 1940 and 1948. During these years he wrote or rewrote the majority of the surviving oeuvre. By this time, it was unmistakably clear that

Franz's main achievement was in the field of lyrical poetry, in the face of which everything else was of secondary importance, even if after a few years it became clear that he had been called to another important task, which I will discuss in due course. Franz was never directly exposed to German influences, because, apart from his time in Vienna, he never lived in a German environment, and Vienna is not Germany anyway. Franz had very little time for Austria, for intellectual Vienna, and above all for the literary climate of Vienna. He even hated it. The important literary achievements which emerged during his time in Prague and Bohemia, with Kafka and Rilke to the fore, hardly counted as Austrian in his view. With the exception of Canetti, he did not consider the Viennese literati to be worthwhile, not even hard-working, and it is surely the case that Franz's poetry shows little influence of the Viennese mind. For Franz, Germanness and Jewishness in German guise were always associated with Prague, whose particular dialect he certainly did not like. Franz said to me that he had first heard proper good German, in particular the intonation, from German emigrés in England. In his lifetime, Franz only got to know a small number of actual Germans who were not Jews. So the only 'German' influences on him were a rejected Austria, the isolated province around Prague, and an experience of Germany based on hearsay, whilst Switzerland lay beyond his horizon (not beyond his knowledge). He regarded the literature written in German by his own generation to be past its best, backward or unimportant, even the Jewish-German poetry. That was at least the case with lyric poetry. So Franz only gave credence to a critically evaluated German literary past which stretched from the *Minnesang* to the *Duineser Elegien* [Duino Elegies]. Consequently, he was only directly influenced by the rhetoric of the German language medium, but otherwise he was, as a Jew and a foreigner in a non-German country, free of almost everything German. This was how he perceived it and that is more or less how it was. Of all the Jews who have contributed to German literature, he was perhaps the least German, even less German than Kafka. This never prevented Franz from liking German poetry and from understanding its nuances and meaning with a particular insight. He did not only attempt to get to know the greats but also valued many less well-known poets. As far as his own work was concerned, if one takes everything into consideration, there are notable influences of Hölderlin, Goethe, Klopstock, Rilke, Mombert, Heym, and Trakl; most noticeably, Hölderlin and Rilke in their later works. The longer Franz spent in England, the more progress his own work made, the less German it became. In terms of achievement, he took German language poetry beyond the position reached by the late Rilke, Heym, and Trakl, which to my knowledge has certainly not happened otherwise in published German poetry. What I said about Franz's relationship with England and his own 'English' characteristics was significant for his poetry. He was repeatedly influenced by old and more recent English poetry, which he knew very well. Of the more recent poets who contributed to the development of his work, it was Yeats, with his later works, Hopkins but also Eliot, although Franz did not really like him. If his understanding of the personal in extreme individual form did not come directly from these poets, then it certainly found its confirmation there. Franz was extremely open in his willingness to absorb new stimuli and influences, even if he also liked to hide these sources again and spread their flow throughout his own work. Ancient Greek poetry became important and even more so the old poetry of Spain. He owed least to the French, whose newer poetry he barely touched. Yet, more important than tracing all the possible sources which might feed a poet's imagination is his own work, if it is indeed solely his own – and Franz's work is his own. He sought to obscure the immediate and that is how the reader must interpret it. This work is particularly full of allusions, it is an educated poetry of the sort which one took for granted until the time of Hölderlin, until the romanticization of the poet in the nineteenth century, and which one saw as a merit, never as a fault. Conversely, it was a criticism in Franz's eyes when he described an otherwise admired poet, such as Rilke or Yeats, as uneducated. Franz was probably the first sociologist and ethnologist who was at the same time a poet of note. This furnishes his verses with an unusual colour and a wealth of surprising images and distant allusions, which constitute the very charm of his poetry. All of this is, however, incorporated appropriately, not merely for adornment or crass dramatic effect. Franz was never happy to just shine through the use of enticing detail, even although he is a master of such detail. He almost always begins working on a poem with one or more details, which often depict a nucleus recorded years before, around which the poem, combined with other details, is set and slowly expanded. Later, particularly in the last four years of his life, given that he began practically nothing new, newly discovered details were worked unexpectedly and for the most part successfully into old poems, which, as a result of, and in combination with a simultaneous general reworking, acquired a new and far more meaningful appearance. Franz's poems have been compared to some modern paintings, almost more than with other modern poems. I do not know whether this comparison is appropriate for it only superficially describes the colour and perhaps a little better the art of precisely ordering all the elements, no matter how disparate they might appear at first. Beside, or rather below the glittering, multicoloured surface there is also a span, by means of which this creativity is organized, ordered, and not just arranged: a foundation of biblical and post-biblical Jewish tradition, oriental wisdom, classical Greece, and the great Western past. Usually such elements are only fully visible for a brief moment, sometimes they are merely hinted at, but they remain effective. However different the desired outcome might be, Franz's way of working reminds one of Beethoven and Hölderlin, who also begin with isolated notes. Franz's poems are always put together with care and reserve, one is barely aware of the laborious processes involved, particularly in the case of the best and most developed pieces. They have the effect of carefully drawn lines on an oversensitive, shining (not flat) surface; they are always more reflective than celebratory, more probing warnings than rousing exhortations, impressions which arise from the aloof severity and crystal clear succinctness which they possess and which force the reader to maintain a carefully considered distance. As such, the poems fit visually with Franz's copper-plate handwriting – he was one of the few people of our time to have good handwriting in the old-fashioned sense, a style not just for the graphologists but for the aesthetically appreciative eye. Franz's poems cannot then be described as elementary natural phenomena, they never rush violently in, they do not roar, they fear nothing more than the torrent of words, they are for this reason short in structure, apart from certain exceptions. Franz also deemed the great lyric form to be impossible in our time, although he did make what I consider to be a particularly valuable contribution to the field. But when considered carefully, even this exception is a thoroughly and artistically intricate mosaic, which can therefore remain purely lyrical in expression and composition and requires no epic aides of elongation whatsoever. This poetry therefore always has a quiet quality to it; it is not hymnic, it is not usually song-like either. Put in positive terms: this poetry makes its mark with every detail and in its careful flow is constantly guided by an exceptional understanding of art and a contemplative intellect. The choice of theme is rich and astounding, the scale extends from poems which punish and mock to restrained confessions and symbolic comparisons. In later years, as indeed in his youth, Franz only used rhyme occasionally. On the other hand, he was not averse to using onomatopoeia, indeed he sometimes loved it and, using his astounding knowledge of linguistic possibility, thought up the most diverse ways to give his poems that final touch. He was just as unlikely to reject rare words of German origin as he was unusual foreign words, nor did he spurn archaisms and he also often used new forms, in particular compounds. More important than this were the changes and shifts in meaning, which Franz could achieve in mundane words. The meaning was enriched, etymologically refreshed, and unexpectedly and ingeniously emphasized by the context. Franz could manoeuvre daringly with syntax too, although he did not tend to go as far as Rilke had done before him. He would often even settle for simply constructed sentences. His rhythm, which he deliberated over a great deal, is very complex. He recognized that the free rhythms used by Rilke and lesser German poets were, like the free verse used by the French and Anglo Saxons, a highly questionable art form and attributed this to the fact that all these authors, tired of the rhyming poem with its rhythmic, usually simple verse structure, began to write 'freely' without having laid the foundation necessary for their venture. Franz also recognized that the creators of free verse in German,

Klopstock and Hölderlin, were only successful with it once they had mastered the hexameter and the classical ode form. The more recent exponents of the free form after Platen, however, had neglected this training and settled for a more or less misguided adoption of Hölderlin's method, from which even Rilke could not be absolved. Even worse was the fact that since Rilke, the *Duineser Elegien* had been used as a model, which are themselves dependent on Hölderlin's hymns. The result was a rhythmic inadequacy in this free verse, they were no longer verses (one recognizes the verse by the repetition of rhythmic units, which are repeated precisely or are related to one another correlatively), it was prose which more or less reminded one of verse. It was with this in mind that Franz made a study of metre, of which something has indeed survived. He found rhythmic freedom in the rhythmic rigour of the ode, for which he adopted a prosodic, innovative way of working, which Franz elaborated upon in an appendix to his poetry. He did not simply take the natural long, half and short German syllables as his starting point, but instead above all the natural dynamic of the spoken sentence, which he analysed in terms of rhythm. This was, in combination with prescribed strophic metres, a consciously new process, which to my knowledge had never been used intentionally before. After 1943 Franz wrote no more odes and refrained from restructuring old poems in ode form after 1942, but by now he had worked out the rhythmic basis which ensured the legitimate rhythmic rigour of his free verse.

I have nothing further to add here concerning Franz's contribution to lyric poetry, and I must also refrain from characterizing individual works or the development of his art. As I already mentioned, the surviving lyrical oeuvre was more or less ready by the late summer of 1948. Only a few short poems were added in the last years of his life, amongst which were of course pieces of particular maturity and depth. However, the work would not have been nearly so complete in its 1948 form as it is presented to us now. There are two reasons for this. During the last four years Franz first of all carefully reordered the poems and grouped and prepared them for the publication of the collected works in three volumes, as well as for suitable selections. As well as this he devoted himself with tireless energy to the refinement of old and new verses, whereby a considerable number were remodelled so substantially that they could be seen as new creations. His poem 'Über dem Tod' [Above death] was restructured on the day before he died. He did not regard this revision process as being in any way complete, as comments he made and written notes prove. Franz had a high opinion of his work which he placed above the achievements of contemporaries, not just German-speaking, whose work he knew, but this did not prevent him from only being satisfied with a few of his creations or only with individual sections. This meant too, that there were many minor problems with the final editing of the text, which were, as far as publication was concerned, nevertheless

surmountable. The final titles of the volumes were: 'Vorgärten und Läuterungen' ([Front Gardens and Purifications] 1929–1943), 'Mündungen und Geleise'
([Estuaries and Tracks] 1943–46) and 'Sorge, Bild, Begegnen' ([Anxiety, Image,
Encounter] 1947–48 and 1952), in total some 300 poems. As well as these a large
number of preliminary pieces, some juvenilia, and some abandoned poems
have also survived. Of the major, coherent cycles which Franz planned, only one
work came to fruition, the result of long and laborious effort (in particular between 1940 and 1946), after many preliminary and intermediary phases, the
Eroberungen [Conquests]. Of the 13 planned pieces, numbers 9 and 11 remained
unwritten. The basic theme of this work is a symbolic, transposed (that is, not
necessarily transparent) autobiography, which employs a lyric-hymnic means
of expression; no narrative thread is provided. The title is intended to convey
that the individual life phases of the conscious subject are conquered in activity
and suffering. This poetry is also a compendium of the author's knowledge, a
poem depicting character development in the true sense of the term. Prefatory
pieces are placed at the beginning, amongst them the saying from Pythagoras
which is so characteristic of Franz: 'Verzehre nicht das Herz' [Eat not the heart].
The *Eroberungen* are undoubtedly the most significant lyric cycle in German
since the *Diuneser Elegien*. Just as Franz strove in his early years for a renewal of
the ballad appropriate to the age, so he remained interested all his life in a revival of the narrative poem and experimented with some fables between 1944
and 47. He valued them quite highly himself but I do not believe that they would
generally be regarded as a success. Every now and again Franz would translate
an English poem. The most successful is his rendition of Eliot's 'Marina'. Franz
ignored nothing in his quest to be a poet. It is one of the many tragedies of his
life that he was never given enough encouragement and rarely received the
recognition he deserved. It is certainly true that the timing was particularly poor
but this does not adequately explain his lack of success in practice with the English, Jewish, and German literati, as well as with publishers and newspaper editors. The only poet of any note or significance to take up his cause was Elias
Canetti, who at one point at least seemed to be about to achieve something major
with the publication of a volume of poems, but this hope too came to nothing. A
Munich publisher took on a selection entitled *In Babylons Nischen* [In the Niches
of Babylon] in 1948 and pressed on as far as a second proof the following year
before getting into difficulties. The completed print setting was melted down,
only a few copies (with no contents list and some errors) have survived. A newspaper published by the same publishing house was forced to close and this
blocked all publication plans. It was not until the year of Franz's death that some
success could be achieved, something which, even if it was rather modest,
brought him a great deal of joy. One must add to this, however, that after the
unfortunate incident with the publisher, Franz himself was in no fit state of

health to pursue further publication possibilities with any energy; almost all the initiative had to come from friends and acquaintances. The fact that after 1948 Franz hardly began anything new has, apart from his health, for the most part to do with this unfortunate event. He said as much himself. We are now of course able to acknowledge a more profound reason for the discontinuation of production in the short lifespan which he had been granted. The completion of the work had to take precedence over new creation. At the time it took months before one could even speak to Franz about his poetry. Due to his very poor health, the unfortunate incident with the publisher had to be kept secret from him for a long time and was finally only revealed to him gradually. Once he was aware of the situation, he declared that he would write nothing more until a decent volume had been published. He then concentrated instead on drawing and painting and even wanted to take lessons but these never took place. Even during his schooldays Franz had spent dreary hours in school or even day-dreaming at home creating garlands and decorative fancies in ink with many faces and hideous figures. He still did this occasionally in later years. It re-minded one most of certain Polynesian or even West African carvings. Now, however, he wanted to take his drawing more seriously; his usual materials were pencil, charcoal, coloured pencils, and pastels. These were to be followed by experiments with watercolours and oil paints. Some two hundred pages, perhaps even more, have survived, faces, complete figures, scenes, and also landscapes, which are at times really quite expressive but always without excep-tion betray the hand of an amateur. Occasionally Franz would also cut a pretty asymmetrical ornament from paper. I will now provide a bibliography of all the poems which were published during Franz's lifetime: 'Schweigsam in der Sonne' [Taciturn in the Sun], 'Das Weib des Uriah' [The Wife of Uriah]; 'Küste im Krieg' [The Coast in Wartime], 'Heimweg' [Homeward Bound], 'Bald wird der Nebel sinken' [The Mist will soon part] (in *Poetry*, X, London 1944 – English translations of the German texts were provided by [Brian] Miller and G[eorg] Rapp; a review by Stephen Spender described Franz's poems as a 'revelation'); 'Begegnen' [Encounter], 'Herbst vor dem Gasthof' [Autumn Outside the Inn] (in *Literarische Revue*, III, 1, Munich 1948); 'Sommerstille' [Summer Calm] (Ibid., III, 2); 'Herbst der Liebenden' [Autumn of the Lovers], 'Die Wahrheit' [The Truth], 'Die Muse der Verstummten' [The Muse of the Silent Man] (Ibid., III, 5); Eliot's 'Marina' in translation (Ibid., III, 9); 'Fern von Ithaka' [Far from Ithaca], 'Taucht ein' [Dive in], 'Der Mund der Macht' [The Mouth of Power], 'Manchmal noch befremdlich' [Sometimes Still Strange] (Ibid., IV, 5. Munich 1949); 'Unter den Kiefern' [Under the Pine Trees], 'Schweigsam in der Sonne', 'Lied vom Sturzbach' [The Song of the Cataract] (in *Sinn und Form*, II, 3, Potsdam 1950); 'Im Anfang' [In the Beginning] (in *Neue Lit[erarische] Welt*, III, 2, Darmstadt 1952); 'Gebet im Garten' [Prayer in the Garden] (in *Eckart*, XXI, April-June 1952, Wit-ten/Berlin – Franz's most important religious poem, also his longest poem – he was also particularly happy with Michael Hamburger's English version in the autumn of 1952); 'Vom Kriege schweig' [Do not speak of the war] (a longer fragment from 'Conquests'), 'Boote vor Sonnenaufgang' [Boats before Sunrise], 'Herbst-Fragment' [Autumn Fragment] (in *Hochland*, LIV, Munich and Kempten, June 1952); 'Boote vor Sonnenaufgang' (in *Neue Lit[erarische] Welt*, III, 12, Darmstadt 1952); 'Prüfung der Lehrerin' [The Teacher's Examination], 'Das neue Märchen' [The New Fairytale], 'Fern von Ithaka', 'Die Sirenen' [The Sirens] (in *Merkur*, VI, 6, Stuttgart 1952). In addition to these there was the aforementioned volume of translations from Lešehrad and, if I am not mistaken, two or three poems which appeared in the thirties in the Sunday supplement of the *Prager Tagblatt*.

In the obituary he wrote for Franz (*Man*, LII, London, December 1952) Prof. Evans-Pritchard described him as a 'scholar of monumental learning'. This statement very aptly describes Franz's scholarliness and should also be applied to Franz's non-lyrical and non-scientific achievements, to the many volumes 'Allerlei Feststellungen und Versuche' [Sundry Discoveries and Experiments], in which his artistic and scholarly sides are found side by side and eventually combine. It concerns a number of short articles, essays, aphorisms, and notes, not yet assessable, which he compiled between 1943 and his death. He wrote them at home, at university, in libraries, whilst travelling or on trips, he even wrote them whilst receiving visitors or when he came to visit you. The initial stimulus for this creation came from Canetti, but Franz must take full credit for the final outcome. The topics are so diverse, just like his own interests: sociology, literature, language, culture, religion, art, contemporary issues, psychology, profound and humorous observations, word games, political views, observations on people and nature, and many other things. The longer Franz went on making these notes, the more dense and refined the statements became, until he succeeded in distilling them to almost the pure essence of the idea, which he was sometimes able to reproduce in two words. In the last year of his life he was eventually able to create what I would like to term the literary aphorism. In two or three words is attained the very germ of poetic expression, which encapsulates perspective and reflection in the most minute work of art possible. A great deal of what is to be found in these treasures was a by-product of his scholarly thought and activity, but for us it will often be its substratum, that which alone survived, which Franz did not complete, and which would have been impossible to complete even in a far longer lifetime. It is inevitable when preserving things in this way that some trivia, even perhaps some unimportant things may remain which Franz would have removed before going to press, something already borne out by hand-written notes. The notes, mostly hand-written and unfortunately often very small and sometimes barely legible, are ordered chronologically and accompanied by an additional volume of various essays from the first years of this creative process. Only the majority of the material from 1943 to 47 was written up and also partially reworked in a particular but not definitive (and as a matter of fact unnecessary) order during Franz's lifetime – three impressive volumes. At least another three or four volumes might still be compiled. Franz found that this part of his work, one which I regard as being particularly valuable, was even less appreciated than his poems. He spoke about it very little during the last years and hardly let anyone see anything. Only a few aphorisms were published in the *Literarische Revue* (IV, 1, Munich 1949). Franz's essay 'Rilkes Weg zur Beschwörung' [Rilke's Path to Incantation], an excellent study from 1943 which deserves a place of honour in the already over-rich Rilke literature, would fill a slim volume of some 60 pages. The apparent reason for writing the piece was as a lecture for the 'Oxford Refugee Club' and the 'Oxford German Literary Society'. As a favour Franz wrote a short introduction in English to 'Extracts from the Work of Robert Musil' (in *The Wind and the Rain*, VI, 2, London, 1949).

An interesting essay on Heine remained in fragment form and a commissioned review of the poems of a certain Fritz Marnau remained unpublished due to its overly critical tone. – In addition to the bibliography of poems, I must also mention the three translations, Blake's 'The Lamb', Yeats' 'Oil and Blood', and Eliot's 'Marina', which appeared in *Die Lyra des Orpheus* [Orpheus' Lyre], Poems of the People translated into German, ed. by Felix Braun, Zsolnay, Vienna 1952. Franz put together three volumes full of poems and other literary gems from various languages which were unusual, little known or important to him for some other reason, out of which one could compile a most unusual reader, if .... yes, if there were only a publisher to be found.

Franz suffered from a heart condition. He died from a broken heart – in relation to him, that is no cliché. The heart became the central symbol for his life, his thought, and his poetry, and eventually, for his death. The mystical teaching of the circumcized foreskin of the heart, as it was developed in the Kabala, preoccupied him greatly. The third canto of *Eroberungen* is entitled 'Das Herz' [The Heart]. Here is where beginning and end should be:

Das herz, das erschaffene innensein
In einem leib, der durch abende eilte
(es achtete nie die brust
Der arme, leicht und hilflos angehängt).
Das den enteilenden menschen erhält, [AsP: 348]

Nicht verschließen in ihrem reifen die zeiten das herz.

Der einsame verschloß sein herz der hoffnung.
Der sterbende verschloß sein herz dem kummer. [AsP: 350]

[The heart, the created interior being / In a body, that hurried through evenings / (the breast never heeded / The arms, lightly and helplessly attached). / Which preserves the fleeting person, [...]
The times do not close the heart in their ripening. / The lonely man has
closed his heart to hope. / The dying man has closed his heart to sorrow.]

When Franz wrote these verses it would be years before he would know of the
evil which was destroying him. Perhaps he never realized that both intellectually and physically, the heart was his fate, his defining central symbol. Franz
did not take his delicate health into consideration; I have perhaps already
pressed the point too much. Up until the end of the war he was spared the
pains which he must have found particularly disturbing. There seemed to be
repeated periods of weakness, but he took them to be the consequence of over-
work, and if he rested a little, then he could carry on as before. Following an
accident in Dalmatia in 1929 which almost cost him a leg and could have been
much worse, he contracted neuritis, which continued to bother him from time
to time and went into an arm. Franz suffered from a painful over-sensitivity to
cold and a lack of sensitivity to heat, particularly in his fingertips, which affected him most when things were going badly and caused him to burn himself on several occasions. I mention this, because for a long time these and also
other rheumatic symptoms misled him, because his diseased heart and a vas-
omotor disorder manifested themselves with the same kind of pains. He insisted on blaming the familiar complaint or nervousness and some annoying
consequences of undernourishment during the war. In 1946 he suffered a
nervous breakdown which he struggled to overcome for at least six months.
Up until then he had, in spite of everything, kept reasonably good health. Outwardly he seemed to have coped well with discovering the awful truth of his
parents' demise and many other horrific things, but eventually it all became
too much for him. The hopelessness of his existence, his future, his work, his
not being married (like Stifter and Kafka, he held marriage and fatherhood to
be a sublime goal – he would never have coped with it), his unbounded loneliness, being in demand with people he barely liked or disliked altogether, the
rejection of others whose approval he sought in vain, the strict religious beliefs
which he did not know how to realize, the torturous desire for pleasures great
and small, which could not be contained – this was all far too much for him.
He suffered as a result of his diminutive build, of the composition of his face
(he was only happy with his forehead, and also his unusually small hands and
feet which were very well proportioned), he suffered in the face of people, of
their stupidity, their chatter, the noise that they made, he suffered in the face
of everything which might possibly distress an over sensitive being. He suffered perhaps most from a seldom conceded fear of life. And he struggled

repeatedly to confront all these difficulties, even if he could not overcome them. He never fully recovered from the nervous breakdown and was often unfit for work for weeks on end. On such occasions he read – oddly for him – detective novels, of which he must have got through thousands in his lifetime. The number of these which he could read and absorb in one day was amazing. He was himself the very embodiment of the intellectual, a type which he utterly condemned and held to be the evil of all civilization. That he could be so critical of it whilst being that way himself is part of his greatness. In 1948, Franz finally gave in to my constant pleas for him to find a good doctor and this revealed dangerously high blood pressure and vascular spasms. Franz underwent a course of treatment, had to put up with all sorts of instructions which he hated. Against all good advice he continued to smoke heavily and drank more than he could really cope with. The enforced rewriting of the study on slavery in 1948/49 finished him off completely. In the summer of 1949 he felt worse than ever. He had not been living with Cookson for some time, but instead as the neglected lodger of people whose moods he could do nothing to avoid. Although the doctor had told him to be particularly careful, he behaved in a most reckless fashion and eventually hastened the onset of a coronary thrombosis around 1 September 1949, with which he was taken to hospital with almost no hope of survival. There, a number of complications followed, his lungs and costal pleura were affected and a treatment involving injections into the veins was almost impossible as all veins had thrombosis. He had to suffer up to 30 attempts to inject at each treatment at the hands of even the most experienced doctors. No one knew what to do but Franz behaved nobly. Four months spent in hospital and sanitarium brought Franz a recovery of sorts. In January 1950 he was able to take a ground floor room and even begin the teaching which should have begun in the autumn. He did not need to lecture before Easter and was allowed to tutor students at home. At Easter 1950 he was even allowed to travel to London, a great treat for him, because life in Oxford was difficult to bear if he could not see his friends and acquaintances in London at least once a month. He had had a room of his own there in the home of his friend Kühnberg since the spring of 1945, where he could also house his ever-increasing library, and was no longer reliant on uncomfortable lodgings. However, Franz was and remained an ill man, even if he did now more or less follow medical advice and had given up smoking and drinking altogether. The situation even improved steadily up until the summer of 1952, when Franz finally no longer required a stick for walking and could make more demands on himself, something which the doctors even permitted. However, it became too much for him again, and particularly in his final months, during the second trip to Spain and during the last six weeks in Oxford, he undoubtedly overstretched himself again and even smoked and drank, which he had been forbidden from doing 'forever'. The final year of Franz's life was influenced by his friendship with the Oxford Philosophy lecturer, I. M., an Irish woman born in London. She is the most estimable and probably the most important woman ever to get close to him. Franz became a new man, although this relationship, which at least cast warming shafts of light on the final weeks of his life, also developed with difficulty and made demands on him which would have been enough for a healthy man, and more to the point, someone other than Franz, whereas this too was all too much for him. His tired heart, his broken soul simply could not cope with this final upturn. This had nothing to do with a lack of consideration on the part of I. M., it did not even have anything to do with Franz, it was the fault of a combination of fateful events beyond all human control. If a person is be fulfilled, then he is handed over, no longer his own master, in to the hands of the law which determines his existence beyond and against his own will. The truth of this became clear at the end of this life. Although Franz did not feel at all well in October and November 1952 and observed with horror an increase in the symptoms which had heralded his first severe illness, the doctors did not regard his condition as life threatening. If Franz was not really poorly, then he simply ignored his condition, made great plans for the future, marriage to I. M. seemed likely to him, he was on the verge of seeing an improvement in his circumstances with a salary increase, he had been promised a subvention for field work in East Africa, his entire being seemed to have been transformed by an optimism which was quite rare in him. Of course, there were also very depressing days and hours, and especially in the summer Franz was aware of his impending demise and made a will before his trip to Spain. A naive egocentric all his life, his love for I. M. taught Franz a new mode of behaviour. He was almost consumed by consideration and reproached himself harshly for any little thing which seemed to contradict this. I do not believe that I am employing poetic licence or misrepresenting the profound tragedy of Franz's life in any way when I say that our friend was reconciled and resigned when he died. He was certainly as loved as a person can be when he died and Franz knew this. On bad days, when he suffered an attack, he would recite funeral prayers. He continued to work until the middle of November. Then he had a few very bad days, during which he was looked after by I. M., who had, in recent days, spent as much time a possible with him. After a few days in bed, he recovered enough to get up and even go out. He spent the evening of 22 November with friends until almost midnight, on 24th he delivered his lecture, on 25th he still taught a student at home. Afterwards he felt particularly unwell. Nevertheless, he got up again on 26th and worked on his poems and read. On Thursday 27 November 1952 he was visited by I. M. in the morning, Franz was in a good mood, relaxed and enjoying a hearty breakfast. After I. M. had left, he began to feel quite ill. When the doctor arrived at 10 o'clock, having been called by the owners of the house at his request, he found Franz dead in bed. The cause of death was coronary thrombosis. A few days later Franz was buried in the Jewish cemetery in Oxford. It was a clear winter's day with blue sky and sun, the ground covered in snow.

Five years earlier our friend wrote his poem 'Rotherzige Dämmerung' [Red-hearted Twilight]:

Wenn vornüberhängt
Des schweigens gesicht aus der öffnung kalten schlafs:
Rotherzige dämmerung.

Und die bäume auf dem rasen strenger geordnet sind;
Frostige einfalt behütet den hohen eigensinn.

Mein nächster, mein nächster:
Der seelenkundig wird und trocken,
Herbstlich zur kälte ein andres,
Daß ein neues schweigen sich artlos unterbreitet,
Gebaut aus dem steilen in der zeit und hingelegt,
Unsanfte geborgenheit, nah am tod … [AsP: 277]

[When the face of silence / Hangs over the aperture of cold sleep: / Red-hearted twilight. // And the trees on the lawn are more rigidly ordered; / Icy innocence guards lofty obstinacy. // My neighbour, my neighbour: / Who grows knowledgeable of the soul and dry, / Another takes the autumn chill, / That a new silence simply spreads out, / Built from the steepness in time and laid down, / Harsh security, close to death …]

Dear Dr Rabin, I did not want to write a treatise when I sat down to answer your letter. But that is what it has become and please forgive me for forcing such a long document upon you, and for sending it to you just as it came into my head, without any preparation. You will sense what Franz meant to me and will always mean to me and – I don't know why – it is a comforting feeling and really good to know that you are the hopefully forgiving reader of these pages. Please use whatever seems useful to you; I have no objection to those who are seriously interested in Franz having access to this document. I very much hope that you will indeed visit us one day. You are, of course, welcome to visit us with your wife too. The number again: LAD 2039. Yours,

21.3.1953

MEMORIES OF F. B. STEINER

ESTHER FRANK

RECORDED BY H. G. ADLER (4–8 MAY 1964)[1]

Dr E[sther] Frank came to Oxford from Cologne in March 1939. The reason for this choice was the link with an Engl[ish] teacher at the Jawne School in Cologne who found a position for E[sther] with his grandmother with a Domestic Permit. They gave German lessons and English for refugees and found a room at 203 Woodstock Road where Dr Heinrich Meinhardt lived, a German Ethnologist with a Jewish wife. The friendship with Franz, who was often there, began in the autumn of 1939. At first neither made much of an impression on the other. Their first proper conversation took place in the synagogue at a lecture by Walter Ettinghausen (later Eytan), the Zionist, then lecturer in Middle High German at Queen's College. Mutual surprise at Jewish and Zionist interests. Then no close contact for some time. A few months later, Franz knocked at my door because Meinhardt, whose study was next door, was not there. As he entered my room and saw my library (Judaica, philosophy, German lit[erature]), he was very interested and stayed right there. I was inwardly frozen and had no interest in my own books, therefore also indifferent towards the visit. These visits were often repeated. He recounted a great deal about his life, which I did not take in at all due to my state of mind. He arrived unannounced, which he would also tend to do in the future, because he thought it self-evident that one would have time for him, whatever time of day it was. He made himself at home in my room even when I was not there. This was how he behaved until the end. Sunday morning, the day of the big clean, did not bother him either, he strode right into the middle of all the chaos. He never helped, though, and would not have known how to go about it. Only during a removal did he take care of the library which he took out of boxes in the new flat and put them on the shelves. It later became evident that he had slipped a number of books he did not like, mainly German text books, behind the rows of books. Erich Unger also lived for some time in Meinhardt's house, without his wife. He often came to my room too, the three of us often held

---

[1] Although seeking to record Esther Frank's memories as a discrete document, Adler occasionally lapses into self-reference. These instances are indicated in the text with (*). Adler also shifts from a third to a first person narrative in his rendition of Frank's words, a further consequence of the rough nature of the document, which was never intended for publication.

discussions about Jewish issues and philosophy. Franz and Unger argued about Zionism and Franz did not like it if I laughed at this. At the time Franz was unreservedly Zionist with sympathies for Paole Zion (a member for a while), he also went to meetings. Franz never recommended me as a teacher with one exception. It was of no interest to him how I earned my living. During the first years he did not ask about my past. What was important to him was my present and that I shared his interests as well as my books which he read in my room and also borrowed.

For several years (circa 41–45) Franz received an annual sum of £350 from the Czech government, earned nothing besides, and did not apply for anything else. All the money went on books. Mr Cookson advised in vain that he should save and paid for his travel around the country. He did not want to spend anything on clothes and accepted what Evans Pritchard offered him. He was obsessed by books. Franz never helped in the Cookson household. During the war he looked after the lawn at Cookson's request. The housekeeper patched and mended everything for him, could not do anything right however. He had two rooms, was well fed.

Cookson introduced Franz to Magdalen College.

In 1941, he showed me a small volume of poems by Willi Schenk (MS) which I did not think was anything special. Then he turned up with a collection of his own poems on pink copy paper, which we discussed. That set the contact going. At that time the Bible was discussed a great deal, esp[ecially] the Pentateuch. He was afraid of the Psalms because they were poetry. The weekly Sidra was discussed.

In 1942, the incident with the suitcase was a terrible shock. Almost all the material for the work on slavery. The work itself had not commenced. He never recovered from the shock. He spoke [of it] for years. He was distracted from the shock by concern for me. I fell ill in April 1942, inflammation of the lungs, seven weeks in hospital. He visited me regularly. He brought me his only copy of *Eroberungen* [Conquests] and left it with me, although he knew that I was unable to read due to my weakness and that the preservation of the copy was in danger. From then on our relationship was friendly.

I moved to Park Town once the war was over.

During this illness, Franz arrived with a mountain of books to give me something to read. He simply could not imagine how one could exist without books. It was a very touching characteristic.

During the illness I suffered heart failure. Franz came the next day. He looked at me and said 'One should not make the end difficult'. Shortly before he brought me his favourite book, Schröders *Bhagavadgita*. He spoke with the doctor and the nurse and worried about me. Then I was sent to a convalescent home for three weeks where he did not visit because it was inconvenient for him. As soon as I returned home he appeared again straight away. It was a great sacrifice as he was not allowed to smoke in my presence. As I was unable to live alone, I moved in with my sister in London until Nov[ember]. During this time he wrote and sent poems. He came and visited me once. Slowly I was able to speak with him as before. From then on the contact continued unbroken until my departure for America at the end 27 March 1951 [*sic*]. It was made more difficult towards the end, however, due to his illness. On the day of his first heart attack there was an 'intimacy of death' between us. This powerful sense of proximity remained throughout the period of serious illness. Once he felt better I had the feeling that he wanted to get away from this proximity. At that time I began to think of emigrating to America, it could not go on the way it was. When I went away, E[lias] said 'Whatever will become of Steiner when you are no longer there?' He even gave up his strict reserve and asked F[ranz], why I was leaving. He would have preferred to say that he did not know but I said she is going to her relatives (*).

In 1942, F[ranz] spoke at the Institute of Anthropology 'On Superstition'. This aroused a lot of interest.

In 1943, at the home of the Jungian Gerhard Adler where F[ranz] often went. He was very interested in F[ranz] and wanted to make him known at least amongst refugees. He put on a grand evening with invitations. The top emigrés were invited, at least fifty. *Eroberungen* with explanations. Franz liked [G.] A [dler], Jung was left out. Reading was beautiful. It was a great success. Present were the Germanist Craig from Westfield Coll[ege], [George] Rapp, [Willi] Schenk, [Paul] Senft.

1943 or 44 Lecture on Rilke in the 'German Club' of Oxford Uni[versity]. It made an impression. He repeated the lecture in a refugees club in Oxford.

R[adcliffe]-Brown advised F[ranz] badly with the work on slavery. He said I should study the legal systems of slavery. F[ranz] then lost himself in the legal systems. Attempt to collate once more the material. He lost himself in the material, could never limit himself. He was hardworking in his way. He split off from himself, suddenly began to write poetry. He travelled to the British Museum to work and then studied Germ[an] literature. He lacked economy.

In 1945 at the end of the war the search for a publisher for the poems began. Oprecht in Zürich: F[ranz] said to himself and Esther, if O[precht] does not answer in 2 or 3 months, then I am asking for the MS back. Pressure to complete the dissertation from E[vans]-P[ritchard]. In 1948 in Belgium, Joseph lecture at the anthropology congress. The achievement impressed. The advice to provide a theol[ogical] basis was abandoned.

In 1946 attempt to work on the thesis. Mr Cookson once sent someone to my house towards evening to enquire as to the whereabouts of Franz, who had not returned for his evening meal. We knew nothing. We asked the police and the hospitals. During the night the police found him well outside the town on the country road suffering from total amnesia and brought him to Mr Cookson. He immediately called for a doctor. He examined him thoroughly and found nothing, Franz was back to normal too. Mr C[ookson] was very concerned. F[ranz] was given two weeks of 'house arrest' and was spoiled. No doubt about it: fear of work. F[ranz] then said one day 'I am going to start writing poetry again.' And with that everything was alright again. Then Franz continued to look for material but did not work on the thesis. The work was not written until 1949. It was barely completed when the severe attack happened, it was too much for F[ranz]. The stay in the Radcliffe was taken care of by E[vans]- P[ritchard] and Hevesi. After the illness he was made lecturer for Social Anthropology. He was not happy with that. I was to influence E[vans]-P[ritchard] so that he would be given a fellowship of a college. I went to E[vans]-P[ritchard] to discuss it with him. He promised to think about it, it was very difficult. He promised to keep it in mind but it would only be possible after several years as a lecturer. I got to know E[vans]-P[ritchard] during the illness as I had to let the Inst[itute] know. The oral exam a few days before. The lectures were excellent, oratorical too. He took them seriously, good visit. The students held him in very high regard. He wore himself out far too much in tutorials. I was at Woodstock Rd. almost every evening.

Residences after Cookson: Newton Rd. – Woodstock Rd. –

One winter three of us, myself, F[ranz] and Miss Feit (daughter of a Viennese bookseller) learnt Spanish together. – Fernando was the name of one of the lessons. Another was called autumn = Brumal. That led to the otherwise meaningless title Fernando Brumal. Great strides with the grammar. Reading of 18th c[entury] fables for translation. Then the poetry of Saint Teresa. Then Luis de León 'The Perfect Wife' [La perfecta casada] (Directions for the happy life of the housewife), by then it was already easier in the Spanish. León promoted a sociology of class, influenced by Aristotle. F[ranz] was interested in this and wanted to write about it. He loved Jorge Manrique inspired F[ranz]'s poem to the father with his own. He valued Lucanor, translation the 'Celestina' in Engl[ish]. The literary critic Menéndez Pidal was read (relatively easy Spanish).

Circle of friends in Oxford. Prof[essor] Malik gave lectures on general philosophy. Franz belonged to the inner circle here. People from different faculties, nations, and religions. F[ranz] was to speak about Judaism there which he did not do due to his perfectionism. From approximately 1942. Many Indians there. Radakrischnan also came, very impressive man, who was on good terms with F[ranz]. Following his time at the consulate in Moscow, F[ranz] wanted to find out about Stalin and Russian pol[itics] from him, and was surprised to discover nothing. The contact remained friendly, however. Franz set up a discussion between four Zionists (amongst them Aba Eban) and Rada-krischnan in Oxford, which made an impression on the Indian, who was to be shown that Judaism and Christianity did not belong together. Franz thought a great deal more about pol[itical] J[ewish] questions and presented the leading Zionists with various suggestions. He also considered missionary work, in order to balance out the loss of reserves caused by Hitler. In this way the Galla were to become Jewish. Srinivas was an anthropologist, went to India a few years before F[ranz]'s death and became a professor. Spalding, an Englishman, also in this circle, not a scholar. Cookson stood up when the national anthem was played on the radio, Franz avoided being there.

In Oxford Schenk, lecturer in Modern History, in Prague a lawyer. Dissertation on the Congress of Vienna. Link was Prague, no friendship. University: Malinowski was valued as a teacher in London, scarcely a personal relationship. Cookson set up the Oxford relations. He liked Radcliffe-Brown. No private contact with any of the gentlemen. He admired E[vans]-P[ritchard]'s style (F[ranz] was perhaps in his house once). Collegial relationship. F[ranz] tried to make him friendly towards Jews as he was on the side of the Arabs. Meyer Fortes, studies on family relations. F[ranz] valued him but did not have a personal relationship with him. F[ranz] liked Peristiani [Peristiany]. He planned a sociolinguistic study with him, also a lecture. [Godfrey] Lienhardt, African specialist, F[ranz] liked him (now prof[essor] in Oxford), was anglicized. He was young, talented. The Bohannan couple from the USA, they were doing fieldwork, F[ranz] had an ambivalent attitude towards them. He wanted to translate Simmel's *Sociology of Money* for them, also the Sociology. F[ranz] was good at translating from German into English.

Parents. At first spoke about his mother a lot, later only about his father. Chiefly about the atmosphere, on the subject of both. To think of his parents carried too much of a burden. At the beginning a lot about Suse, facts too. With a great deal of love. Detailed descriptions of illness and death. Speaking about Uncle Paul, whom he excused, as circumstances meant that he need not bother about him. F[ranz] recounted: Before his father signed up, he went up a mountain with him, his father was serious, F[ranz] had the feeling, that his father wanted to sacrifice him as Abraham had Isaac. They went up in silence. When they reached the top, he thought his father would gather wood to make a fire etc. When they went down, he was very relieved. The impression was so strong that F[ranz] planned to write about it in later years. F[ranz] described the ear-boxing incident. Wanted to write something with Willi Schenk in memory of Eugen Lieben.

F[ranz] spoke of me (*) as a friend, gr[eat] joy at the news of my survival, worry over my accommodation here. I was the only person from Prague he mentioned.

He spoke about the year in Palestine. Living with an Arab family, with Hugo Bergmann (here he discovered Bach). Great love of music in the final years. Of Deller, whom he did not like at first: he treats his voice like an instrument. In Jerusalem he read the *Bhagavadgita* which opened up religion for him.

Year in Vienna. He mentioned [Pater] Schmidt, Heine-Geldern. He got to know the capital of the empire.

Judaism. He became a Jew in Jerusalem. He had always regretted his lack of knowledge of Judaism. Great love of Pentateuch. He planned a sociology of the Pentateuch. 'Das Leib des Jahres' [The Body of the Year] is from the tract Pessachim. My orthodoxy was important to him, he wanted to know a great deal (*). Strong pull towards orthodoxy, indecision: 'In a few years I'll be that far.' He liked reading [Scholem's] *Major Trends of Jewish Mysticism* and Buber's Chassidic writings. A few years before the illness he went to the synagogue on holy days. Followed the liturgy in the prayer book. Contact with Dr [Chaim] Rabin, other Zionist things. In Oxford a Paole Zion group was established, Franz member. This gradually waned. At first regular attendance at the meetings, slackened off due to illness.

Christianity: a heathen-Jewish religion, cobbled together. He found the N[ew] T[estament] worrying as a literary document, contradictory and lacking in depth. When Christians asked him what he thought of the founder, he answered 'Nothing'. He spoke of Islam with reserved recognition, the Koran was a gr[eat] work of art.

Particularly loved Koheleth. He intended to read the Prophets later. He avoided Psalms: If one truly absorbs the Psalms, then one can no longer write poetry. To him they were a great work of art which he avoided. He said: The Psalms would overpower me and then I would be empty. He liked to recite Job on the end [of the world]. He had the feeling, that he scarcely understood it but hoped to later. Judges: sociological interest. The less refined books to which Esther also belongs depicted reality. The correct structure for life without disguise or pretence is depicted. His own aphorisms nothing in comparison to Mischle. Lines and lines of Schirhaschirim by heart, the greatest love poem.

He found Plato too heathen. Aristotle as scholar and creator of sociology, not as a metaphysician. Hegel as a sociologist (*Phenomonology*) in the later period.

Judaism: Lewertoff (converted Jew) wrote a book about mystical Zionism. The poem 'Auf dem Felde' [In the Field] influenced by this.

Relationship to Engl[ish] lit[erature]: preferences: Bacon's essays (as lit[erary] achievement), all the Elizabethans. He rarely spoke about Shakespeare. Interpretation of Hamlet??? Hamlet basically a rough oaf who destroys everything that he comes into contact into with without intending to; like a golem. He valued Wyatt, Herbert, Vaughan, Donne, Traherne, Milton. From 19th c[entury] Mrs Gaskell. Blake (later lost interest completely). Yeats very much (F[ranz]'s 'gelbes Haar' literally from Y[eats]' 'yellow hair'). Eliot: lyric poetry yes, criticism no (not thorough enough). Joyce. Smart. Auden. Melville. P[iers] Plowman.

East[ern] religions: valued very much the translations by Arthur Wayley. F[ranz] once began Chinese. Valued Genji very highly.

German lit[erature]. He was basically interested in every line ever written. Preferences: Jung-Stilling, the Brothers Grimm (he read whatever he could find in the British Library), correspondence Grimm-Arnim, all German Baroque poets (whether good or bad), every line of Klopstock, Haller (unjustly forgotten, hoped for a selection of his works), Hamann, Jacobi. Schiller was the ruin of the Germ[an] language because of his 'military music' (just as unmusical people love military music, so unpoetic people love Schiller, he valued his philosophical writings, however, Sch[iller] belongs in the 18th c.). Lessing was highly regarded, better as a stylist. Preference for medieval works, Walter but also other things. Hölderlin: 'Every new gen[eration] creates a new image of H[ölderlin] for itself.' He wanted to create the new image for his generation. He scarcely spoke of Goethe. Did not mention Jean Paul. Kleist ditto. No interest in Novalis, nor Büchner, Grabbe. Mörike a minor poet. He wanted to edit an anthology of lyric poetry, beginning with the Baroque (Gleim, Wieland, Pfeffel included) up to circa 1945/50. Next to the pictures of his parents there was a picture of Stifter as an old man and a picture of Kafka as a young man. Bohemia also played a role here. Wittiko was one of his main books. Stifter's Letters.

England: loved and read everything to do with Keats. He wanted to get to know his entire circle of friends too.

Germany: No mention of Grillparzer and Lenau. Mörike a *poeta minor* with a few good poems. Nothing on Hebbel, at the very most a reference to the Diaries. He valued Immermann, informative descriptions of manners. He valued Arndt, Adam Müller. He loved some of Eichendorff's poems. He was interested in some of Arnim's correspondence. He rarely mentioned Heine, alien to him. From the modern period he valued Trakl, the later Rilke. Musil *Der Mann ohne Eigenschaften* [The Man without Qualities] (pref[erred] the funnier sections). Of Broch he probably only knew the 'Der Tod des Vergil' [Death of Virgil]. He did not like Th[omas] Mann.

International literature: Positive Proust. Gogol 'Dead Souls'. When in hospital he asked for [Ovid's] 'Tristia'.

Franz came to know Hevesi through Prof[essor] Waismann. H[evesi] published a book on French.

Mary McCann from the Oxford area. She was at Westfield College in London, evacuated to Oxford. During the war she came to a kosher kitchen and met Franz there.

Franz never showed any interest in Esther's financial situation, Hevesi also took everything for granted. Hevesi was very clever and erudite. He had a knowledge of literature and very good taste. He admired F[ranz] almost as a master. First name and book?

Canetti. Franz said of him 'a very important man', highly regarded. A quarrel for some years. He said a great deal about Canetti. He also spoke quite a lot about Veza. When F[ranz] was in Spain, his excuse for not having written much was that he was spending the time there 'on behalf of Canetti.'

Parting. Emigration announced quite some time beforehand. Franz did not take it seriously. I told him once the final word came from the consulate, which he did not take quite seriously either. 6 weeks before, when the visa arrived, I told him on the telephone. 'When are you leaving then?' 'In 5–6 weeks time.' He was speechless. Then the contact was a little spoiled. It seemed so unlikely to him that I would not be there that he went to London for the last fortnight. I was very happy about this as I had so much to do and the whole thing was wearing me down. Leaving hurt me too, because of Franz as well. I began to pack. All at once Franz appeared. 'What are you doing here?' 'Well, I thought you were leaving tomorrow.' This was a few days beforehand because he had muddled it up. I was spending the last 2 days with my sister in London. He sat down in the middle of my packing, circa 9pm. He looked at me: 'It's probably better that I go.' I said 'Yes'. This distressed him deeply. Then he travelled back to London ('I just can't bear to be with you'). He saw that I looked awful. Promised to meet at my sister's. During those two days he was there almost all the time. Hevesi came too and Canetti. F[ranz] and C[anetti] stayed to dinner on the first day. Second day very lively, F[ranz] came at midday and stayed until late evening. I was so tired, exhausted and agitated, which F[ranz] could not understand. The next morning my sister accompanied me to Waterloo. Canetti came on the last afternoon for 1 or 2 hours.

1940 something like a Quaker lecture for refugees. F[ranz] spoke along with Meinhardt. First M[einhardt], then F[ranz] on Carpathian Russia with pictures.

Lore Salzburger occasionally visited me in Oxford, she was nice. Her book on Hölderlin is rather pretentious. I did not have any special contact with her. She was a let down when Franz was ill. She visited once. 'What can I do for F[ranz] then?' I mentioned some purchases. 'I can't do that, I need my money for myself.'

F[ranz] sometimes wanted to appear important with his female acquaintances. He wanted to emphasize his masculinity. Once he said: 'I have still not written enough love poems, a poet must write more love poems. They belong in a poet's oeuvre.' I said: 'The mod[ern] Fr[ench] poets don't write any love poems at all.' Franz scarcely mentioned his early poems, but he let people see them. He did not expect me to say anything about them.

Germany: He read a lot of Meister Eckhart. Great preference for Droste [Hülshoff], esp[ecially] short prose fragments, compared her to Emily Bronte, impressed by *Das geistliche Jahr* [The spirit[ual] Year]. He could not understand why she had fallen in love with L[evin] Schücking. F[ranz] found my tentative objection that good poems had been created as a consequence inconclusive. This was said repeatedly. He was pleased that Schücking had then married a young woman, even if she did not write any notable poems. He repeatedly read Gutzkow, whom he found historically very interesting. After his illness he was interested in Tieck's dramas. He found Franz Baader interesting.

England: He valued anthologies of light verse and wanted to prepare [one] in German too.

Through me he got to know [Max] Scheler, whose sociological writings he valued, he ignored his philosophy.

High regard for Barth's sociology (there was only one volume), Mark Bloch: Feudalism. Henri Pirenne: Charlemagne and Mohammed. Negative towards [James] Frazer.

He gave me (in the early days) his poetry folder, so that I could browse through it and a new poem was hidden in the middle. He took a mischievous delight when I found it and read it aloud to him. Then he was happy. Once, he borrowed a volume of Goethe's poetry and found the poem 'Vogelscheuchen' [Scarecrows]. It seemed odd to me, he wanted to persuade me that Goethe had [really] written it. G[oethe] also wrote poetry which was different from what I imagined. Finally I rejected it for not being Goethe-like, at which point he admitted he had written it himself.

[He] was always enticed by the figure of Sindbad.

F[ranz] said that the word 'gentle' was to be found in the oddest places in Proust, which he liked. He used it in lyric poetry in this sense. It expresses something which cannot be achieved with any other word: le mot just. That is what he always wanted to achieve.

Poem 'Herbstmorgen an der Moldau' [Autumn Morning on the Moldau] he was proud of 'wir sanften fische' [we gentle fish].

On rare words in poems: In response to objection: There are dictionaries after all. He found an objection to it banal.

Favourite words 'karg' [barren], 'genau' [precise].

Franz liked 'Bald wird der Nebel sinken ins herbstliche Tal' [Soon the mist will sink into the autumnal valley]. He often quoted it and knew it by heart. Others he seems to have known partially. A few years later he stopped quoting.

F[ranz] also liked 'Das Weib des Uriah' [Uriah's Mistress].

The cycle 'Läuterungen' [Purifications] was no longer important to him, but because he could not throw anything away, he had kept it.

F[ranz] once said on the subject of attempts to order his poetry: 'I am not up to it.'

I and my whole family were 'his family' to Franz, he was interested in everyone too.

Second volume of poetry 'Scarecrows' I was to negotiate for a poem by Goethe.

'Wallern' dedication unclear.

'Am Kanal' [On the Canal] = the Oxford Canal. F[ranz] asked if it (the canal) really existed again? The little dog, Mr Cookson's dog.

'Taprobane'. This poem refers to Franz's Singhalese girlfriend. The title perhaps paraphrases her name, otherwise unexplained. The dedication 'for K. K.' refers to her but not decipherable in full. 'Schon zur Erinnerung' [Remembered already] refers to Staverton Rd in Oxford. F[ranz] liked the arrival of the baker's boy in the afternoon.

'Mädchen in einer Leihbücherei' [Girl in a Lending Library] 'for Norma Ford' = librarian in the public library in Oxford, she spoke very little German, F[ranz] cannot have had a relationship with her. I asked why? 'Why shouldn't I. I'm there so often…'

'Kalter Garten' [Cold Garden] = Mr Cookson's garden in Staverton Rd.

'Vor dem Auftreten der Sängerin' [Before the Singer appears]. Refers to the Icelandic singer Engel Lund, but not quite certain.

'Heiterer Heimweg' [Fair Weather heading Home]. F[ranz] and I had read something haggadic in the Talmud about the hair of Absalom and Sampson. F[ranz] was pleased that the two men were mentioned together. The next morning he brought the poem. All elements of the poem have a real basis.

'Das Blei' [The Plummet] (first version) was poor according to F[ranz].

'Das Leib des Jahres' [The Body of the Year] refers to the tract Pessachim. On the things created before the creation of the world = miracles. Miracles created before creation. Franz was never quite satisfied with it, was meant to be something especially good. He gave up improving it because it was not working. Comment: When he read from the Talmud, he found inspiration for poems. After reading a passage he said: 'Now let's clarify things a little.' That made him happy, he was in his element.

'Die Zigeunerinnen' [The Gypsy Women] F[ranz] worked intensively on it again and again. He did not want to leave it as a fragment.

'Tod der Hoffnung' [The Death of Hope] F[ranz] liked a lot. He said he had put many secrets in it.

'Auf dem Felde' [In the Field] F[ranz] considered a complete success.

'Lied vom Sturzbach' [Song of the Cataract] F[ranz] liked especially.

Amongst the folk song variations there was one piece in early Chinese which is clearly missing from his papers.

'Erinnerungen an den Neusiedler See' [Memories of the Neusiedler lake] C[ompare] 'Schwesterlich ähnelnd versargte Gesicht' [Sisterly similar entombed face] = Suse.

It was difficult for me to ask about the meaning or allusions in poems. F[ranz] was too reserved to give information willingly. If I did not understand something, there was the danger that F[ranz] would think the poem was a failure.

'Der Sänger' [The Singer] refers to French-Swiss song patterns. After reading a book. 'Mahnung' [Admonition] 'Vagula, blandula' Lat[in] poem to which F[ranz] alluded.

'Am Kamin' [By the Fire] refers to Kae Hursthouse.

'Im Mondlicht' [In the moonlight] F[ranz] often quoted the final line, when something had affected him deeply. He liked the line very much. Otherwise he rarely quoted himself.

'Erinnerungen an den Pentlandberge' [Memories of the Pentland Hills] written in one go at my home (*), whilst Nelly Wolffheim lay seriously ill in the next room (previously E[rich] Unger's) and Esther looked after her. I made the point that I could not look after him. His answer: 'That doesn't matter.' It did not bother him that I was constantly running back and forth.

'Traum von einem Abschied' [Dream of a Departure] Fernando = refers to the imaginary Fernando from the text book.

'Spaziergang' [Walk] refers to the Second World War. F[ranz] was silent and the others spoke. One can only cope with this terrible event through silence. This was F[ranz]'s view. In Thersites is seen the one who tells all. He who actually knows what has happened is the one who has fallen. The poem certainly does not refer to Canetti. This poem, if one may say so, is F[ranz]'s war poem.

F[ranz] showed the poems to very few people in Oxford. Apart from me occasionally Schenk and latterly Hevesi regularly.

'Herbst vor dem Gasthof' [Autumn Outside the Inn] refers to Kae Hursthouse ('Katharina').

The 'Fabeln' [Fables] were a convalescence for F[ranz]. He found them very easy, he could have written dozens. 'Die freieste Wahl' [The Freest Choice] was his favourite piece.

'Nach der Wüstenschlacht' [After the Battle in the Desert] was inspired by the poem by an unknown poet from North Africa in the collection 'De Profundis'.

F[ranz] admired Kierkegaard's capacity and ability for work, that he had written such a great oeuvre in relatively few years. Of himself he said that he could not do this.

'Spätere Jahre des Dichters' [Poet's later Years] admittedly refers to Franz himself.

'Dichters Grabschrift' [Poet's epitaph] refers to himself.

1947 F[ranz] wrote a series of what are objectively his best poems, which he did let people see but for which he sought no approval because he was sure of their quality. These poems also remained for the most part in their original version.

'Leda' inspired by a Yeats poem on the theme.

'Ritt durch die Farme' [Ride through the Ferns]. In Park Town in Oxford there lived a lame academic, his wife was nice to him. The daughter was in a college, a young, slim, shy thing. F[ranz] scarcely knew her. That should show just how many relationships he had with women.

'Erker und Freundin' [Oriel and Girlfriend] dedicated to Eithne Wilkins.

'Zwei Ränder' [Two edges]. Written when he discovered that Kae was pregnant. He came back from London horrified and brought with him this poem, which he had written in the train. He came to see me unusually late, looked like death and laid this poem on my table. He left the poem lying there. I was concerned by his appearance. I asked, he said: I met Kae Hursthouse and was horrified by her appearance. Then he told me that she was pregnant. Then he left and left the poem at my house. We never spoke about it. – Before Kae went to Australia, after F[ranz]'s illness, she came to see me and asked after him. At first she thought that I was keeping Franz from her. I gave out the address where she found him. F[ranz] said to me afterwards: She said goodbye to me.

'Wandlungen des R. Jeffries' [R. Jeffries' Transformations]. A couple, he a social anthropologist. Franz didn't know the pair well. These dedications are not borne of true attachment but snobbery. Those honoured in this case (as per usual) do not know anything about it and I would not name them in print.

'Junia' = Kae when she gave birth to her child in June 1948.

The Ceylonese girlfriend was called Mrs K. Kalenberg, was at the Ladies College in Colombo and lived at 13 Arthur's Lane, Bambalapitiya, Colombo.

Kae Fearon Hursthouse came from Christchurch, was described by Franz as a fiancée in 193[?]. She was married before he got to know her. She was a nursery school teacher. When she went back before the beginning of the war, the affair was more or less over. When she came back after the war, she was pregnant, he said 'She is blooming towards her forties'. He was horrified, she wanted to marry him but he no longer wanted to.

On the day that I found out that my sister Bertl and her son Rafael had survived, F[ranz] received the news that his parents had been killed. We had both heard early in the day and we told one another. He visited me in the afternoon and brought me a bunch of flowers which he had picked from Mr Cookson's garden. He brought them shyly and did not say a word.

'Feststellungen und Versuche' [Essays and Discoveries]. Approximately 1942 Franz began to talk about literary criticism (Kafka, Rilke), also odd things, aperçus etc. Sociology too. He said things quite freely in conversation. Whole theories. I thought it was a shame that he was telling this to a person who might forget it. I suggested that he might like to write it down. At first he resisted: everyone knows that, it's old hat. I kept insisting and one day I bought him a little black notebook. He was annoyed that I was pressuring him, went away sullenly. After a few days he came back and had already written something down. At first somewhat crude and longer pieces. I was soon copying the things for him. Then he got used to it. Later he enjoyed many things. F[ranz] had so many ideas himself. Canetti said to me before I left that F[ranz] had 'taken' a great deal from him, esp[ecially] on division of labour. I said: F[ranz] had so many ideas that he did not need to borrow any.

Canetti: During the war there was a temporary break in their relationship.

4–8 May 1964.

FRANZ STEINER

ELIAS CANETTI[1]

There is so much to say about him. Where do I begin?

His life was determined by his figure, he had none. He was small and so slight, that one almost overlooked him. His face was particularly ugly: low, sloping forehead, powerless eyes in constant involuntary motion. His voice was tearful, even when there was nothing to complain about. There cannot have been a less winning human being.

But then you talked to him, and, in his slow and apparently passionless manner, he always had something to say. It was always clear and concrete and free of any rhetoric. It was always original, never reliant on any means of expression. When you had grown accustomed to the slightly plaintive tone and ignored it (you could not help but notice it which is why I use the word 'ignore'), you noticed a second and no less constant thing, the question, one so modest that it did not really demand an answer. You really had to know your way round a little in the intellect of this person, in order to know, that he was only interested in immense answers. These are so rare, that a sensible person does not even expect them.

You can ask about laws without being punished. The wording is laid down, and in the end, for many, there remains nothing more than to ask for the precise wording of the laws. That was really Franz Steiner's way. He increasingly opted for obedience to the law in matters relating to his faith.

But he never tried to win me over to his way of thinking. He never dared to touch the drive for freedom which shaped my character. He was thankful for the fact that I took him seriously in conversation despite his increasing concentration on a historically established faith, as if he were free, as free as I felt myself to be.

There was one way in which he was and always would remain free, something to which he would never have admitted in the final years of our friendship. He found freedom in myths. He was the only person I have known, with whom I could speak about myths. Not only was he familiar with a great number and just as able to surprise me with them as I was able to surprise him: he did not touch them, he did not interpret them, he made no attempt to order them according to scientific principles, he left them alone. For him they never became

---

[1] This memoir first appeared in *Akzente* 42/3 (1995), 204–209. It was reprinted in Elias Canetti, *Aufzeichnungen 1992–1993* (Munich: Hanser, 1996), pp. 17–24.

253

a mere means to an end. For him too they represented the highest and most precious human achievement. We could talk with each other for days on end about myths, both of us thinking of new ones to offer the other, and they had always been the most important thing in the life of a particular group of people, they had always been valuable and influential. Neither of us, neither he nor I, would have dared to invent anything in the course of these conversations.

These conversations centred on myths which were rendered precisely, myths according to which people had organized their lives, not his or my playful inventions. The trust which reigned between us was grounded in the respect for myths with which we both, each for himself, spent a good deal of our time. One would like to think that this it not at all rare, and overlook the fact that almost all experts in the study of myths abuse them for some end, in order to support some theory or system of classification.

Innocent admirers and observers of myth are rare. Even amongst poets, I have myself only known those who briefly took an interest, mostly to support a piece on which they were working.

His feel for everything worth living. His quiet shining knowledge of it. It was unattainable for him, he *dreamt* of it. He dreamt of a family, of a wife and children. He loved his sister, whom he lost at an early age. It was the ultimate proof of his trust in me that he showed me the picture of this sister. All women whom he later courted with indescribable patience resembled this sister. For others, whom he might have won – despite his ugliness – he felt contempt. He became angry if you tried to help him and was probably never conscious of just how in need of help he appeared to be. In his notion of a family, he was the *man*, and his anger was directed towards any woman who wanted to care for him like a child. Something must be said about his appearance, in order to understand why he was never able to achieve something as mundane as a family.

He died just as a woman agreed to become engaged to him. It was the English writer Iris Murdoch who knew him in Oxford and was intellectually overpowered by him. She entrusted him with the manuscript of her first novel. For years he had been threatened by a serious heart condition and was reading it when this overcame him for the final time. The last letter he ever wrote to me was about this novel: he asked me to read it quite insistently, something which he would not normally have done. It was 'Under the Net' and he must be recognized as truly having discovered Iris Murdoch.

She resembled his sister. Lying ill in bed, he asked her to marry him. She agreed and considered herself to be engaged. The condition of his heart did not leave much hope for him. But it is possible that the joy brought by this engagement was the cause of his death. Were this the case, then this otherwise unhappy man would have died in a happy frame of mind.

Steiner was a great lover of the truth and never flattered. Veza,[2] who was a terrible flatterer, must have seemed uncanny to him. His adoration of beauty was so great that he could never interpret anything which a woman said to him as flattery, he always took it to be the truth.

The 'Prayer in the Garden on my Father's Birthday', which I read again yesterday after forty years, moved me greatly. It is written under the influence of Jorge Manrique and never was an influence more legitimate.

Steiner would really have liked to be with me in Spain and really he was there for me.

His letters from Spain contain the most beautiful words he ever wrote me.

In our conversations about peoples – many so-called primitives amongst them – I emphasized myth, he early poetry. In letters he often wrote poems about tribes on which he was working at the time, not, or at least more rarely, I think, about myths. He felt I possessed a power to uphold the veracity of things, something which he envied. He did not hesitate to employ me for this purpose. As he only courted in earnest – he wanted to marry and start a family, it was the thing he wished for more than anything else and almost all the time – he could not see anything rash in having someone intercede on his behalf, someone who valued him, knew his high intellectual worth and reliability and who could convey this to the person concerned with a fire which he did not possess.

He did not claim to know better than words know and he did not always try to read between the lines. As such he was free from psychoanalysis. He could calmly and critically assess a suggestion which came from that quarter without being taken in by it. Testing things out was very much his thing. For him, writing poetry was a way of testing words. He never read without writing down words which he liked. That he did this in many languages, also in those which he approached from outside as an anthropologist, does not detract in any way from the validity of the German words which he used to write his poetry. It was impossible for him to misplace or waste anything of value, that is to say, a word. He spoke slowly and with reserve, he had always thought about what he said. You were never near to an origin when you listened to him speak but always near to a result. Work was almost a ceremonial word for him. He equipped himself to work, could spend days on end preparing himself for a task. He dreamt of places and rooms in which one could work well, he saw them as – work landscapes, without putting it so clumsily and without being in any way proud of hard work as a virtue.

He took it very much amiss that I only answered every third or fourth letter. I found it difficult to maintain a regular correspondence; to me letters were outbursts for which I had to wait and which I did not want to force.

---

[2] Elias Canetti's first wife.

He must have known that and as a good observer he cannot have failed to notice it for long, but as he did not only live in letters, but rather always *wanted* something, I took care not to respond to his every whim. When complaints did not help, then he threatened to cut contact altogether, but settled for the threat when he saw that it served no purpose.

When he came to Oxford from London, we met over several years, while the war was still going on, in the Student Movement House in Gower Street. That was the place where students of all origins met, from Africa and India, but also from the white Dominions. There were emigrés from all over Europe and Arabs, Chinese, Malays. It was a club devoid of prejudice, the only entrance requirement was a connection with the university. As such it was frequented for the most part by young people, but people who had long finished their studies enjoyed coming too. You could start up a conversation with anyone, you introduced yourself, took a seat, chatted, and got up again whenever you wanted to or when you felt drawn to someone else. It was the freest, least prejudiced atmosphere I have ever known. Of course, people were as they had always been, but during the hours they spent in the club, they cast their prejudices effortlessly aside, it is unforgettable how comfortable they were doing this.

Steiner, who had come to England some years before me, introduced me to this club. For him as an anthropologist it was paradise, and to choose this place for our conversations was the most wonderful present he could give me. When his obligations allowed it, we spent three or four hours here together, in serious and always concentrated conversation, interrupted by meetings with a great variety of people who approached us or who he wanted me to meet. Just imagine what it meant when, just as we were discussing Ashanti proverbs, he was able, in the middle of our conversation, to introduce me to Kessi who was said to be an Ashanti prince. Not that we then learnt much about these proverbs as a result, but we could imagine the lips which spoke them, and if it were not the somewhat arrogant laughing Kessi himself, but rather another student from the Gold Coast, such proverbs were recited for our pleasure. You could really rely on the marvellous collections by English scholars.

Both, he or I, liked to surprise the other with a book which he had been looking for for some time but did not yet know. It became a competition which we did not want to give up. The bookshops around the British Museum were inexhaustible and we spent as much time searching for antiquarian books as we did in our conversations. In the midst of all these days of searching, came the one when I was able to show him a copy of 'Specimens of Bushman Folklore' by Bleek and Lloyd, one of the wonders of world literature, without which I would no longer like to live. I had found it just before our meeting in the club, he could not believe it, I handed it to him, he leafed through it with – literally – trembling hands and congratulated me – just as one would on the occasion of one of life's important milestones. There were also moments of generosity when one of us was able to present the other with a duplicate copy of something the former already owned.

Our conversations were an exciting combination of books from all over the world, which we carried with us, and people from all over the world, who surrounded us. There were lawyers, future politicians, linguists, anthropologists, historians, philosophers, less frequently medical doctors too. No one forced his subject area onto anyone else, but you were then always particularly pleased when someone asked about your field in detail. I have never experienced an intelligent society which was more tolerant. Everyone was noticed, even the most lonely or withdrawn person merited interest. Anyone who was normally afraid of others was able to thaw out here with the help of his neighbours' tactful curiosity. There were of course those who tried to make an impression but as there were so many others there who were just as worthy, they soon quietened down or disappeared.

As far as Steiner is concerned, it is true to say that he was never in a bad mood in this place. He, who suffered so greatly from the lack of a family, and who always complained about it – here he was calm, clever, observant, so enthralled by others or in demand that he did not see himself as being any more unhappy than anyone else and did not feel sorry for himself.

CHRONOLOGY

CHRONOLOGY

1909   Born 12 October, Prague.

1913   Sister Suse born.

c. 1915   Friendship with H. G. Adler.

1920   Deutsches Staatsgymnasium, Stephansgasse.

1925   Staatsrealgymnasium, Heinrichsgasse. Friendship with Wolf Salus.

1926   Joins 'Roter Studentenbund' (Red Student Association).

1928   Matura (school leaving certificate).
         First poems.

1928–35 Studies Semitic languages and general linguistics, briefly Indian Studies, then Ethnology at the German University in Prague.

1929   Serious accident during a holiday in Dalmatia.
         Public appearance with the 'Freie Gruppe Prague' (Prague Free Group) (with Paul Leppin jr., Friedrich Ost, Wolf Salus).

1930–31 Studies Modern Arabic at the Hebrew University in Jerusalem.
         Lives with Shmuel Hugo Bergmann.
         Conversion to Zionism. Rejection of Marxism.
         Continues writing poetry.

1932   Death of sister Suse.

1932–38 Early novellas.

1933   Public lecture with Heinz Politzer.
         Publishes first poem, 'Der Bruder' (The Brother), *Prager Tagblatt*.
         Translates Blake's 'The Lamb'.

1933–36 Novel projects: 'Der Friedhof von Turschau' (The Cemetery at Turschau), 'Die Pickiade'.

1935   Completion of doctoral thesis, 'Studies on the History of Arabic Roots'.
         Steiner's translation of Emanuel Lešehrad's *Die Planeten* (The Planets) (from the Czech) is published by Orbis-Verlag, Prague.
         Studies Ethnology in Vienna.

1936   Continues study of Ethnology in London (in the British Museum and under Bronislaw Malinowski).
         The essay 'Orientpolitik' appears in the periodical *Selbstwehr*.

1937   Research trip to Carpathian Russia.
         Prague: first lecture series 'Die Kunst der Primitiven' (The Art of the Primitives).
         Vienna: friendship with Elias Canetti.

1938   Leaves Prague for the last time. Resumption of studies in London. Acquires refugee status following the Munich Agreement in September.

Gives paper at the second International Ethnology Congress in Copenhagen.

Failed engagement to Kae Faeron Hursthouse.

Failed attempt to travel to the USA.

Moves to Oxford.

1939   Renews friendship with Elias and Veza Canetti.

Possible return to Prague blocked for good by the Nazi occupation of the city.

Moves into the home of Christopher Cookson in Oxford as a houseguest. Affiliated to Magdalen College.

Studies at the Institute of Social Anthropology under A. R. Radcliffe-Brown; begins work on a second doctoral thesis on the Sociology of Slavery.

1940–45 Main phase of work on *Eroberungen* (Conquests).

1940–50 Friendship with Esther Frank, Anna Mahler, Eva Erdélyí, Radrakrischnan, Aba Eban, Chaim Rabin, Georg Rapp, Michael Hamburger, David Wright, Nikos Kazantzakis, Erich Fried, and others.

1941   Stipend from the Czech Government in Exile.

1942   April. Loss of thesis and all related materials.

July. Parents deported to Theresienstadt.

October. Death of parents in Treblinka.

1943   Begins recording 'Feststellungen und Versuche' (Essays and Discoveries).

Lecture: 'Rilke's Weg zur Beschwörung' (Rilke's Path to Incantation). Gives a reading from *Eroberungen*.

1944   Five poems appear in *Poetry London*.

Translates two poems by James Joyce. 'On the Process of Civilisation'.

1945   Learns of parents' death.

1946   Nervous breakdown.

E. E. Evans-Pritchard takes over supervision of thesis.

'Letter to Mr Gandhi'.

1946–52 Member of the group around Evans-Pritchard, which changed the character of modern British social anthropology. Friendship with Mary Douglas, William Newell, and M. N. Srinivas; subsequently also Paul and Laura Bohannan and Julian Pitt-Rivers. Collegial relations with Meyer Fortes, J. G. Perestriany, and Godfrey Lienhardt. London circle of poets with Erich Fried, H. G. Adler, Hans Eichner, Hans Cohn, Georg Rapp.

'Gebet im Garten' (Prayer in the Garden).

Translates T. S. Eliot's 'Marina'.

Publication of the pamphlet *Gestade* (Shores), edited by Erich Fried.

1948   Death of Christopher Cookson.

Willi-Weismann-Verlag (Munich) agrees to publish the selection of poems *In Babylons Nischen* (In the Niches of Babylon). Correspondence with Rudolf Hartung.

1948–52 Publication of poems in *Literarische Revue, Sinn und Form, Neue literarische Welt, Eckart, Hochland, Merkur*.

1949   Completion of doctoral thesis 'A Comparative Study of the Forms of Slavery'.

1949–50 September-January. Hospitalized due to coronary thrombosis.

1950   Graduates with doctorate. British citizenship. Appointment as University Lecturer for Social Anthropology. Begins teaching career.

Friendship with Ilse Aichinger.

Publication of *In Babylons Nischen* abandoned due to publisher's financial difficulties.

1951   Beginning of friendship with Iris Murdoch.

Trip to Spain.

1952   'Taboo' lectures.

Second trip to Spain.

Autumn. Falls ill.

27 November. Steiner dies.

28 November. Buried in the Jewish Cemetery in Oxford.

1953   Memorial service, Club 1943 and Exil-PEN, London.

NOTES ON CONTRIBUTORS

Jeremy Adler is Professor of German at King's College London. He has published a book on Goethe's *Die Wahlverwandtschaften* (1987), a catalogue of visual poetry (with Ulrich Ernst), and edited the collected works of August Stramm. With Richard Fardon he edited Franz Baermann Steiner's *Selected Writings*, and brought out Steiner's collected poems, *Am strürzenden Pfad*. His most recent book is a life of Franz Kafka.

Peter J. Conradi is Professor Emeritus at Kingston University and Honorary Research Fellow of University College London. He is author of *The Saint and the Artist: A Study of the Fiction of Iris Murdoch* (2001), of *Iris Murdoch; a Life* (2001), and of monographs on Fowles, Angus Wilson, and Dostoevsky.

Richard Fardon teaches social anthropology and African ethnography at the School of Oriental and African Studies, where he is Chairman of the University of London's Centre of African Studies. He has written and edited books on anthropological theory and on African issues, both contemporary and historical. His next book will concern the fusion of human and animal images in West African masquerade.

Rüdiger Görner teaches Modern German Literature at the University of Aston in Birmingham and has been Director of the Institute of Germanic Studies, University of London since 1999. Recent publications include: *Nietzsches Kunst. Annäherungen an einen Denkartisten* (2000), *Unerhörte Klagen. Deutsche Elegien im 20. Jahrhundert* (2000), *Literarische Betrachtungen zur Musik* (2001), and *Grenzen, Schwellen, Übergänge. Zu einer Poetik des Transitorischen* (2001).

Katrin Kohl is Lecturer in German at the University of Oxford and Fellow of Jesus College. Her publications include *Rhetoric, the Bible, and the Origins of Free Verse: The Early Hymns of F. G. Klopstock* (1990), *Friedrich Gottlieb Klopstock* (2000), and articles on German poetry and poetics. She is currently working on the role of metaphor in German poetics since the Middle Ages.

Michael Mack is Amos-de-Shalit/Minerva Fellow at the Franz Rosenzweig Research Center for German-Jewish Literature and Cultural History, Hebrew University, Jerusalem. He is the author of *Anthropology as Memory. Elias Canetti's and Franz Baermann Steiner's Responses to the Shoah*, published in 2001.

Robert B. Pynsent teaches at the School of Slavonic and East European Studies, University College London. He has published several books and articles on European literature and history, especially Czech and Slovak. His next book concerns woman, the Devil, and nationalism.

Ines Schlenker gained her MBA at the University of Tübingen, Germany, before going on to study Art History at the Courtauld Institute of Art in London. Her doctoral thesis on official National Socialist art was completed in 2000 and is currently being prepared for publication. She is now a researcher at King's College London and is working on a catalogue raisonné of the artist Marie-Louise von Motesiczky. Her research focuses on 20th century German and British art.

Erhard Schüttpelz is based at the Collaborative Research Center 'Media and Cultural Communication' at the University of Cologne. His research area is literature and anthropology and he has published *Figuren der Rede* (1996), *Signale der Störung* (with Albert Kümmel, 2002), and *Die Kommunikation der Medien* (with Jürgen Fohrmann, 2002).

Pavel Seifter has been Ambassador of the Czech Republic in London since 1997. He studied at universities in Czechoslovakia and France until the Soviet invasion of 1968. Subsequently, he played a central role in the dissident movement of the 1970s and 1980s and served as a member of the Civic Forum during the Velvet Revolution of 1989. Combining his diplomatic and academic interests, he has published widely in the field of Political Studies.

Carol Tully is Lecturer in German at the University of Wales Bangor. Her research centres on German-Spanish literary relations, chiefly in the nineteenth century, and German women's writing. She has also translated an anthology of German Romantic fairy tales. She is currently working on a major study of the German Hispanist Johann Nikolas Böhl von Faber.

Nicolas J. Ziegler studied in Göttingen and at King's College London, where he completed his thesis on Steiner's cycle *Eroberungen* in 2001. He is now employed by BBDO Consulting as a Senior Consultant and contributes to periodical publications in both the academic and business fields.

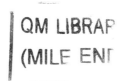